Paulus and Stalingrad

PAULUS
AND STALINGRAD

....

A life of
Field-Marshal Friedrich Paulus
with notes, correspondence and documents
from his papers by

WALTER GOERLITZ

With a preface by
ERNST ALEXANDER PAULUS

Translated by
COLONEL R. H. STEVENS

The Citadel Press   *New York*

FIRST AMERICAN EDITION 1963
LIBRARY OF CONGRESS CATALOG CARD NUMBER 63-21199
MANUFACTURED IN THE UNITED STATES OF AMERICA
PUBLISHED BY THE CITADEL PRESS
222 PARK AVENUE SOUTH, NEW YORK 3, N. Y.

*The maps for this edition
have been specially drawn
by W. H. Bromage*

First published as
Ich Stehe hier auf Befehl
© Verlag für Wehrwesen Bernard und Graefe,
Frankfurt am Main, 1960
English translation © 1963 by Methuen & Co Ltd

Contents

•••

PART II (DOCUMENTS)

Contents

Illustrations

PLATES

MAPS

XXXXX		XXXX		XXXX		XXX	
	Army Group		Army	∞	Air Army		Corps

Flagstaff indicates HQ locations

XX		X		III		II	
	Division		Brigade or Brigadiers Command		Regiment or full Colonels Command		Batt./Regt. or Lieut. Colonels Command

Army Group Boundary ▬XXXXX▬ Army Boundary ▬XXXX▬

Tactical symbols from Division downward also include arm of service

⊠ Infantry	⊘ Cavalry	⬭ Armoured	∞ Air force unit

Airborne	Mountain	☐ Enemy formations

KEY TO SYMBOLS USED IN MAPS

Preface by Ernst Alexander Paulus

Today, the name of the town Stalingrad holds a special significance for every German. The battle of Stalingrad is one of the most bitterly controversial engagements of the Second World War. In the many discussions regarding the downfall of the Sixth Army, conducted for the most part with sincere or insincere passion and prejudice rather than with any real knowledge of the facts, particular significance has naturally been attached to the handling of the operations by my father, Field-Marshal Friedrich Paulus, the Commander-in-Chief of the Sixth Army. Of merciless critics there is no dearth. And it is, I think, undeniably essential that we should strive to achieve clarity in our own minds regarding the causes of this heavy defeat and how much of it was due to error and how much to the blows of fate. But in all the stories, memoirs and 'eye-witness' accounts that have so far been published, this has hardly ever been achieved. All they have done is to give birth to a host of legends about Stalingrad, which are of no value from the viewpoint of historical research.

Although in the summer campaign of 1942 I was on service as an officer in a Tank Regiment of the Sixth Army, I can give no first-hand report on the battle of encirclement, as I had been wounded shortly before the commencement of the operation. Like so many of those belonging to units besieged in Stalingrad, I followed the fortunes of the Sixth Army from a distance at home. Still indelibly fixed in my mind is the contrast between the vague and often misleading communiqués issued by Supreme Headquarters of the Armed Forces and the accounts emanating from well-informed circles or from eye-witnesses who had broken out of the ring of encirclement. And the more gloomy the trend of events appeared to me at the time, the more determined I later became to do my utmost to discover the truth.

I also know – only too well – the bitterness which overwhelmed my father when he returned from captivity in the Soviet Union regarding the many irresponsible and prejudiced verdicts that had been passed on the events of 1942–3. What worried him was not any anxiety about his own reputation, but the question as to how the German people could possibly arrive at any correct appreciation of the history of the Second World War, if it had to content itself with legends, myths and sensational reports.

In the course of the many conversations I had with him in Dresden after his return in 1953, my father repeatedly expressed his intention of writing his own views on the war against the Soviet Union and the responsibility for the Stalingrad disaster. But painful illness and a premature death prevented him from doing so.

In the interests of research into historical truth, I feel that now, when more than a decade-and-a-half separate us from the events, the time has come for me to publish the notes made by my father during his captivity as a prisoner of war. These he was able to bring back with him when he was released in 1953. Some of them he gave me to read for myself during our talks between 1953 and 1956; the remainder I found among his papers after his death on 1 February 1957.

The whole collection of notes is now in my possession. In addition, there is also a series of documents regarding my father's military career, which have been preserved by the family, and such portions of the official correspondence for the years 1940–42 as were flown out of Stalingrad after the Sixth Army had been surrounded. Furthermore, of noteworthy importance is a collection of notes I myself made on the conversations I had with my father and on the lectures he delivered during his years in Dresden. I felt that I could not do better than entrust the collation of all this material to Herr Walter Goerlitz. He has already studied many of the problems of the Second World War and, before I had decided on this present publication, he had made a special and meticulous study of 'Stalingrad'. He knows the facts and the problems involved, and he is personally acquainted with a number of survivors who played leading parts in these events. (Cf. his treatise on 'Stalingrad', published in the volume entitled *Entscheidungsschlachten* [Bernard & Graefe, Frankfurt].) With the help of Herr Goerlitz and thanks to the co-operation of Dr Hans-Adolf Jacobsen, I have further been able to supplement my father's notes with the contents of other, hitherto unknown, files.

As a result, in both the biographical introduction and in the documented portion of the book there emerges a completely new picture of events.

In addition to Herr Goerlitz and Dr Jacobsen, my thanks are due to all those who, out of friendship for my father, have contributed much very valuable information, and in particular to General Hermann Hoth, Lieut-General Heinrich Kirchenheim, Colonel Wilhelm Adam and Colonel Hans-Guenther van Hooven.

I am also grateful to all those who, at the request of Herr Goerlitz, have come forward with information. I am especially indebted to Colonel Thomas Young, Aquasco, Maryland, USA, for sending me the confidential reports on my father from the files of the German Adjutant-General's Branch, which are still in American safe custody.

I am quite sure that this book will bring forth much new comment, and no one will welcome objective criticism and discussion more than myself.

Each and every reader must pass his own judgment on the personalities primarily involved. Apologia serve no purpose whatsoever, and nothing was further from my father's mind than to indulge in them. The endeavour to establish the historical truth is of far higher importance and was, indeed, regarded by my father as a solemn duty. So, in all reverence, I dedicate this book to the memory of the Sixth Army.

Viersen/Rhineland
March 1960

Introductory Note by Walter Goerlitz

The documents and letters published in the second part of this volume fall into two categories: firstly, the memoranda and notes written by the Field-Marshal while a prisoner of war in Soviet Russia and found among his papers by his son, Ernst Alexander Paulus, after his death in 1957; and secondly, such remnants as remain of the Field-Marshal's correspondence, private and official, before he was taken prisoner. Captain Paulus is of the opinion that of the former nothing of importance has been retained by the authorities of Eastern Germany, though copies or photostats of them were kept in the Soviet Union. At the beginning of 1959 the Russian *Journal of the History of the War* announced that it proposed to publish a number of memoranda written by Paulus, and extracts appeared for the first time on 7 January in the Russian military journal, *Red Star*.

The second category, from which extracts are published here for the first time, consists of copies or photostats of the files of the German Military Mission to Rumania, the diary of Field-Marshal v. Bock for 1942, teleprinter correspondence between Sixth Army and Army Group, Don, and parts of General Halder's diary – all of which were collected by Dr Hans-Adolf Jacobsen (Koblenz) in the course of his study of the battle of Stalingrad and all of which he kindly placed at my disposal.

It is, then, with great pleasure that I acknowledge my indebtedness to Dr Jacobsen, author of a number of surveys of the western offensive of 1940 and of the battle of Dunkirk, and a comprehensive documentation of the Second World War.

My thanks are also due to General D. Deichmann, Curator of the Archives of the War in the Air, who kindly allowed me to study the diaries of the Commander-in-Chief of Air Fleet 4, General Freiherr v. Richthofen, and Field-Marshal Milch, as well as those of General Pickert (GOC 4 Flak Division) and General Fiebig (Commander VIII Flak Corps).

I must further express my gratitude to all those who willingly came forward with information and answered such questions as I put to them. Particularly do I wish to thank the former Chief of Staff, Sixth Army, Lt-General Arthur Schmidt, who was given the opportunity of comparing his own notes with Sixth Army War Diary, preserved in the United States Historical Division; to Freifrau Jutta v. Richthofen, the widow of the Field-Marshal, and to Generals Hollidt, Blumentritt, Heim, v. Lossberg, v. Drebber, Colonels Huenersdorff, Laicher, v. Zitzewitz, Majors Luttitz, Cantacuzene, v. Rappard and Dormeier; and to the Rumanian Library in Freiburg, without whose help the biographical introduction could not have been written.

PART I

1. Friedrich Paulus, his life

Since the days of the revered Derfflinger, the old Brandenburg and Prussian Army has afforded innumerable examples of the fact that every courageous and gifted officer, though he might be of humble origin, carried a Field-Marshal's baton in his pack. The social circle from which the highest leaders of the Prusso-German Army were drawn was much more of a rigidly demarcated preserve in the days of Bismarck and Wilhelm than it had been in the old Prussian days, when Frederick the Great's dictum held sway – that a soldier must have luck, but that luck must also earn its own reward.

The lower boundary here was the lower level of the cultured and prosperous landed gentry. The owner of a shop – even if his shop were the most elegant of fashion houses or a very select provision or wine merchant's, even if it were a vast general store which brought in more money than any Junker of Pomerania could possibly have earned – was not eligible to become an officer of the Reserve. And whether his sons could become officers was also very doubtful. All this may well have been justified in the age of limited armies and unlimited rule by a well-defined social upper class; but time does not stand still, and the social order and standards change.

In the years before the First World War, in the debate on the General Staff's demand for a strengthening of the Army, the Prussian Minister of War, General von Heeringen, declared that an unlimited increase in the strength of the Army would 'ruin' the Corps of Officers. These were the controversies that characterized the time at which Paulus began his career as an officer.

The Paulus and Rosetti-Solescu families

Friedrich Wilhelm Ernst Paulus was born at about half past nine on the evening of 23 September 1890 at house No. 95 in the parish of Breitenau-Gershagen. His father, Ernst Paulus, was at that time Treasurer of a corrective establishment, or, as we should now say, the accountant and book-keeper of an approved school. His mother, Bertha, née Nettelbeck, was the daughter of the Chief Inspector and Director of the same establishment. Friedrich Wilhelm Nettelbeck stood as godfather for his grandson, who was baptized in the evangelical church on 16 November 1890. Breitenau, which in the older Army Lists appears as Breidenau, was in the Melsingen district of the province of Hesse-Nassau. It was an ancient part of the province, which, at Bismarck's instigation, was annexed and joined to Prussia in 1866. During the National Socialist era, for as long as the Commander-in-Chief of the Sixth Army, General Paulus, enjoyed the privilege of being regarded as 'a valuable asset' by 'the Fuehrer' and the Reichsminister for Propaganda, Dr Joseph Goebbels (a short honeymoon!), the Field-Marshal was described as 'a scion of the finest Hessian yeoman stock'.[1]

In the nineteenth century one of Paulus' forebears was Bürgermeister of Lohre. Most of the Paulus's were agriculturalists, dairy farmers and teachers, while some, like this Ernst Paulus, were minor civil servants. Physically, this typically respectable family of Hessian middle-class yeoman stock produced upstanding men with a fine presence. One of the Field-Marshal's uncles had been given the nickname of 'the gnarled oak'.

Ernst Paulus remained a civil servant for the whole of his life. In 1904 he was appointed Chief Treasurer of the province and worked in Kassel. Later the family moved to Marburg. The wife, Bertha, née Nettelbeck (a family from the vicinity of Solingen in the Rhineland) bore him three children – two brothers, Friedrich and Ernst, whose respective careers followed very different paths, and one daughter, Cornelia ('Nelly'), who remained a spinster. There was nothing remarkable about the father. He was a conscientious official and a man who, in all modesty, had an exact appreciation of his station in life. The mother has been described as 'a fine, calm and patient woman', who enjoyed indifferent health but bore her 'many trials and sufferings' without complaint.

The son who was later to become a famous and fiercely controversial figure was born at a time when the lower and middle grades of the civil service were in the process of ameliorating their social

---

[1] From an undated newspaper cutting of 1943(?), now in possession of the Paulus family. The photograph shows the F-M's father with his six brothers.

standing. Young Friedrich Paulus was educated at the Wilhelms-Gymnasium in Kassel. In 1909 he passed the examination for his leaving certificate, and in his final report it was noted that 'the recipient of this certificate, Paulus, wishes to make the Navy his career'.

The young Imperial Navy seemed in those days to be opening the whole world to Germany. But this ambition of the son of a modest, middle-class family proved to be too optimistic. The Navy, the new, young Service, painfully but zealously striving to acquire status equal to that of the traditional Corps of Officers of the Army, laid great store on an exclusive officer intake. The son of some minor civil servant in Hesse did not seem to fill the bill. What they wanted were the sons of noblemen or of rich and distinguished financiers and the like!

Notwithstanding his excellent physique and his undoubted mental ability, Friedrich Paulus was not accepted. There is nothing to show what effect this had on him. It is nevertheless certain that the realization that he belonged to a generation and a social class which would firstly have to fight for its place in society and then prove itself in its new environment, had a very considerable influence on his general outlook. It would otherwise be difficult to explain, for example, why so naturally handsome a young man (his brother officers later dubbed him 'The Lord' and 'The Major with the Sex Appeal') should have attached such exaggerated importance to his external appearance, to absolutely correct and immaculate uniform, to collars and cuffs of the precise height and width laid down by regulations – all to such a degree that even his wife and children smiled lovingly at his little foibles.

Friedrich Paulus, rejected by the Navy, then decided to study law at Marburg University, where he started to read jurisprudence in the winter term of 1909–10.

Even so, his real love and his secret ambition was soldiering. The Army needed officers. The Army was much less petty in its outlook than the Navy, and when it was found that the traditional sources of supply for the Corps of Officers was proving inadequate, the Monarchy turned, naturally enough, to the social strata of the civil services, to men traditionally imbued with the concept of service and devotion to duty.

On 18 February 1910, the young law student reported for duty as a cadet officer to the Markgraf Ludwig Wilhelm (3rd Baden) Infantry Regiment No. 111 stationed in Rastatt. The Prussian Army was rather inclined to turn up its nose at regiments 'with high numbers' and with officers from the middle classes. But the Baden Regiment had already been in existence for three-quarters of a century and was not without repute in Baden.

The young ensign from Prussianized Hesse found himself in a regiment which, as a result of the military agreement between Baden and Prussia, formed part of the XIV Prussian Army Corps. His career followed a normal course – Ensign 18 February 1910, 2nd Lieutenant 18 October 1910, and, after a course of instruction at the military school in the old castle built by Count Philipp Walderdorff, Archbishop of Trier, in Enger, he was duly gazetted Lieutenant in August 1911.[1]

During this part of his career the personal aspect is of more interest than the purely military. Serving with the Regiment were two young Rumanian brothers, Efrem and Constantin Rosetti-Solescu, sons of the former Rumanian Consul-General, Alexander Rosetti-Solescu (1859–1910) and his wife, Ecaterina, née Ghermani (1863–1940). Alexander Rosetti-Solescu had served in the diplomatic corps of the young Rumanian kingdom. His brother, Gheorghe, had for some considerable time been Rumanian Minister in St Petersburg and had there married a Russo-German lady of the Tsarist household, Olga v. Giers.

Alexander, thanks to a series of unfortunate circumstances, had lost a goodly portion of his fortune in Rumania and had retired to his property, Copaceni, in Wallachia. His wife, a Serbo-Macedonian, had left him and had settled in Germany with her five children – two sons and three daughters. While on furlough in Raumünzach in the Black Forest, young Lieutenant Paulus was introduced by his Rumanian friends to their eldest sister, Elena Constance Rosetti-Solescu, who was then twenty-one years of age. On 4 July 1912 the handsome young Lieutenant and the beautiful Rumanian married.

For both parties, this was an unusual alliance. The German

[1] Vide Prussian Army List, 1912. The 111th Regiment was in the 56th Brigade, 28th Division, XIV Army Corps.

Lieutenant had chosen his bride from the foremost of the Rumanian princely Houses. The proud, immensely wealthy Ecaterina Rosetti-Solescu, born and bred in the feudal and patriarchal traditions of the Balkans, at the outset presumably regarded this young Lieutenant of German middle-class origin with no small measure of scepticism. On the other hand a Lieutenant of Infantry, the brother officer of her sons, whose upbringing she had elected to entrust to the German Army, was obviously perfectly acceptable socially.

The family of Friedrich Paulus' mother-in-law, the Ghermani, claimed to be descended from the legendary Germanos, nephew of the Emperor Justinian (AD 527–65). They owned the castle of Leurdeni in Wallachia. Caterina's father had been a Colonel in the Serbian Army and his mother came from the Serbian Royal House, of Obrenovic. As far as the Rosetti-Solescus were concerned, they regarded themselves, with the Princess Mavrokordatos, as members of the oldest and most distinguished indigenous nobility of Moldavia and Wallachia, the two Principalities from which, under the rule of Prince Alexander Cuza (1859–66), the new Kingdom of Rumania had emerged. Prince Cuza, originally Stadthalter of Galatz, had married Elena Rosetti-Solescu, a great-aunt of Lieutenant Paulus' bride. And her grandmother was a member of the princely house of Stourdza, which had many times produced the Hospodars of Moldavia, the sovereign Princes under Ottoman suzerainty.

The Rosettis, then, who most probably migrated from Genoa to Rumania towards the end of the Middle Ages and who flourished in two branches – the Rosetti-Solescu branch, after the ancestral estate of Solescti in Jassy, and the Rosetti-Tetzeanu of Bacau – really did belong to that small upper-class of great Rumanian landowners who were immensely wealthy – at least up to the beginning of the twentieth century. The great peasants' revolt in Rumania in 1906–7 and the agrarian reforms which followed it admittedly destroyed the economic foundations of this upper-class. Nevertheless, families like the Rosettis, the Stourdzas, Ghikas, Cantacuzinos and Stirbeys continued to play a leading part in Rumanian affairs right up to 1944, when the Red Army marched in.

His marriage to Elena Constance Rosetti-Solescu, known in the family as 'Coca', was destined to be of very much more than merely social significance in the life of the future Field-Marshal. For as chance would have it, his duties in the Second World War brought him into close touch with the Rumanian Army. The marriage not only bore him upwards into the great world of an aged Europe already tottering to its end; it also gave to his private life a character quite different to that of the average officer. In the Third Reich under the domination of Hitler, the People's Tribune, it brought him, too, face to face with the implacable, aristocratic antagonism towards the vulgar dictator who trampled rough-shod over God, justice and every accepted traditional social order.

Elena Constance Paulus, born on 25 April 1889 in Bucharest (with a Prince Cantacuzino as a witness of the birth), by religion a member of the Greek Orthodox Church, must have been a remarkable woman in every way, not only blessed with material advantages, but also endowed with a natural intelligence of a high order. Educated as a child in the French manner at the Convent of Notre Dame de Sion in Constantinople, she spoke French far better than German when she first came to Germany with her mother. But she quickly became completely at home there. In Karlsruhe she attended the exclusive Victoria Lycée under the ægis of the aged Grand Duchess Luise, and in due course, like the rest of her family, was accepted into the social circle of the Court.

The marriage of the young Rumanian aristocrat and the German officer from the middle-classes stood firm through all the tempests of the times. Three children were born of it, a daughter, Olga, in 1914, who later married a Baron v. Kutzschenbach, and twin sons, Friedrich and Ernst Alexander, born in 1918 and both combatant officers in the Army of the Third Reich. Friedrich Paulus fell as a Captain at the battle of Anzio-Nettuno in February 1944; Ernst Alexander, also a Captain and destined for a General Staff career, found himself in *Sippenhaft*, corporate detention, at the end of the war[1], as the result of his father's having declared himself to be anti-Hitler while in a Russian prisoner-of-war camp. Elena Constance Paulus, who died in Baden-Baden in 1949, turned a contemptuous back on the Gestapo officials who, on the orders of the

[1] This refers to Hitler's policy of placing under arrest not only the individual who incurred his displeasure, but also every other member of the family he could lay his hands on.

'All Highest', promised her that not a hair of her head would be touched if she would renounce the name of Paulus, which the 'Fuehrer' himself had condemned as infamous. That occurred in the late autumn of 1944, when the old Rumania was dying, and death had already pointed his finger at the Hitler régime.

The First World War, 1914-18

The year 1914, which brought the outbreak of that First World War that was destined to destroy the old Europe, found Lieutenant Friedrich Paulus as Adjutant of the 3rd Battalion of the Markgraf Ludwig Wilhelm v. Baden Infantry Regiment. The Officer Commanding the Regiment was Colonel Oskar v. Lorne v. St Ange, a member of a French family which had emigrated in 1789 and taken service under the Grand Duke of Baden. The battalion consisted of the 9th, 10th, 11th and 12th Companies. OC No. 10 Company was Captain Johannes Blaskowitz (later Colonel-General), the son of an East Prussian clergyman and a friend of very long standing of Friedrich Paulus. In Nos. 9 and 10 Companies, Paulus' brothers-in-law, Lieutenants Efrem and Constantin Rosetti-Solescu, were serving as Company Officers. On 6 August 1914 the battalion paraded in field service order and then proceeded on service.

The salient feature of his activities during the First World War, during which he was employed for the most part first as a Regimental and then as a General Staff Officer, is characteristic of the whole of the rest of his military career. As has already been said, he was a conscientious worker and an assistant greatly valued by his superiors.

In 1915 we find Lieutenant Paulus serving as a Regimental Staff Officer with a crack unit, the 2nd Prussian Jaeger Regiment, which formed part of an élite formation, the Alpenkorps. The burden of most of the staff work fell on Paulus. His primary virtues were his conscientiousness, his skill in getting on with his superiors and his ready adaptability. Even at this early stage, it was obvious that he had all the makings of a General Staff Officer. In point of fact, this son of a generation that had thrust its way into the ranks of the professional Army officers was predestined (both as a man, and as a result of his marriage into the aristocracy) to gain for himself a place among that company of officers, whose position in the scheme of things was assured by tradition, but who nevertheless were adapting themselves to the changing times.

In 1918, decorated with the Iron Cross, Class II and Class I, he was promoted, in that dark September sinister with foreboding, to the rank of Captain. During 1917 he had already served for some time in the Operations Branch of the Alpenkorps General Staff. Four years previously he had participated in the sweeping victories on the Western Front, he had learnt the trade of war at Verdun and in Rumania; and to him, too, might well have been applied the phrase coined by General v. Seeckt: the man who knows war as it really is wants to see no more of it.

Captain Paulus lived through the revolution of 1918. What he, as a regular officer, thought of the collapse and of the flight of the Supreme War Lord, The Emperor of Germany and King of Prussia, we do not know.

Though he derived great pleasure from his desk work as a methodical student of the art and science of war, and was, indeed, often over-meticulous in his devotion to duty, Paulus was never a great letter writer or a diligent keeper of diaries. A man who ponders every factor thrice before deciding what is to be done is not usually inclined to lay bare his innermost thoughts. And Field-Marshal Paulus was just such a man – more is the pity, from the viewpoint of historical research!

The years of revolution

There is one thing, at least, that is known about this General Staff Officer of the 48th Reserve Division – he remained in the Service. Among the late Field-Marshal's papers is a memorandum, dated 1 July 1937, from the Deutsches Kriegerbund, which stated that Captain Friedrich Paulus, Berlin-Friedenau, took part in the battles fought by the Freikorps, Grenzschutz Ost. What form this participation took, whether he was personally on the eastern frontier in 1919 or whether he merely took part in the raising of this Freikorps, is not clear.

In 1920 he became Adjutant of the 14th Infantry Regiment, stationed in Konstanz and commanded by Colonel Blaskowitz.

In the possession of the Field-Marshal's son, Ernst Alexander, is a note, dated 4 May 1957, from the late Chief of Staff, SA, Major-General Otto Wagner (retired), on Paulus' attitude towards the Kapp Putsch in 1920. The writer thinks he remembers meeting Paulus in those days while the latter was serving as Adjutant to Colonel Steinwachs in Karlsruhe; and he goes on to say that in his opinion it would be inadvisable today to go in any detail into Paulus' attitude at that time. The only possible inference that can be drawn from this is that Paulus supported Kapp and his attempted conservative *coup d'état* – an attempt that was, admittedly, ill-timed and politically badly planned, and an act which, of itself, should not have been the cause of political repercussions. If this were so, then Paulus was one of a small minority. The statement leads to the assumption that this officer of the shattered Imperial Army, like most of his brother officers, regarded the revolution as a shameful and disgraceful act.

The report on Captain Paulus as Adjutant of the 14th Infantry Regiment is illuminating: 'A typical General Staff Officer of the old school, of good physique, extremely well turned out, modest (at times over-modest), a pleasant young man, with excellent manners, and a good mixer. He is, admittedly, at pains to avoid making enemies, but he is an exceptionally good and enthusiastic soldier. He is slow, but very methodical in his office work and is passionately interested in war games, both on the map and the sand model. In these latter he displays marked tactical ability, though he is in-inclined to spend over-much time on his appreciation, before issuing his orders. His health has been indifferent, and he seldom spares himself as he should. He is too fond of working at night and sustaining himself with coffee and cigarettes.'

It is perfectly true that he always liked to study every situation minutely and to work out his orders to the last detail. He would spend hours on the drafting of his orders in order to ensure that they were as well worded as it was possible to word them. That his papers for the period 1943 onwards do not all bear the hall-mark of such polished endeavour is due to the fact that long before he had completed his work, the deadly disease that was to kill him had already struck the pen from his hand.

Lieutenant Dormeier, who first met Paulus when they were

serving together on the Staff of the 2nd Jaeger Regiment in the First World War, remembers how, when he himself was with the Staff of the Sixth Army in 1939–40, Paulus of an evening used to go in detail over the whole events of the day in a sort of muted conversation with himself.

General Heim recalls that once, on manoeuvres in the middle 'twenties, the Director suddenly put the Officer Commanding the Regiment out of action, and his Deputy, the Adjutant – Paulus – had to take over. He found himself confronted with 'a precarious situation', in which a swift decision was essential. . . . The Director passed his verdict: 'This officer lacks decisiveness.' Heim adds that in those times that sort of thing was an everyday occurrence, and no one really took such remarks to heart, any more than Paulus himself later took exception to the nickname of Fabius Cunctator bestowed upon him by some of the more irreverent of his pupils when he was an instructor at the Staff College. Whether and to what extent this meticulous thoroughness in forming his appreciation of the situation proved to be a disadvantage or not during the Second World War will be examined later.

It was during these years that there came to light a most striking example of contrast between two great war Commanders of the future. While doing his tour of regimental duty with the 13th Infantry Regiment, of which he was OC No. 2 Company, Paulus made the acquaintance of the already much bemedalled Commander of the MG Company, Captain Erwin Rommel, a proven soldier, a typical Swabian and a real thruster in action. Later in the Third Reich, Rommel was hailed everywhere as 'The People's Marshal', until, charged with treason against 'the Fuehrer', he committed suicide by taking poison sent to him by Hitler via 'a General on the Fuehrer's personal staff'. Paulus and Rommel were the exact antithesis of each other. But Paulus noted, with no small degree of quiet satisfaction, that his No. 2 Company invariably beat the MG Company at both work and play. A General Staff Officer is not always and of necessity a rotten Company Commander!

Regimental duty, for all that, was not really of paramount interest to him, any more than he felt the need, later, as an Army Commander, to shine in the eyes of his troops, in the manner of Field-Marshals Reichenau, Model or Rommel. This must not be taken to mean in any way that he was lacking in sympathy for the trials and hardships of the ordinary soldier, crouching in his fox-hole, or choked by the summer dust, or frozen by the icy winter winds of the storm-swept steppes. Those were things he knew all about – he had had some, and he was constantly going round the front lines; but to him it seemed that a Commander's place was in the map-room and on the end of a telephone at his battle headquarters, and not up in front with the armoured vanguard. As an operational planner and a Commander in battle, he was exceptionally talented, and for these duties he cherished a deep, though concealed passion. In the more fictional literature and the more popular type of mem-oirs of the Second World War, these characteristics have, it is true, been depicted in a critical and unfavourable light. In many of them he is painted as a remote and unworldly individual, supinely obedient, beset with doubts and anxieties and seeking refuge in the music of Beethoven, rather than emulating the deeds of a Yorck. No picture could be more false.

Its painters, admittedly, are not wholly to blame for their error. As a Commander-in-Chief in war Paulus was still a quiet, even, one might say, subdued man, a thinker and certainly no thrusting swashbuckler. Hardly anyone ever saw him excited, scornful or in a rage. The only thing which even his friends confirm is that from time to time he showed a certain bewilderment and a measure of helplessness when confronted with ill-bred boorishness and un-becoming conduct in others, and he hated blatant, uninhibited brutality with an exaggerated fastidiousness. Even so, he never showed his real feelings, but remained always completely self-possessed. He was, therefore, ill-equipped to offer opposition to a man of Hitler's type. In this respect Reichenau and Model were far superior to him in self-assertiveness.

Reichswehr and Reichsheer;
the raising of the Panzer Arm

In October 1922, Paulus, together with Hollidt, was detailed to attend one of the so-called 'R' courses for General Staff Officers at the Ministry of Defence in Berlin. In addition, he took a course in topography and land survey which necessitated a year of previous study at the Technical High School in Berlin-Charlottenburg.

According to the Army List of 1923, he was posted as a Captain to the General Staff of Reichswehr Group 2 in Kassel. From 1924 to 1927 he served as a GSO in Stuttgart; after that, as has already been mentioned, he did a two-year tour of regimental duty with the 13th Infantry Regiment in Stuttgart, and then for a further two years he was with the 5th Division in the Württemberg-Baden District as an instructor in tactics to what was at the time called 'candidates for appointment as junior leaders' (the training of General Staff Officers being at that time forbidden by the Versailles Treaty).

In the autumn of 1931 he was transferred to Berlin, where he was employed in the Ministry of Defence as Chief Instructor in tactics and military history to another class of 'candidates' – in other words, of embryo General Staff Officers.

Among the Field-Marshal's papers and now in possession of his family is a number of those somewhat frivolous periodicals in which all students delight, produced by the younger members attending the courses. It is of interest to note, in parenthesis, that among these students were several Soviet Russian officers, and that the Red Army asked whether Paulus could be seconded to take over the post of Chief Instructor in a school for junior leaders in the Soviet Union. To this request the Ministry of Defence did not, of course, accede. Among the instructors on these courses were Herefurth, Adam, Scherff, Schmundt, Busse and Brennecke, all of whom later rose to the rank of General and most of whom came to a tragic end during the rise and fall of the Third Reich.[1]

For Germany, these were indeed dark days. The young Subalterns and Captains nevertheless maintained a light-hearted attitude *vis-à-vis* the senior officers instructing them. To them, Paulus still remained 'The Major with the Sex Appeal', 'The Noble Lord' and 'Our Most Elegant Gentleman'. And, though the words were spoken

[1] Major-General Otto Herefurth, CGS, Wehrkreis III, Berlin in 1944, was executed for complicity in the July 20th plot; Lieut-General Rudolf Schmundt, Adjutant General of the Wehrmacht, succumbed to wounds received in the bomb explosion of July 20th; Lieut-General Walter Scherff, Official Historian at Supreme Headquarters of the Armed Forces, committed suicide in 1945.

in jest, this must have been the impression he made on them. Though he could lay no claims to blue blood, he was, in every essential, an aristocrat. And the impression he always gave was that of a well-educated, highly trained man, typical of that school of constructive thinkers whom the German General Staff of the previous generation had produced in such profusion.

On 1 Feburary 1931, with his seniority ante-dated two years, Friedrich Paulus, now a Major on the General Staff, could well be regarded, on Seeckt's definition, as a typical example of the highly trained but completely a-political Staff Officer such as Seeckt himself desired ('General Staff Officers have no names'). Although Seeckt himself and General v. Schleicher, 'the Cardinal in politics'[1] of the Ministry of Defence, were both most certainly very active in the political field. But the Reichswehr itself was expected to remain aloof from party strife, political activity and the menacing danger of civil war. It was neither republican nor anti-republican. It stood in reserve, with its arms at the order. And in the midst of all the want, the great economic crisis and the general feeling of hopelessness, its officers watched, with more or less sympathy according to their rank and generation, the rise of a new national movement which was in favour of a strong Army.

Then Hitler took the centre of the stage. To decent people like Paulus, his uncouthness must have been repellent. His wife, an aristocrat as little interested in politics as her husband himself, was merely disgusted by the bragging vulgarity of these oafs in the brown shirts. The alternative, that the Reichswehr should be called in to suppress the revolt of the masses, was admittedly never even mooted. And when the aged Field-Marshal v. Hindenburg, albeit with the greatest reluctance, appointed Hitler Chancellor of the Reich in 1933, and a General of the Reichswehr became Minister of Defence, the Corps of Officers accepted the situation. What else could they have done? Officers had always been urged not to bother their heads about politics; and the new Chancellor seemed to be showing considerable understanding with regard to the requirements of the Army. Who, among all the officers, could have dreamed of the devil that was hidden in Hitler?

For the small, professional and, in many instances, highly quali-

[1] Groener.

fied Corps of Officers of the Reichswehr, who in a few years' time would be called upon to perform a gigantic task, the raising of a new conscript army with completely new types of formations – armoured units, smoke screen troops, mechanized artillery and the like – the rapid expansion of the next few years was achieved at the expense of esprit de corps and homogeneity; and the decisive factor in their subsequent attitude towards the phenomenon of Hitler and National Socialism was based as often as not on the manner in which this new era appeared to them from the purely military point of view.

On 1 April 1934 Lieut-Colonel Paulus took over command of Motor Transport Section 3 in Wünsdorff, which was then transformed into an armoured and motorized reconnaissance unit and became the prototype of the many motorized units to follow; and this was the last time that he was in active command of troops until he assumed command of the Sixth Army in 1942. On 30 June 1934, the day of the Roehm Putsch and the murder of the former Chancellor, General v. Schleicher, his unit, like all the other units of the Reichswehr, was alerted and proceeded to the gates of Berlin, where they were told that the SA were planning a *coup d'état*; but they were not called upon to take any action. As far as is known, their Commander accepted the official version, and there were no further repercussions. At that time a very great number of people accepted the official version.

On 1 June 1935 Paulus was promoted to Colonel, and the decisive turning point in his career came in September of that year, when he was appointed Chief of Staff to the newly constituted Headquarters, Mechanized Forces in Berlin, which became the centre for the raising of the Panzer arm and all its ancillary formations. The GOC of this new Command was General Oswald Lutz, of the Bavarian Mechanized Forces, and his satisfaction with his new Chief of Staff was not confined to purely military matters. Paulus' predecessor, Colonel Guderian, who had held the appointment only for a short while from July 1934, became GOC 2nd Panzer Division in Würzburg. Guderian, a passionate apostle of the Panzer arm, very much doubted whether Paulus was the right man to carry on the fight with sufficient verve on behalf of his revolutionary ideas against the orthodoxy of the General Staff and the traditional wishes of the numerically very strong Cavalry branch of the Service. His

Captain Paulus on manoeuvres, 1926

Capitulation of the Belgian Army, 28 May 1940. Centre, Col-Gen v. Reichenau, on his right, the King of the Belgians, on his left, Maj-Gen Paulus

Invasion practice, St Malo, August 1940

Fighting on the steppes

doubts were soon allayed. Paulus in his eyes quickly became the personification of the wise, enterprising, enthusiastic and conscientious General Staff Officer of the modern type, whose sincerity was beyond all doubt a pearl of great price.

A number of officers who later achieved well-merited fame as Generals of the Armoured Forces found themselves gathered together at this focal point: The Ia (GSOI) was Lieut-Colonel Nehring, Ib (GSO II) was firstly Captain Walther Huenersdorff and then Captain Einck; IIb was Captain (Cavalry) Smilo v. Luettwitz, and the Administrative Officer was Captain Kurt v. Huenersdorff, a brother of the Ib.

It does not come within the scope of this book to go into the enormous difficulties and the innumerable bitter controversies (particularly within the Inspectorate of Cavalry) which accompanied the formation of an effective Panzer arm, organized in large formations and with tanks, armoured reconnaissance units, anti-tank artillery and motorized escort units. Nor is this the place to dwell upon the fact that at hardly any stage was the arming of this new Panzer army properly co-ordinated with the general military and civil motorization in progress or with the productive capacity of the German motor industry.

There are two points worthy of attention: Hitler, in this respect up to date in his views and displaying considerable technical understanding, showed the greatest possible interest in the new arm. He could be counted on, when it was a question of developing the thesis that armour would be the decisive weapon in the battles of the future. And the small band of General Staff Officers of the Panzer Army found themselves to a quite considerable degree in objective disagreement on points of fact with the conservative Army General Staff under Beck, who were far more sceptical in their appreciation of the potentialities of the Panzer arm.

These facts can very easily lead to misconceptions. Beck, who resigned in 1938 as a protest against Hitler's war plans (and Hitler forbade the publication of the news of his resignation), has often been reproached on the grounds that his opposition to the development of the Panzer arm was actuated by political considerations. That is quite untrue. Beck's quarrel in 1938 was not with Hitler's political aspirations, but with the objectives at which military planning seemed to be aimed. All the planning of the old General Staff had been based upon a limited, defensive war to ensure the security of the German Reich in Central Europe. And until 1938, this, too, had been the basis of all Air Force planning. But if the units of the Panzer Army were now to be grouped together in large formations, this could only denote that large-scale offensive operations were being envisaged. The men on Beck's General Staff continued to regard the Panzer arm primarily as an auxiliary weapon of the conventional army units – and, in any case, certainly not as the decisive weapon in battle, as Guderian thought. This equally does not mean, however, that the General Staff Officers of the Panzer Army deliberately planned this treacherous war of aggression or even participated in the planning of it. Nothing was further from their thoughts. All they felt was that the Panzer Army should be an independent branch of the Service and not, as in the First World War, an ancillary weapon to the infantry and cavalry.

Notwithstanding their different backgrounds, Beck and Paulus were in many respects similar characters, although their personal relations were cool without being antagonistic, and in spite of the rumours later current that, in view of what happened at Stalingrad, they must have acted in tacit unison – Beck as a sort of embryo Head of the State and Paulus as a somewhat curious edition of Yorck. Both were Hessians, both came from middle-class families, and neither had been intended for the General Staff of the Prusso-German Army. Both were intelligent, conscientious – above all, conscientious – and astute military thinkers, of a type which the old Prusso-German Army was only too seldom able to produce. Both were *a priori* devoid of any political interests: Beck acquired political insight late, Paulus in a bitterly controversial manner and after a great catastrophe.

There was nevertheless one man serving as Oberquartiermeister I[1] on Beck's Staff, who possessed a precise and up-to-date appreciation of the potentialities of the Panzer arm – Lieut-General Eric v.

---

[1] In the German Army, the three Principal Staff Officers under the CGS were designated, in order of priority, Oberquartiermeister I, II and III, rather in the manner of the Adjutant General, the Quartermaster General and the Master General of the Ordnance in the British Army, though not with the same functions.

Manstein, who, later, in the tragic and decisive phase of the battle of Stalingrad, was Paulus' direct and highly revered Commander-in-Chief; under Beck, too, another Oberquartiermeister was coming to the fore, General Halder, who, as Chief of the General Staff in 1940, selected Paulus, the former 'Chef' of the Panzer arm, to be his Oberquartiermeister I and Deputy CGS. And by the most progressive thinker among the Army Commanders-in-Chief, Field-Marshal v. Reichenau, Paulus was regarded as a proven General Staff Officer, a wise councillor and a good friend.

It is advisable that considerable thought should be given to all these matters before subscribing to certain verdicts which were popularly accepted for a long time, without there having been any real scrutiny of the facts on which they had been based. One thing is incontrovertible – in all the differences of opinion between the the old General Staff and the group of Panzer Army General Staff Officers, politics played the least important part of all. Indeed, it would be more accurate to say that politics played no part at all. It was simply a conflict regarding a purely theoretical military problem. And although politics, in the person of Hitler, played into the hands of the supporters of the Panzer arm, neither of the contesting parties realized the hidden pitfalls inherent therein. That Halder, who regarded Hitler with such scepticism and personal revulsion and whose brain was as fertile as that of his predecessor, Beck, should have been the man who, when the decision to invade the Soviet Union was finally taken, chose Paulus as his Deputy does not seem to indicate that Paulus was 'a tremendous admirer of "The Greatest War Lord Of All Time" ' – as one very popular version insists!

Paulus and Hitler

In the process of reviewing the career of Field-Marshal Paulus, it has repeatedly become apparent that it is not enough to measure the actions of a senior officer of the Third Reich solely by the yardstick of 'resistance'. Anyone who, between 1934 and 1939, was involved in the raising of the new Wehrmacht had little time for reflection or surmise; and to none did this apply more than to the General Staff Officers engaged upon an enthralling and responsible task, under such seniors as Lutz, Guderian (from 1939 'Chief of the Mobile Units'), and Hoepner, the G O C-in-C XVI Panzer Army Corps, formed in 1938 – all men of action who were only too pleased to have a devoted and conscientious Staff Officer prepared to work day and night and relieve them of 'the General Staff bumf', as Hoepner put it. Unless, of course, he were a man of overweening ambition, or one inspired with the desire to engage in politics; and that, Colonel Paulus was certainly not.

This Colonel who, as a General Staff Officer, made a contribution to the organization, system of command and tactical employment of the new German Panzer Army as important as it has remained to this day unappreciated ('General Staff Officers have no names') stood aloof from National Socialism. It is true that in Hitler he saw 'the Leader' and in conversation never alluded to him otherwise than as the 'Fuehrer'. With General Freiherr v. Fritsch, appointed Commander-in-Chief of the Army in 1934, he was conscious of a measure of affinity. What he thought of that officer's unworthy downfall in February 1938, which resulted also in the dismissal of General Lutz, is not known. But it is safe to say at least that, like all the more senior General Staff Officers in the Reich, he had the feeling of having been taken unfairly unawares. It is true that he regarded Fritsch's Chief of Staff, Beck, with some misgiving, although all three of them, Fritsch, Beck and Paulus, possessed certain characteristics in common – they were all very thorough, conscientious and zealous workers, endowed with strategic and didactical ability; they were all averse to publicity and limelight, and were reluctant to admit that, in this era of 'politically-minded officers' demanded by Hitler, the professional soldier, fashioned to the noble ideal of chivalry, could no longer remain aloof from the events of the day.

Nevertheless Paulus, mindful of the exclusive, aristocratic clique of the old Reichswehr, which caused him, a son of the middle classes, to regard these aristocrats with some misgiving, certainly regarded the 'Fuehrer' as a patron. Here in his eyes was a man, who not only showed full appreciation of the potentialities of the Panzer arm, but who also gave it his passionate blessing and support; and, still as a son of the German (not Prussian!) middle classes, he was present during those great hours which seemed to be presaging the realization of the pan-Germanic dream – the *Anschluss* with Austria in 1938, and the annexation, in the teeth of deadly danger and the threat of a world war, of the Sudetenland in the autumn of 1938. Nor must it be forgotten that very large sections of the German people greeted these bloodless victories with great enthusiasm, even though they were achieved by blackmail.

The Second World War : Reichenau

War came in the sultry summer months of 1939. Elena Constance Paulus, the Rumanian aristocrat, regarded the attack on Poland as an unjust act. Her husband's thoughts were confined to his duty as a German officer. But he must, of course, have known only too well that the Reich was armed for, at the most, a restricted conflict and was not prepared for a world war.

On 26 August 1939, Paulus (a Major-General with effect from January 1939) was transferred from the post of Chief of Staff XVI Panzer Corps to that of Chief of Staff of the Tenth Army, which was being raised in Leipzig in the course of the unproclaimed mobilization. Commander-in-Chief, Tenth Army was General Walther Reichenau, up till then Commander-in-Chief, Army Group, Leipzig. After the Polish campaign, the Tenth became the Sixth Army and was destined to play a fateful role in both Paulus' career and in the swift rise and fall of Reichenau.

Paulus once said jokingly that Reichenau was keen on all the things for which he, Paulus, was physically pre-eminently suited – riding, sports and the like, while he himself preferred to sit at his desk and work. This was not meant to be in any way derogatory. It was the Chief of Staff's duty to take work off the shoulders of his Commander, and Paulus had always been a man who preferred to sit and pore over his maps.

In Reichenau he came into contact with one of the most unusual, most brilliant and most controversial figures among the leaders of the last German Wehrmacht. Walther v. Reichenau came from a Nassau family that had always produced senior officials for the State. Born in 1884, the son of a Prussian General, he was an excellent soldier, up-to-date in his outlook and even, perhaps, with a touch of genius in his make-up. By his marriage to the Countess v. Maltzan of Militsch, he became related both to the magnates of Silesia and to the ancient Prussian noble house of Schwerin. But this old world meant little to him. He was a man of immense ambition.

Although not in reality a student of politics, he devoted himself to political activity wherever and whenever it seemed to be in the interests of his advancement to do so. In 1932, through his uncle Friedrich v. Reichenau, a retired diplomat and the President of the German Overseas League, he came into contact with Hitler, whom the uncle greatly admired. In 1931-2, Colonel v. Reichenau, then Chief of Staff, Military District I, East Prussia, was accepted as being a National Socialist, and when General v. Blomberg, his District Commander, became Minister of Defence in 1933, Reichenau went to the Ministry with him. Twice, in 1934 and in 1938, he was within an ace of being appointed Commander-in-Chief of the Army or, alternatively, of being for ever precluded from such a possibility. In 1934 Hitler asked for his appointment, but was frustrated by the strong objections of the aged Field-Marshal v. Hindenburg, who regarded Reichenau firstly as too young for the post and secondly, quite frankly, as not very sound. In 1938, after the disgraceful dismissal of Fritsch, Hitler again toyed with the idea but was again frustrated, this time by the conservative Corps of Officers. Reichenau himself regarded himself – and no one could blame him – as the only man who firstly could carry out the Army reforms so long overdue since 1919-20, and secondly, who could gain complete, personal control of the Army. It may well be that in this connection the idea at the back of his mind was that he, Reichenau, would then be in a position to lay down the law to Hitler whenever the latter refused to toe the line in accordance with the wishes of Reichenau's Army.

Now Reichenau was a man devoid of all sentiment, at times, indeed, a cold-blooded, brutal man. Before 30 June, cold and calculating and well aware that blood must and would flow, he demanded a show-down with the S A. During the winter of 1939-40 – and this Paulus found utterly incomprehensible – for the maintenance of military discipline in the Sixth Army stationed in the Rhineland, Reichenau ruthlessly ordered to be shot any men who went absent without leave or had been guilty of any other act of ill discipline. He was also possessed of an unbridled passion to shine when and wherever there seemed to be an opportunity to do so – as a sportsman, at tennis, riding, athletics, putting the shot, swimming, pistol shooting, everything, without any regard for his early physical disabilities; and as a 'War Lord', who was always up with his foremost troops and did not shrink from swimming across a river in Poland or hurling himself personally into the battle in Russia, in order to master some critical situation or other. He was not an attractive personality, but he was certainly a bold and self-willed man, as ruthless towards himself as he was towards others.

Without the backing of an exceptionally conscientious, zealous and loyal Chief of Staff, such a man could not exist. Reichenau had no love for pettifogging routine, paper war and office work. In Paulus he had found a man whom he only had to ask, as he signed his papers, 'Well, Paulus, tell me – what orders am I issuing now?' He knew full well that Paulus invariably acted as he would have had him act.

And in this rough, blunt, untidy Commander-in-Chief with a shining eye-glass in his pale blue eye, his quiet, rather distinguished and sensitive Chief of Staff saw a man of action, a Commander whose delight was deeds, not words.

When asked what he thought of the less likeable features of Reichenau's character – quite apart from his political escapades, his way of life and his ruthlessness could well be repellent to many people – Paulus replied with an air of surprise that with that side of his Chief's life he had nothing to do. It is to Reichenau's credit that he not only appreciated the devotion to duty, the sound military knowledge and the mastery of his profession that Paulus displayed, but also lavished on him the affection of a father for his son. And it is typical of the unquestioning sincerity and guilelessness of Paulus that, regardless of whether he agreed with him or not over details, he saw and admired in Reichenau a supremely courageous Commander, always ready to act and always ready to accept the responsibility for his actions.

Reichenau and Paulus. In many ways this was a typical reproduction of the picture quite often to be found in the history of the Prussian and German Armies, the picture of a naturally gifted Commander-in-Chief in collaboration with a wise and thoughtful Chief of Staff. Bluecher and Gneisenau, Mackensen and Seeckt, Hindenburg and Ludendorff afford classical examples.

On the staff of the Sixth Army

As Chief of Staff, Tenth Army, renumbered Sixth Army, Major-General Paulus was present, under Reichenau's ægis, at the breathtaking victories over Poland, Belgium and France in 1939 and 1940. One of the highlights was accepting the capitulation of the Belgian Army under King Leopold III at the Château Anvaing on 28 May 1940. Still under Reichenau, he had also played his part in the practical preparations for Operation 'Sea Lion' – the invasion of England. The Army Staff was like one large family. Colonel Anton Freiherr v. Mauchenheim (Bechtolsheim), the Ia (Operations), and men like Captain v. Wietersheim, were old friends of Paulus, who also took a personal interest in the amenities provided for the Staff, such as messing and the like.

There is one point worth mentioning at this juncture. Paulus very probably did remark – or at least, he has never denied having done so – that he was 'no Reichenau'. By this he wished to convey that he did not feel himself in any way inferior to Reichenau, but was an entirely different sort of man. For example, he regarded 'playing to the gallery' at the front as something quite uncalled for. He felt, on principle, that a Commander's proper place was at his battle headquarters and that touch with the front should be maintained by regular tours of inspection to the Headquarters of Divisions and Regiments in the front line. In many of the more fanciful books and 'eyewitness' accounts of the second world war this attitude of his has been the subject of frequent adverse criticism.

Deputy Chief of the General Staff

Under Reichenau, the Sixth Army had gained the reputation of being a *corps d'élite*, and it was generally accepted that in its Chief of Staff it had one of the few senior General Staff Officers who had had years of experience in the raising and training of the Panzer Army and was well versed in the tactical employment of armour.

In the late summer of 1940, swayed presumably by the possibility or even, perhaps, the inevitability of a conflict with the Soviet Union, the Chief of the General Staff of the Army, Colonel General Halder, obtained the services of Paulus as his Oberquartiermeister I

– as the senior member, that is, of his Staff and as his Deputy Chief of the General Staff. For a long while, until after the conclusion of the campaign in France, this post had been held by a close friend of Beck, Lieut-General Karl-Friedrich v. Stuelpnagel, who, like Beck and Halder, was no friend of Hitler's. He had been succeeded for a brief period by General Mieth. But at this juncture, Halder, in view of the possibility of operations in the wide open spaces of eastern Europe, felt that his primary need was to have an adviser well versed in the tactical handling of armour. Apart from that, Paulus, like Manstein, was also regarded as a gifted field Commander.

As Oberquartiermeister I, Paulus was the third senior member of Army Headquarters after the Commander-in-Chief, Field-Marshal v. Brauchitsch, and the Chief of the General Staff, Colonel General Halder. Fundamentally and each in his own way, all three were typical examples of the highly trained General Staff Officers of the classical school of the first world war. Halder, reticent man though he was, has clearly shown in the letters he wrote to him that in Paulus he had quickly realized that he had someone who was more than a merely conscientious and trustworthy colleague. He regarded him as a friend at a time when the old school of soldiers was finding itself in continuous conflict with the new type of demagogic senior officer. And when Paulus assumed command of the Sixth Army in 1942, Halder followed his fortunes with the pride of a master for his most gifted pupil.

The post of Oberquartiermeister I of the Imperial General Staff had been a feature of the golden age of the General Staff as it was up to 1918. The post was originally created in the late 1880s with the object of achieving a closer co-ordination and a more cohesive organization of the very numerous branches of the General Staff. At the beginning of the Second World War the OQuI, in addition to being principal adviser and Deputy to the Chief of the General Staff, was also responsible for training and organization. Initially the Operations Branch was also under the OQuI; but when Paulus took over it was transferred to the direct control of the Chief of Staff.

The scope and authority of the post in 1940 could not, admittedly, compare with those previously wielded by, say, a Ludendorff who, as OQuI, to all practical purposes directed the entire war effort. The General Staff of the Army no longer personified the supreme direction of military affairs in the widest sense of the term, as it had done in the First World War, but had been greatly diminished in stature to the function of the directing instrument of just one of the three fighting Services. The major decisions were taken by Hitler who, in the Supreme Headquarters of the Armed Forces under Field-Marshal Keitel and the Directing Staff of the Armed Forces under General Jodl, had created a military organization of his own. Relations between Paulus and Keitel and Jodl remained cool all the time. And the Chief of the Army Branch of the Armed Forces Directing Staff, Lieut-Colonel v. Lossberg, was both a man of the old school of Staff Officer and at the same time a sharp critic of the whole new system of control and direction.

As soon as he took office in September 1940, the new OQuI realized that he was faced with a task which, to a student of the art of war and a planner, must have seemed of enthralling interest – the planning of the invasion of the Soviet Union. He approached his task solely from the purely military point of view, for the planning of a campaign of this nature is one of the most responsible tasks that a Staff Officer can be called upon to perform. At Army Headquarters opinion on the subject was divided. Halder never quite made up his mind whether the Soviet Union was planning an attack on Germany, as Hitler believed – or at any rate said he believed – or whether the very large-scale forward movement of Soviet troops into covering positions, on much the same scale, indeed, as the German concentrations, was a purely defensive and precautionary measure. The fact remains that the Soviet formations stationed on Russia's western frontier were taken completely by surprise by the German attack when it went in on June 22 1941. It is also a fact that a considerable number of senior Soviet officers had their own ideas about this massing of their troops on the western frontier, and not a few of them gave blunt expression to these views, in much the same way as did the officers of the German Panzer Regiments who raised their glasses to the advance on Moscow.

Paulus himself had had some Russian officers as pupils when he had been an instructor. Furthermore, as the result of the international connections of the Rosetti-Solescu family, a number of Russian emigrés had been frequent visitors to his mother-in-law's house – Prince and Princess Vassilchikov, Prince Gagarin, Count

Zubov, the Baroness Hoyningen-Huene and others; and all these had met there the German son-in-law of the house and Captain in the German Army. Bolshevism, as a way of life, was utterly repellent to him, and it remained so, in spite of the fact that, while a prisoner of war (and, in keeping with his character, after much thought), he felt ready to give his support to the 'German Officers' Association in the National Committee of Free Germany', and in spite of the fact that, under the influence of the unjustifiable 'preventative' war of 1941, he had come to regard close co-operation with the Soviet Union as the corner-stone of all future German policy.

But in the winter of 1940-1 all he had eyes for was his duty as a soldier. Details of the concentration of forces for the invasion of Russia will be found in Part II of this book. Suffice it here to say one thing: The deep divergence of opinion regarding operational objectives between Army Headquarters and Supreme Headquarters of the Armed Forces – or, expressed in terms of personalities, between Brauchitsch and Halder on the one hand and Hitler and his advisers, Keitel and Jodl, on the other, was never resolved until, in the crisis in the autumn of 1941, Hitler decided, against all the advice and plans of Army Headquarters, that the ultimate decision should be sought not by a thrust on Moscow but on the flanks.

In preparing the General Staff plan for Operation 'Barbarossa', Paulus had done all that mortal man could do. But he, like his Chief, Halder, was of the opinion that the decision, in so far as Britain, the principal adversary from 1939-40 was concerned, must be sought in the Middle East.

It was inevitable that while Paulus was engaged on this great planning task at General Headquarters in Zossen, the problem should also have been mentioned in the family circle in Berlin, greatly though the OQuI disapproved of such a thing. But he often found himself compelled to take home with him files which were not top secret, and such things as maps of the Middle East and Russia – for time was pressing. And occasionally he could not avoid using them in front of his family. His two sons, who were but rarely at home and for very brief periods at that, had long ago heard rumours that 'the balloon was soon going up against Russia'. Elena Constance, on the other hand, who was not merely a wife and a mother, but a woman of independent mind and sovereign judgment, had already come to the conclusion that the war against Poland had been unnecessary. The war against Russia, which was about to break out thanks to Hitler's hallucinations that the Soviet Union was the last continental bastion of a Britain still unconquered and obviously difficult to defeat, she regarded as demonstrably unjustified.

To these ideas, though discussions of the sort were distasteful to him, since they offended against his canons of professional secrecy, Paulus retorted that all these things were matters for political decision, in which the individual could expect to be granted no hearing; but that, in point of fact, there were also sound, purely military grounds for the undertaking of such a campaign. But what, Elena Constance objected, would become of them all and who would survive to see the end? There was quite a chance, countered Paulus, even a strong hope, that a victorious decision could be achieved in 1941 itself. One could not say for certain, of course, and could not categorically prophesy victory. But that was always so in war. Nevertheless, as he saw it, the situation was as follows: If a swift and energetic thrust were made into the heart of Russia, it was by no means impossible that the whole Bolshevist system, and with it all military resistance, would swiftly collapse. 'It is possible even,' he said, 'that the campaign will be all over in from four to six weeks. The whole structure may well collapse like a pack of cards at the first onslaught.'

At that time, Paulus, Deputy Chief of the Army General Staff, obviously accepted the thesis that the attack on the Soviet Union was the ultimate means by which Germany could enforce a reasonably satisfactory outcome to the whole war. Be that as it may, in those rare discussions in the family circle he never once put forward the argument that it was a question of forestalling Soviet aggressive intentions.

Even so, in an address to a restricted circle, which included the Fuehrer and the Commanders-in-Chief of the Armed Forces, he took as his theme the possibilities which would present themselves once Soviet Russia had been defeated. Then, he pointed out, the Mediterranean and the Middle East would become the real theatre of operations against Britain. This was once again voicing the old divergence of view in the choice of the strategic objectives in this war – should the war against Britain be waged directly by land, sea and air in the Mediterranean, the Near East and the island kingdom itself, or should the choice fall on the astonishing and fantastic detour via Soviet Russia?

The African Mission

The short space of time between his assumption of the duties of OQuI at Fontainebleau on 3 September 1940 and the launching of the surprise attack on Russia on 22 July 1941 was for Paulus a period of intense planning activity. Anyone who had been brought up as a soldier and taught to regard politics as a field of activity inappropriate for a man of his profession had no time to ponder over political combinations – and still less over internal political events. The Reich created by Adolf Hitler stood at the zenith of its might. These are things which people today, after the catastrophe, are very prone to misjudge and to assess wrongly.

Apart from the planning of Barbarossa,[1] Paulus was also engaged, albeit indirectly, in the negotiations being conducted with the Finnish General Staff on the possibilities of joint military action. At the end of March 1941, the *coup d'état* of the Jugoslav Army against the Prince Regent Paul and his pro-Axis cabinet completely upset the calculations for the eastern campaign. Paulus was sent to Budapest to discuss with the Hungarian War Minister and the Hungarian General Staff the question of joint operations against Jugoslavia.

Thanks to his irreproachable manners and his quiet air of self-possessed authority, both Hitler and Halder obviously regarded Paulus as the ideal man to handle delicate military negotiations of this nature, particularly as, in addition, through his wife he had influential connections with the new ally, Rumania. At that time a cousin of his wife was Lord Chamberlain at the Court of the by no means pro-German Queen Mother, Helene of Rumania.

The campaign against Jugoslavia and Greece in April 1941 not only caused a fatal postponement of the eastern operations, the opening of which had been planned for the middle of May, but it also raised new problems regarding the main thrust in the attack against the Russian colossus.

As a result of the defeats suffered by the Italian Army in North Africa, it was regarded as essential that an Army Corps under General

[1] Vide Part II, Chapter 2.

Rommel (Paulus' former brother officer in the 13th Infantry Regiment in Stuttgart) should be sent out to help the Italians. The commitment of German armoured and motorized forces in North Africa, dependent upon very insecure sea lines of communication, raised the question, in Halder's view, whether, having regard to the 'Barbarossa' plan, Germany possessed the means to mount yet another great offensive campaign, Operation 'Sonnenblume', in Libya and Western Egypt. Was it in any way possible, by means of careful planning which gave full consideration to the man-power, the material and the armament resources available, to mount two offensive campaigns – one against the British forces in Egypt, and the other against the eastern giant, which stretched from the Vistula to the Pacific Ocean? Halder's appreciation led him to the conclusion that North Africa (and with it the Mediterranean) would have to be treated as a secondary theatre of war, if the overthrow of the Soviet Union were accepted as a firm and positive objective. In this, however, he was frustrated firstly by the fact that each new theatre of war develops its own conditions and demands, and secondly by the fact that in the open spaces of the Libyan desert a man of Rommel's dynamic character was in command and imposed his own will on the course and scope of operations.

On 23 April 1941, General Halder noted in his diary: 'It is therefore essential to get a clear picture of conditions in North Africa as soon as possible. After due consideration, I decided not to fly there myself. I cannot go on a purely fact-finding mission; if I turn up there, I shall have the right to give orders. Army Headquarters on the other hand is nervous about this, as they say it will lead to difficulties with the Italian High Command. The real reason, of course, is something very different, and it is therefore perhaps better to send Paulus, who is an old and good friend of R(ommel) and is perhaps the only one who might, by his personal influence, succeed in putting the brake on that madcap!'[1]

This unduly harsh verdict on 'that madcap, Rommel', made in a moment of sudden, great and perplexed anxiety, throws a vivid light on the divergence of view between the bold offensive plans of the Panzer Gruppe, Africa, and the ideas of Army Headquarters.

[1] Halder Diaries: 23.4.41. It looks as though Halder put too high a value on the good relations between Paulus and Rommel.

The latter were, of course, very much more in the general picture than Rommel, who had no inkling of the vast and imminent operations in eastern Europe. On the evening of 23 April 1941, Paulus, accompanied by a few officers from the Operations and Administrative Branches of GHQ and from the Quartermaster-General's Branch, set off for Rome, *en route* to North Africa.

There he found that the Italian Army and Rommel's Afrika-korps, at the conclusion of their first offensive in East Libya, were in a precarious situation. The attack had been brought to a standstill at Sollum on the Egyptian frontier, with the stubbornly defended fortress of Tobruk in British hands in their rear. Paulus here ran into an old friend of his Alpenkorps days, Lieut-General Kirch-heim, who had been on a fact-finding mission to North Africa and was now in command of an armoured detachment of the 5th Light Division and about to launch an attack on Tobruk. On 1 May Paulus followed the whole operation from a forward position. The attack, made with inadequate forces, was repulsed.

Paulus remained in North Africa for two-and-a-half weeks. On 4 May, Halder noted in his diary: 'On my orders, sent by tele-printer, Paulus has remained in N. Africa. I'm very pleased that he can thus continue to hold a watching brief for our views, with which the Fuehrer agrees.' On 11 May he wrote: '1700–1930, Paulus. Report on his two-and-a-half week stay in Africa. Returned via Rome. Saw Mussolini. Situation in North Africa unpleasant. Ro[mmel], by exceeding his orders, has created a situation with which present lines of communication can no longer cope. Ro. is not up to the job.'[1]

After very searching discussions with Rommel, which had not been easy to conduct, Paulus, by virtue of the powers vested in him as Deputy Chief of the General Staff, gave strict orders that for the time being Rommel was to remain on the defensive and at all costs to hold on to Cyrenaica. Back in his own family circle he rather let drive about 'this thick-headed Swabian', who, he said, showed plainly that he wanted advice from no man, but who, equally, had no conception of the general situation. He found it extraordinary that, for publicity purposes, Rommel allowed himself to be surrounded all the time by a horde of war correspondents and Press photographers.

[1] Halder Diaries, 4 and 11 May 1941.

He regarded Rommel as 'an enterprising leader of men', but he rather doubted whether, taking the long view, he had correctly appreciated the situation in the North African theatre of war (a viewpoint which, to say the least of it, is open to controversy!)

Paulus, who for a long time had been hankering after an appointment at the front, debated in his mind whether he should not recommend to Army headquarters that a change be made in North Africa and that he himself should take command of the Afrika-korps. His wife's comment on the idea was cuttingly unsympathetic: 'Keep your fingers out of that pie! It won't do you any good to get put in the bag in Africa!'

Opposition to inhuman orders

The last five weeks before 22 July 1941, when the German armies poured into Russia, were fully occupied with final preparations, which included a visit to the Commander-in-Chief, West, Field-Marshal v. Witzleben, to discuss what deceptive measures could be initiated in the west (Operation 'Haifisch', or Shark), which, by creating the impression of an imminent offensive elsewhere, would serve as a screen for the real intentions in the East. On 16 May Halder noted in his diary: 'OQuI's branch seems overburdened with work at the moment, but I see no reason for any drastic changes.'

In his notes, Paulus has made no mention whatever of his views, either at the time or during the two years up to the fall of Stalingrad, on two orders which, together with the unsolved controversy on strategic objectives between Hitler and Army Headquarters – Moscow or the two flanks as the decisive factor – cast their shadow over the coming campaign and which, far more than the launching of an unjustifiable preventative war, branded the aggressor with the odium of conduct contrary to the terms of international law.

The so-called Commissar Order was issued as early as March 1941. Under it, the political commissars who accompanied all Soviet units were to be separated from the troops and not treated as prisoners of war, but were to be shot out of hand. On 13 May 1941 a further order, entitled the Barbarossa Jurisdiction Order, was issued, which decreed that civilians in the occuped eastern zones would not have the right to appeal to a Military Court and that misdeeds committed by members of the Wehrmacht against such civilians would not automatically be regarded as a Court Martial offence. Both clauses constituted a flagrant breach of international law; both were contrary to all the accepted traditions of the Prusso-German Army; both led to severe internal conflict within the Corps of Officers and to a latent conflict between Army Headquarters and Hitler. Field-Marshal v. Brauchitsch did at least try to circumvent the second clause by issuing a further order to the effect that the maintenance of strict discipline was the bounden duty of every soldier.

What Paulus thought about it can only be surmised from his actions as Army Commander. When he assumed command of the Sixth Army, he again reminded those under him that the Commissar Order was not to be carried out. Further, he cancelled the unfortunate and oft-quoted 'Severity Order', which Field-Marshal v. Reichenau had issued to the Sixth Army on 10 October 1941, 'Attitude to be adopted by troops in the eastern theatre.' This order contained, among other things, the following paragraph:

'There appears to exist a great deal of misconception regarding the attitude to be adopted by the troops towards the bolshevist system. The most important object of this campaign against the Jewish-Bolshevik system is the complete destruction of its sources of power and the extermination of the Asiatic influence in European civilization. In this connection, there devolve upon the troops tasks which go beyond the confines of normal military duty. In this eastern theatre, the soldier is not only a man fighting in accordance with the rules of the art of war, but also the ruthless standard-bearer of a national conception and the avenger of all the bestialities perpetrated on the German peoples. For this reason the soldier must learn fully to appreciate the necessity for the severe but just retribution that must be meted out to the sub-human species of Jewry....'

As has already been stated, this order by Field-Marshal v. Reichenau, which ended with an exhortation to the troops that it was their duty to 'destroy the fallacious, bolshevist teachings, the Soviet

State and its armed forces', and to 'exterminate' its repellent treacheries, was cancelled by an Army Order issued by Field-Marshal Paulus, in spite of the fact that the 'Fuehrer' had found it 'an excellent order' and had recommended that others should follow Reichenau's example. In the same spirit Paulus remained loyal to an old friend, the first Commander-in-Chief, East, in occupied Poland, General Blaskowitz, when the latter fell into disfavour for having written a memorandum protesting against the excesses committed by the SS in occupied territories. And from the evidence of what has survived of Paulus' correspondence, it is obvious that it was just those very officers who were imbued with the traditions of their Service – Field-Marshal v. Witzleben, Commander-in-Chief, West, General Oswald Lutz, dismissed in 1938, and that sharp critic of Supreme Headquarters of the Armed Forces, General Rudolf Schmidt, who never wavered in their trust and confidence in him. It is true that they all believed that the OQuI exercised more influence than he really possessed or himself thought he was justified in having.

At Fuehrer Headquarters and at the Front, 1941

On 22 June there began the great offensive against the Soviet Union, extending from the Black Sea to the Arctic Ocean, in the preparation of which Paulus had played so important a part. Did he still believe that, in certain circumstances, Stalin's kingdom would collapse like a pack of cards? Or had he some inkling of the severity of the struggle that was to follow?

At the beginning of the Russian campaign, he received a visit from Lieut-General Kirchheim of the Special Branch (Tropics), who had been attending a series of conferences at the new Army Headquarters, 'Fritz', in Mauerwald near Rastenburg. Kirchheim agreed with Paulus that in the North African campaign lines of communication constituted the decisive element. Now he asked Paulus whether he did not think that the same applied to the eastern theatre, particularly in winter? Paulus said that the difficulties which would have to be overcome during the winter were causing the greatest possible anxiety at Army Headquarters, particularly as the campaign had opened later than had originally been envisaged. But Hitler, he added, had in his particular manner brushed all this aside.

For a while he remained silent, then, controlling himself with an obvious effort, he said that when he himself had personally submitted on behalf of Army Headquarters a note on these difficulties to Hitler, the latter had flown into a rage and replied: 'I won't listen to any more of this nonsense about the hardships of our troops in winter! There's not the slightest need to worry about it, for there is not going to be a winter campaign. That you can confidently leave to my skill as a diplomat. All the Army has to do is to hit the Russians a few hard cracks. Then you'll see that the Russian giant has feet of clay. I herewith formally and emphatically forbid anyone to mention the phrase winter campaign to me again!'

Kirchheim was greatly taken aback. Then he started to talk about an article in the *Völkischer Beobachter*, which had waxed hilarious over a map published in the American newspapers showing a picture of the Russian Trans-Ural armament industry. Paulus brushed aside a number of maps lying on his desk and pointed to the one that remained there. It corresponded to the map which had caused such mirth among the publishers of the leading newspaper of the Third Reich. In his dry, objective manner, Paulus remarked: 'This is an accurate map of the Russian armament industry.'

'But that's the map that the *Völkischer Beobachter* is passing off as an American invention!' exclaimed Kirchheim.

'Yes – the American map agrees with our own latest information. And as far as I am concerned, I must say that the Fuehrer is wrong when he says: "Hit the Russian a few cracks and he'll collapse".'

After the first few weeks of the campaign and the tremendous successes achieved in them, Halder, it must be admitted, wrote in his diary on 3 July 1941 that the war had been won, though it had not yet been ended. And as regards this ultimate end, his Deputy very early had, to say the least of it, grave misgivings – though that does not mean that he was completely pessimistic.

This gives rise to the question of what he really thought about Hitler's leadership and of the principles underlying the creation of this new system of command, the functioning (or non-functioning) of which he was now admirably placed to observe from his post as one of the senior Staff Officers at 'Fritz' Headquarters on the eastern front.

Paulus cannot be described as either a National Socialist or an anti-National Socialist. For him as an officer, Hitler was the Head of the State and the Supreme Commander of the Armed Forces – no more and no less. Paulus thought that this man, though no trained soldier, had assessed the powers of resistance of the Western Powers more accurately than had the old General Staff. Like Reichenau, he had been greatly impressed by Hitler's address to the Chiefs of the Armed Forces on 23 November 1939. Among the Field-Marshal's papers is a note written by v. Reichenau and containing the most striking sentences of the Fuehrer's speech. The Second Reich, he had said, had missed the opportunity to gain *Lebensraum*, living space, and now here was another and unique opportunity. Reichenau had also found quite convincing the arguments on which Hitler based his moral right to march into the neutral States of Belgium and the Netherlands. Reichenau had added his own comment: 'I myself have learnt something and I agree with his (i.e. Hitler's) point of view, but the Wehrmacht – not yet.' His final comment is: 'Victory certain – of that I am quite convinced.' And at that time Paulus must have shared his conviction.

Paulus was also firmly convinced that, although he was a layman in military matters, Hitler had nevertheless displayed ability. His leadership, thought Paulus, had been cautious but sound – at Dunkirk in May 1940 and in his handling of the problem of 'Sea Lion' (the invasion of England).

Typical of his reactions is the attitude Paulus adopted during the great command crisis in August 1941, when the point at issue was whether a decision on the eastern front should be sought in a direct advance on Moscow, or whether it would be wiser firstly to clear up the situation on the flanks. On 4 August Halder wrote in his diary: 'Conference with Heusinger [Chief of Operations Branch] and Paulus, and in the evening with the C-in-C [Brauchitsch] on much the same lines. Instead of giving our Army Groups clear directives and leaving it to them to carry them out, we are confining the whole of our activities as controllers of the war effort to details, which in reality should be left to the Army Group Commander to decide. But if we are to do the former, we must be given a

clear exposé of what our political master regards as the correct objective. The alternatives are either to occupy the Ukraine and the
Caucasus as quickly as possible for economic reasons, or to concentrate on destroying the enemy. The former entails a demand for
complete liberty of action in the means available to us. Only in that
case we must not be subjected to interference. . . .' In this connection it should be noted that Halder and Paulus were of one
mind: the main objective of the eastern campaign must be the
capture of Moscow. But they realized equally that they would have
to obey if Hitler decided otherwise!

On 6 August, according to Halder's diary, a conference with
Hitler took place at Army Group South Headquarters (Field-
Marshal v. Rundstedt), at which Paulus as OQuI represented the
General Staff. At Halder's request, Paulus made some comments on
'questions of high strategy', during which he emphasised the sig-
nificance of Moscow. Halder notes in his usual laconic style: 'The
Fuehrer once more rejected the whole idea. He still sticks to his old
gramophone record of: 1 Leningrad (to be the task of Hoth), 2 The
Eastern Ukraine (forces for this to be reinforced by Guderian), and
3, only as a last resort, Moscow.'

If General Hoth's Panzer Group 3 and General Guderian's
Panzer Group 2 were turned north and south respectively, Army
Group Centre would find itself robbed of the armour it required for
its thrust on Moscow. To Halder (and undoubtedly to Paulus
as well) it had in the meanwhile become abundantly clear that they
had under-estimated the strength of the Russian colossus.

But after it had been decided, on Hitler's orders, to seek a decision
in the Ukraine in the south and to detach Guderian's armour for
the envisaged battle of encirclement in the vicinity of Kiev, Paulus,
while on a visit to Panzer Group 2, agreed with Guderian that his
forces were insufficient for the task. He telegraphed to Halder, recommending that the remaining corps of the Panzer Group should be
sent to Guderian and that his force be then placed under the command of the Second Army. This angered Halder, who noted in his
diary on 28 August 1941: 'Paulus has unfortunately allowed himself to be persuaded by him [Guderian]. I've no intention of
giving way. . . .'

Although Paulus did not agree with many of Hitler's military decisions (and there is ample evidence to show that he did not), he still acknowledged that 'the man had ability', and because he was convinced that the 'Fuehrer' did not issue directives or orders frivolously he was prepared to grant that Hitler had the right, in special circumstances, to demand that the German people at home should face hardship and sacrifice and still remain steadfast in their determination. He had for a long time felt secure under Hitler's leadership (a feeling that probably remained with him even during the first two months of the siege of Stalingrad), provided always that Supreme Headquarters, thanks to the excellent means of communication available, was kept precisely informed regarding the situations of the armies under its command. To give any consideration to the political implication that this might well be the crucial moment to come out openly 'for' or 'against' Hitler never entered his head. As a conservative officer of the old school, such an idea would never have occurred to him; and apart from that, to what, if indeed any, extent would it have been possible for a Commander-in-Chief on the eastern front and faced with a critical situation to take heed of the exortations of some anti-Hitler opposition and turn rebel? As far as Paulus was concerned, his one idea was to do the militarily correct thing in the military situation that confronted him.

In this he was, of course, a typical Staff Officer of that purely objective school, the Moltke Institute of a couple of generations ago – if, that is, one accepts as the last generation the 'Young Turks', Staff Officers of the type of Count Claus Schauffenberg, Henning v. Treschkow and Hans-Ulrich v. Oertzen, who showed great political courage such as had been displayed in byegone days by a Gneisenau.

Paulus' relations with Supreme Headquarters became cooler and cooler; and in this connection the influence of Elena Constance Paulus was not without considerable effect. She had nothing but haughty contempt for men like–Field Marshal Keitel, and she was constantly telling her husband that he was too 'good' – meaning too easy-going and too decent – for such people. Even his relations with so good a soldier and fundamentally so honest a man as General Jodl, Chief of the Supreme Directing Staff, suffered the same fate; and this was not solely the outcome of the latent rivalry between Army Headquarters and Supreme Headquarters of the Armed Forces, which had its origins in professionally objective divergencies of opinion, but as a result also of Paulus' own rather hypersensitive nature.

He had always displayed a certain measure of helplessness in the face of bad manners. Once, when he was delivering one of his addresses (which, he being the man he was, were always long and ranged far and wide) Jodl yawned rather obviously. Paulus was deeply offended, but he lacked the courage to tell Jodl to his face that that sort of thing was 'not done'. Instead, he later complained long and bitterly about it to the Army representative on the Directing Staff, Colonel v. Lossberg. Then again, as Hitler, with the connivance of his Supreme Headquarters, intervened more and more in the direct control of operations and his Staff Officers, in direct contrast to the scepticism and doubts that reigned at Army Headquarters, expressed loud optimism and lofty contempt for the enemy, Paulus' resentment grew stronger and stronger.

It has often been suggested that of all the Army Commanders Paulus, with his experience as OQuI, should surely have been the one man who should have been ready to make his own independent decisions, for with his own eyes he had seen the 'insanity' of Hitler's leadership. In point of fact, however, directly the reverse is the case. No one knew better than he how the eastern campaign was now being conducted – as the result of a meticulous planning of the preliminary concentration of force within the framework of the war as a whole, of exact calculation of frontage and precise distribution in depth, and of a co-ordinated distribution of Armies and Army Groups in the fabric of the general plan. Modern means of communication, telegraph, wireless, telephone, teleprinter, the shortening of space by means of air courier and regular inspections by air, seemed to make it possible (and the emphasis is on the word 'seemed') to control armies of millions precisely, indirectly and yet personally, in much the same way as in the Thirty Years War Count v. Tilly was confident that he could keep a firm hold of his squares of Walloon infantry and exercise close and direct control over them from his command vantage point on a nearby hillock.

Moltke once expressed sympathy for the Field Commander who found himself at the end of a wire. Nowadays, however, there is no such thing as a Field Commander. He has been replaced by senior officers in the framework of a functionally directed organization, a vast conglomeration of wheels within wheels. The great masterpiece of the Moltke school (for which, admittedly, the brains of Gneisenau had paved the way) had been the introduction of *Auftragsweise Führung* (Command in accordance with the given task), under which, while all had been put through a rigidly uniform course of instruction, each individual senior commander was allowed complete liberty, within the framework of the general plan, to carry out the task allotted to him as he saw fit. From this point of view, the old Prussian General Staff, as set up by Scharnhorst and Gneisenau, was undoubtedly the child of that liberal and civic age which inscribed the freedom of the individual and the ideal of universal education as the crest on its banner.

In this mass age, the mass leader has different standards. Even in the First World War Ludendorff had made great use of the telephone in order to be able to intervene directly in the conduct of operations. It can, then, be well imagined how grateful the rabble-rouser, Hitler, was for the invention of broadcasting and other means of news dissemination which, in a nation of sixty million, made it possible for the voice of this demoniacal Tribune of the People to be heard by millions and millions of believers, uncommitteds and downright adversaries simultaneously throughout the country. And this same Hitler undoubtedly had a flair for using these same means in the war against the 'Jewish-Asiatic Power', which he regarded as his primary enemy and the destruction of which, as he saw it, would transform Russia into a 'German India'. Gradually, under the influence of an incessant stream of fatuous flattery from men like Reichsmarschal Goering and Field-Marshal Keitel, he really came to regard himself as a military genius. But at the same time he mistrusted both the highly trained and coldly objective Staff Officers of the type of Halder and Paulus, and the whole of the old, aristocratic class of Army Generals; and, since he was in any case wholly lacking in any mental discipline, he made unlimited use of the technical means of communication in order to be able to intervene personally and directly in the control of operations. In his notes, Paulus points out how completely irreconcilable this method is with the traditionally accepted 'Auftragsweise' system mentioned above.

Hitler's interventions increased in number when in August 1941 he scored a final victory over the Generals in the great controversy on strategic objectives in the second phase of the eastern campaign. They increased further when Operation 'Typhoon' (the dash for Moscow), launched too late and hailed as a victory too early, ended in failure. The Commanders-in-Chief of the Army Groups and Armies now found their hands completely tied by Hitler. He not only forbade them to make any large-scale withdrawals on their own responsibility, but refused to allow them to make even minor and local readjustments of the line; at the 'situation conferences' at his 'Wolfsschanze' Headquarters he reserved to himself the right to control the allocation of reserves and to decide on the precise dispositions of formations down to and including Brigade Groups; and he maintained the same direct, personal control over the distribution and employment of formations transferred from other parts of Europe for service on the eastern front. It was, indeed, not long before he insisted, on some occasions, upon discussing in full conference the tactical employment of a section of tanks or a single battalion of infantry. The wire on the end of which he dangled his puppet commanders and, still more, the facilities offered to him by wireless communications were an irresistible temptation to this unbridled man at the head of affairs.

There is yet another aspect to all this. Right through – from Divisions, Corps and Armies up to Army Groups – the impression became prevalent, sometimes justly and sometimes unjustly, but always, in the circumstances, inevitable, that those 'at the top' were waging the war in a coldly impersonal and heartless manner. For there is a world of difference between a Supreme Commander who issues grim orders, demanding the sacrifice of whole major formations and entailing frightful suffering, impersonally through the medium of a wire, and one who, in the old manner, issues his orders to his subordinate commanders in person, sitting on a prancing charger in the midst of bursting shells or from the vantage point of his battle headquarters.

There is also a third point that should be remembered. The narrow confines of the Reichswehr imposed natural limitations upon the ambition to achieve advancement, and anyone who made an unexpected jump upwards became the object of wary jealousy. Now every soldier should be imbued with ambition, and a good deal of this laudable characteristic had, it is true, been handed on to the Corps of Officers of this new, functionalized form of leadership. Whoever desired promotion had to function conventionally in his allotted sphere of the machine. The era of the independent thinker was coming to a close, quite simply because, often to his own fury, he was never given the slightest opportunity of proving his worth. And it came to be accepted by all concerned that, in accordance with 'Standing Order No. 1 of January 1940', an Army Commander was not expected to bother his head about anything which was not directly connected with the immediate task allotted to him. As a result, the principle that an Army Commander was now nothing more than the commander of a sector whose job was to get on with whatever was under his very nose was put into practice in the Russian campaign of 1942 in a manner and to an extent that were quite grotesque. Paulus himself felt this very bitterly.

It was under this system of command that the OQuI now began to play an active role in the Russian campaign. His own ideal was to exercise broad operational control, while at the same time remaining in proper and adequate liaison with the various major Headquarters at the front. But at the 'Fritz' Headquarters he was nothing more than just one of the higher bureaucratic organs called upon to put into effect the operational ideas of the Fuehrer. And it was his personal tragedy that he, a disciple of the last school of truly operational General Staff Officers, should have enjoyed a relative measure of independence for so short a period.

With the front he maintained contact in his own way. Halder, who trusted him completely and had a high opinion of him, sent him forward from time to time to the individual Army Group sectors South, Centre and North. In August 1941, he saw his old Sixth Army again, in the southern sector under Reichenau, who loved to go careering round in the forefront of the battle and who, in Colonel Heim, now had a Chief of Staff as cautious as he was able. This visit took a heavy physical toll of Paulus. He had never given due consideration to the dysentry he had contracted during the Balkan campaign, and now he went down with the 'Russian sickness', an acute form of intestinal trouble akin to dysentry, which passed off eventually but was to attack him again later in the dry heat of the summer of 1942.

Apart from his tours of inspection, he received a considerable number of letters from the front – from old brother officers and from younger Staff Officers of his own branch, who had gone on service and who now wrote him letters full of grave misgivings and anxiety.

Thus, tied though he was for the most part to his desk, he was by no means out of touch with the front and the world at large. One lesson which he learnt was the enormous value, in this centrally controlled system of command, of meeting the complaints from the front, whether justified or otherwise, and whatever his own feelings may have been, with an outward show of confidence, and of sending explanatory, encouraging and sympathetic replies to his correspondents.

The 1941 campaign petered out in the winter crisis before Moscow. Throughout the whole year and a half that Paulus spent at Army Headquarters, the man with whom, next to Halder, he became most intimate was General Fellgiebel, the Head, first of the Army Information Services and then of the Information and Communications Branch of Supreme Headquarters – a man who had always been a consistent critic of Hitler and seldom made any secret of the fact. Brauchitsch, the Commander-in-Chief of the Army, was dismissed, and shortly after his dismissal Paulus suggested to Halder that things would perhaps become simpler if Hitler himself assumed command of the Army (as, in fact, he did on 19 December 1941). To Lieut-Colonel Lossberg, who tried to persuade him that Manstein should succeed Brauchitsch, Paulus gave an evasive reply, saying that that was a question which did not come within the competence of his official position.

Major Coelestin v. Zitzewitz, a General Staff Officer who later became Army Headquarters Liaison Officer with the Sixth Army in Stalingrad, has stated that at the turn of the year 1941–2, when he went to say goodbye to Paulus prior to assuming the post of Liaison Officer, Ninth Army, Paulus said to him: 'Before the outbreak of war with Russia, on orders of the CGS I ran a large-scale war game, and at the end of it I jotted down on paper what I thought would happen. Everything has occurred exactly as I foretold. It's all in writing in that safe' (pointing to a corner of his office). 'And I'm just wondering whether, when I have the time, I shall just turn in and sleep and sleep, or whether I'll have another go at those notes. I think I'll probably do the latter.'

Zitzewitz felt that before him was a man who had been over-worked to the point of exhaustion. And a characteristic of this man who throughout these years kept so tight a hold on his self-control was the nervous twitching which affected the left side of his face. Even so, this reserved, aloof man would continue to do his duty to the very end.

Commander-in-Chief, Sixth Army

In the meanwhile Paulus' career had already entered upon its decisive phase. The twin shadows of the eastern autumn and winter with their seas of mud, their icy winds and their blanket of deep snow were now dangerously imminent. But Hitler not only persisted too long with his offensive against Moscow, but also ordered Army Group South, under Field-Marshal v. Rundstedt, to advance across the lower Don in the direction of the Caucasus; and at Rostov, where the Don flows into the Sea of Azov, this offensive had ground to a halt.

Rundstedt demanded permission to withdraw his Army Group to a shorter winter line on the River Mius. Hitler mistrusted this grumbling, growling bear of a Junker from Courland (who nevertheless had hitherto always obeyed him!). He rejected the request. Rundstedt asked to be relieved of his command. This struck Hitler as being unseemly in the extreme. It was a General's job to obey his, Hitler's, orders – even if he did not understand the point of them. But – he acceded to Rundstedt's request. On 3 December, Field-Marshal v. Reichenau, Commander-in-Chief, Sixth Army in the Kharkov area, was appointed C-in-C Army Group South (while still retaining for the time being command of the Sixth Army). Reichenau, having completed the withdrawal to the Mius line which by then had become quite inevitable, reported his action, carried out, as he said with blunt and admirable aplomb, 'in anticipation of your concurrence. . . .'

Hitler accepted the *fait accompli*. Like Rommel, Reichenau in his eyes was a 'People's General' and a 'true National Socialist'.

On 3 December, the day on which Reichenau assumed command

of Army Group South, Hitler was at Sixth Army Headquarters in Poltava (the town in the vicinity of which, in 1709, was decided the fate of King Charles XII of Sweden, the first western monarch to declare that the great Power in eastern Europe must be smashed by force!). At dinner, eating his potato puffs with millet and pumpkin, Hitler sat between General v. Sodenstern, Chief of Staff Army Group South, and Field-Marshal v. Reichenau. He spoke quite frankly about the tension that had existed between himself and Reichenau. Brauchitsch had told him, he said, that of the Army Commanders on the eastern front all but two had been in favour of continuing the advance across the Dnieper. 'Had I known that you, Reichenau, had been one of those two, I would at least have asked you why.' Then for half-an-hour he discoursed on the role played by millet in the sustenence of soldiers from time immemorial. Reichenau drew his own conclusions from this frankly expressed tribute to his judgement, for, 'thruster' though he undoubtedly was, he had issued repeated warnings against making too great demands on the troops in one major offensive after another.

Taking the long view, it was obviously impossible for one man – and a man, moreover, who had a complete disregard for his physical disabilities – to continue indefinitely to command in person both Army Group South and the Sixth Army, with two large Staffs under v. Sodenstern (Group) and Heim (Army), even after both Staffs had been concentrated in Poltava. Reichenau recommended that Paulus, his old Chief of Staff, should take over command of the Sixth Army. This suggestion fitted in admirably both with the wishes of Paulus, who for a long time had been yearning for an operational command, and the ideas of Halder, who felt it was only fair that his talented Deputy should be given his chance, sorry though he himself would be to part with him.

With effect from 5 January 1942, in the middle of a most vexatious winter crisis, with the enemy launching simultaneous blows in the Moscow and Kharkov areas, the OQuI, promoted now to full General, assumed command of the Sixth Army. As far as that revered shibboleth, the seniority roster, was concerned, it was a chance that might well have aroused the envy of others. Paulus had never before commanded even a Regiment, let alone a Division or a

Corps; his last active appointment with troops had been that of Chief of Staff, Sixth Army, eighteen months previously; in his new command there were several Generals senior to him – his old friend, Karl Hollidt (a man devoid of envy), was commanding XVII Corps; General Heitz, the former Judge Advocate General, was commanding VIII Corps. And now a young General from the Staff stepped in over their heads.

A good two weeks, it is true, were spent in the formalities of handing and taking over before Paulus assumed actual command. One of those concerned gave open expression to his gratification – Field-Marshal v. Reichenau. Among the Paulus papers is a message of good luck, written on thick, Sixth Army notepaper by Reichenau in merry mood at a farewell party to two departing Staff Officers:

'Dear Paulus!

Good luck! I can think of no one in whose hands I would rather see the Army than yours. Perhaps I shall. In all sincerity,

> Yours,
>> v. Reichenau.'

'Perhaps I shall.' This may mean that Reichenau had not yet received official intimation of Paulus' appointment; but it could, on the other hand, well have been one of those mysterious premonitions, a presentiment that he, Reichenau, would not live to see the implementation of his recommendation. In any case, when he put Paulus' name forward Reichenau knew that his old Chief of Staff was taking over the best Army in the Group. And it was because they were so essentially different in every respect that they understood each other so well.

Three days later, on 12 January 1942, Field-Marshal v. Reichenau went for his usual cross-country run in a temperature of over twenty degrees below zero. When he appeared in the Mess for lunch he looked extremely ill. He admitted that he felt far from well, ate very little, signed a few papers and then, as he was leaving the Mess, he collapsed. It was a severe heart attack, and he was unconscious. The Medical Officer who normally attended him, Dr Flade, happened to be away on duty in Dresden and was summoned hastily to return. Colonel Heim informed Hitler of what had occurred, and the latter immediately arranged that the Reichenau family doctor,

Professor Hochrein, who was serving with Army Group North, should be flown by special aircraft to Poltava. On 17 January, still unconscious, the Field-Marshal was strapped into an armchair and flown to Leipzig for treatment. At an intermediate stop in Lemberg the aircraft crash-landed. Reichenau received severe head injuries, and it is not known whether he had already died *en route* or whether he was still alive when the plane crashed. In any case, however, on the evening of 17 January the Leipzig hospital officially confirmed that the Field-Marshal was dead.

In great haste, Field-Marshal v. Bock, who in the middle of December had relinquished command of Army Group North for health reasons and was now convalescing, was offered command of Army Group South. Bock accepted. But with the death of Reichenau there departed a Commander-in-Chief who was not only the ideal superior for Paulus but also one who regarded Paulus as a man after his own heart. This does not imply that Bock and Paulus were always at loggerheads with one another. But in the relationship between Reichenau and Paulus there had been that extra element, to which personal friendship alone can give birth.

On 20 January Bock assumed command of the Army Group and Paulus took over the Sixth Army. A series of heavy defensive winter actions lay before them. As far as Sixth Army was concerned the order of the day was, quite simply: 'Hold on and stand fast!' No finesse in the art of war was called for; all that was required was steadfast tenacity. Bock, himself ridden on a tight rein by Hitler and Supreme Headquarters, was forced, against his own inclination and experience, to exercise the same rigid control over his subordinate commanders.

Colonel Heim, now Chief of Staff under Paulus, has described the change in Commanders-in-Chief, Sixth Army in the following terms: '*Le roi est mort, vive le roi!* Within a few days the new C-in-C had firmly grasped the reins that had slipped from his deceased predecessor's grasp. I was myself quite happy about things, for I knew we should make a good "two-in-hand". He sat in the same chair as the late Field-Marshal and he used the same pens and pencils; and he was every inch a soldier, with a superb mastery of his profession. And yet, in appearance, how utterly different he was.' Well groomed and with slender hands, always beautifully turned-out with gleaming white collar and immaculately polished field-boots, he presented such a contrast to his rugged and always deliberately battle-stained predecessor.

'Before me there now stood not a massive body on sturdy legs but a slender, rather over-tall figure, whose slight stoop seemed somehow to be a gesture of goodwill towards those of smaller stature. Instead of the fresh face of the Field-Marshal, with his small yet sparkling light blue eyes, were the slender head and features I knew so well. Was it the face of an ascetic? For that it was hardly severe enough. Rather, I would say, it was the face of a martyr. . . .

'And their characters were as different as were their physical attributes. Where before a broad and worldly wisdom had been in command, taking seemingly snap decisions, but decisions which so often turned out to be unerringly correct, there now ruled a trained mind, sober, cool and calculating. In the place of an agile intellect, quick to grasp the essentials of any problem, there was now a brain which examined every aspect from every possible angle, which painstakingly separated the wheat from the chaff, which advanced slowly, logically, step by step, until absolute clarity led it, almost laboriously, to the correct decision. And instead of categorical orders, we now had irrefutable, convincing argument and proof. . . .'

Paulus' first Chief of Staff was destined soon to become commander of XXXXVIII Panzer Corps in a tragically hopeless situation – and thus to join the ranks of the many Generals who learnt to their cost how the Fuehrer and Supreme Commander was wont to set them impossible tasks and then brutally to call them to account on the grounds of 'personal incompetence'. He recalls yet another characteristic of the Army Commander who, he says, having taken some decision in the evening, would sometimes alter it the next morning, saying that he had spent the night thinking over the problem and was now quite clear as to what must be done.

But – and this applies particularly to the second phase of the Stalingrad operations, the encirclement – once this extremely methodical and, at times, over-meticulous man had reached a decision which he knew to be right, he adhered to it and exhibited a 'thick-headed obstinacy' which is normally attributed to the Westfalian rather than to a man of his origins.

It was this same feeling that he needs must examine every problem minutely and from every possible angle which caused him to be un-remitting in his endeavours constantly to obtain first-hand information about conditions at the front – without, however, indulging in the gasconades so dear to Reichenau's heart. He paid regular and frequent visits to the battle headquarters of his formations, down to Divisions and Brigade Groups; and he regarded these visits as essential pre-requisites to his own appreciation of the situation. In the same way as he had done his best, as OQuI, not to lose touch with the troops in the field by means of letters, conversations with men returned from the front and tours of inspection, now, as Commander-in-Chief, he seized every opportunity of talking with officers of all ranks at the front in his determination to obtain a true and clear picture. All this was done very unobtrusively, for Paulus disliked and avoided ostentation in any shape or form.

He showed great consideration for the comfort and well-being of his subordinates, from the Chief of Staff right down to the most humble despatch-rider and batman. As the final authority on matters of discipline and martial law, he displayed a precise punctiliousness towards officers and other ranks alike. Typical is the following case: A young infantry soldier was court-martialled on a charge of feigning an injury to his leg in order to avoid going into action, was found guilty and, as this was 'cowardice in the face of the enemy', was condemned to death. The Medical Officer had certified that the man was fit for service, and the Commanding Officer had pressed for the supreme penalty. Paulus, by whom the sentence had to be confirmed, decided to order an X-ray examination. This showed that the accused had a broken bone in his leg. Then the whole story came out. The young soldier, through fear of being accused of malingering or of being branded as a coward, had done his best to carry on. He was, of course, immediately released and transferred to hospital.

A case like that of the two Generals, Stumme and Freiherr v. Boineburg, which resulted in the latter being reprimanded for improper conduct, affected him deeply. Hitler had accused the two Generals of having committed a breach of security regulations, and Paulus, on the ground that ultimate responsibility rested with him as the senior officer involved, felt that he ought to have demanded that disciplinary action be taken against himself.

Another facet of this picture is provided by the fact, already mentioned, that he had at once cancelled the 'Reichenau Order' of 10 October 1941, which he found revolting in the extreme, in spite of its having been highly commended by the 'All Highest'. And to that may also be added the fact that he refused to countenance any further compliance with the 'Commissar Order' (though, in this connection, it must be admitted that according to Jodl's diary (6.5.42) the order had already been cancelled unofficially).

It would appear, too, that Reichenau himself, fundamentally a brutal man but also a man of very shrewd commonsense, had paved the way for a change of outlook as regards the treatment of the Russian, or rather the Ukrainian population in the occupied territories. Among his effects was found the draft of a memorandum to the Fuehrer in which he suggested that the Ukrainian population should be more generously treated and might by this means be persuaded to make common cause with the Germans in their fight against Bolshevism. As the contents of this memorandum coincided with his own views on the subject, v. Bock sent it to Army Headquarters. That Paulus himself gained the confidence of the Ukrainian population is proved by the message of congratulation, found among his papers, which the Ukrainian notables had addressed to him on the occasion of his victory in the battle of Kharkov at the end of May 1942.

Defensive battles in the snow and ice

The situation which faced General Paulus when he assumed command of the Sixth Army on 20 January 1942 was a somewhat precarious one. The Soviet offensive over the Donets on each side of Isium had made a deep bulge in the southern flank of the Sixth Army. In the Losovaya, Ligovka and Liman sectors the enemy was pressing forward on Poltava. That was the situation as he found it. He moved his command post forward to Kharkov, while Army Group Headquarters remained at Poltava. The most acute danger spot seemed to be the dividing line between the Sixth and Seventeenth Armies, immediately south of Ligovka. Here the enemy's ultimate objective was undoubtedly a break-through to the Dnieper crossing at Dnepropetrovsk. All this was happening in a temperature of thirty to forty degrees below zero. The roads were ice-bound, the railways on the German side had all but ceased to function, fodder for the transport animals was inadequate, and fuel, in all the formations whose mobility depended on it, was in extremely short supply.

Paulus' first consideration was the concentration of reserves behind his right flank. But reserves, like reinforcements from home, were arriving in driblets and their allocation remained in the hands of Army Headquarters, which, in practice, meant that the concurrence of Supreme Headquarters had to be obtained at one of the 'situation conferences' held twice daily before any action could be taken. By the end of January deep snow and the bitter cold, which slowed down all movement to a crawl, caused a further deterioration in the situation.

On 4 February 1942 Field-Marshal v. Bock noted in his diary: 'According to the British radio, Timoshenko is aiming at the recapture of Kharkov and Dnepropetrovsk, with the object of depriving the Germans of the springboard from which to launch their Spring Offensive against the Caucasus. . . .' (Marshal Timoshenko was the C-in-C of the Soviet Army Group South, a soldier of the revolution, a man of 'proletarian', probably peasant, origin, but still by no means lacking in talent as a Commander.)

Bock's diary also notes a report from Paulus, dated Kharkov, 6 February 1942, in which the latter states that Infantry Regiment 208, which had received orders to prepare for a counter-attack on Alexeyevskoye on the northern fringe of the Isium bulge, had lost no fewer than 700 men from frost-bite and exhaustion. Such, then, was the merciless winter war in the east which now had to be endured. And the Sixth Army under its new Commander, without experience of this type of defensive warfare, stood the test admirably. By about the middle of February it was more or less certain that an enemy break-through in depth to the very important Dnieper crossing at Dnepropetrovsk had been circumvented. In some places, indeed, it had even been possible to straighten out the Isium bulge. And in this connection it must be remembered that v. Bock was commanding a front which stretched from the Crimea to north of Bielgorod in central Russia.

Bock regarded with, to say the least of it, critical scepticism the possibility of a new German offensive in the southern sector with the object of capturing the Caucasian oilfields. He assessed correctly the enemy's ability to mobilize large fresh reserves and with them to intervene and disrupt German offensive preparations; and he regarded the building up of strong German reserves in the Kharkov area as a matter of urgency. On the other hand, his Chief of Staff, General v. Sodenstern, was informed by Halder at the beginning of March that the Fuehrer had had but little time to examine plans for extensive operations and had not yet been able to read Bock's memorandum of 30 January. This was the other side of the medal as regards the campaign in Russia. Paulus, too, was becoming acquainted with it from a new angle. But it was not in the power of a solitary Army Commander to put a spoke in the wheels of this vast and queerly controlled machine.

March brought forth a fresh crisis in the Kharkov area between Liman and Volchansk in the north. The frontages covered by the divisions of the Sixth Army were anything from fifteen to twenty miles. Bock noted in his diary on 15 March 1942: 'Tomorrow I shall discuss the whole question of the future conduct of operations with Paulus. The essential thing is to keep calm.' But, in this instance, 'keeping calm' was only another way of saying hang on at all costs, until the effects of the new, local counter-attacks begin to make themselves felt. For a short while, it looked as though the enemy armour might succeed in breaking through to Kharkov. In this situation, Bock, in spite of certain misgivings, allowed Paulus a free hand, confident that he would correctly appreciate the situation. Later it became clear that Paulus had taken too gloomy a view. The planned counter-attack of General Breith's Group (3 Panzer Division and attached units) had been robbed of its striking power by the withdrawal from it, at Paulus' request, of some of its units. Army Group had appreciated the situation more correctly than had Sixth Army. Paulus also learnt several lessons during these months of, as it were, apprenticeship – he was far too conscientious a man not to have done so. Nevertheless, after these events Bock came to the conclusion that some change must be made in the leadership of Sixth Army. In its present set-up, he thought, it lacked the 'holy fire'. Paulus was 'a first class fellow' but, thought Bock, Heim would have to go. In this he did Heim an injustice. But Halder agreed.

At the beginning of May, Heim was relieved by Colonel Arthur

Schmidt, who remained at Paulus' side until the very end in Stalingrad. Schmidt, like Paulus himself, did not come from a traditional Army family. But from the time that he, the son of a Hamburg merchant, volunteered in 1914, he had been a dedicated soldier. And without question he was a man of immense enterprise and mental ability. Exactly as had been the case with Paulus himself, Schmidt, from the point of view of the revered seniority roster, had attained the much sought-after post of Chief of Staff as a comparatively junior officer. Not a few of the Generals, apparently, took this amiss – more indeed than Paulus' emergence straight from the General Staff incubator, as it were, to Commander of an Army.

Instructive crises : the Battle of Kharkov

On 5 April, while the Soviet winter offensive was coming to a standstill, thanks to stubborn German resistance and the fact that this resistance prevailed until the spring thaws made movement all but impossible, the Fuehrer issued his Directive No. 1 for the Summer Campaign, 1942.

The campaign, it said, must bring final victory in the East. The Directive laid down two objectives:

1. Operation 'Nordlicht' – the capture of Leningrad and the creation of a land link with the Finnish allies. (Army Group North.)
2. The main operation envisaged in the southern sector, provisionally named Operation 'Blau', was the break-through to the Caucasus. This operation was divided into four sectors:
(a) Break-through on the Don in the north to Voronezh.
(b) Destruction of enemy forces facing Sixth Army to the east of Kharkov in the Volchansk area and to the east of it. In this operation, Fourth Panzer Army would co-operate by wheeling south from the Don.
(c) Existing Army Group South (v. Bock) to be split into two Army Groups – B (Bock) Sixth and Fourth Panzer Armies, and A (Field-Marshal List) Seventeenth and First Panzer Armies. Both groups to operate in unison in a pincer movement on Stalingrad.
(d) Conquest of the Caucasus up to the line Batum-Baku (Black Sea-Caspian), including the oil-bearing regions in the North Caucasus and Azerbaijan.

The Directive, though admittedly making very heavy demands on the generally inadequate forces available, did lay down a sequence of events that was both logical and carefully co-ordinated. It envisaged, as an essential pre-requisite to the launching of the two major offensives, firstly, the occupation of the whole of the Crimea, including the heavily fortified land and sea fortress of Sevastopol, by Eleventh Army under General v. Manstein, and secondly, the rectification of those heritages from the winter campaign, the two bulges at Isium and Volchansk – Operations 'Fridericus I and II' and 'Wilhelm' respectively.

In April 1942 there arose a sharp controversy regarding the sequence and timing of these three preparatory operations between Bock, a man of very independent mind and great vision, on the one hand, and Army and Supreme Headquarters (i.e. Hitler) on the other. Bock wished to launch 'Fridericus I' from south west of the Donets; Hitler insisted that it should go in from the north east, from Sixth Army area. Bock urged that advantage should be taken of the favourable weather conditions to launch the Volchansk attack at once; Hitler refused even to consider such an attack until at least part of the Crimean operations had been completed and the Kerch isthmus had been retaken. Bock from the outset had a feeling that the enemy might well launch a new drive on Kharkov and thus throw the German offensive preparations completely out of gear; and when he asked Halder bluntly whether such a possibility had been thought of in the Fuehrer's calculations, all that Halder could reply was: 'No.' The German forces concentrated in the Kharkov area, he added, were so strong that the enemy would hesitate to attack them.

Before any satisfactory agreement had been reached, however, all these controversies were rudely interrupted by the enemy. But they do nevertheless shed an illuminating light on the fact that scarcely had the major offensive Operation 'Blau' got under way, than Bock was abruptly dismissed because he was an awkward senior commander with a mind of his own.

The interruption was caused by the massive counter-offensive launched by Marshal Timoshenko on 9 May 1942. It is highly probable – though not certain, since the Russian General Staff has not yet published any official account – that the Soviet Supreme

Command (STAVKA), under Stalin with Marshal Shaposhnikov as his principal adviser, was aware of the objectives of the German summer offensive, which had been discovered either in the course of normal reconnaissance or by their Secret Intelligence Service.

Be that as it may, between the 10 and 20 May Timoshenko extended the Isium bulge and with very strong forces thrust deep into the assembly areas of the German offensives; and though by so doing he did not completely destroy the German plans and timetable, he greatly delayed their implementation.

The course of the second battle of Kharkov, which continued until the end of May, is described in Part II of this volume. For Paulus the battle was a new test, and the most severe that he had so far been called upon to face. Once again the applied art of operational leadership played, initially, a smaller part than the ability of the troops to hold on. The Sixth Army had to check the deeply probing thrusts of enemy armoured, motorized, cavalry and infantry formations and hold them until the counter-measures on the deep southern flank (in reality, Bock's conception of Operation 'Fridericus I') began to take effect. The Chiefs of Staff of both Bock and Paulus were in favour of this 'large-scale solution', while Bock and Paulus themselves preferred localized, temporary expedients as opportunity offered – though Bock in his diaries states that he was originally in favour of the 'large-scale solution' but had been compelled to rest content with the lesser until such a time as Army Headquarters (Halder), with Hitler's concurrence, sanctioned more comprehensive action.

In this instance Halder, whose advice Hitler for once accepted, was right; and Paulus had to admit to himself that Army Headquarters was often able to arrive at a more correct appreciation of the situation as a whole than the individual, functionally-bound Army Commander. On a man who was so essentially logical in all his mental processes and so staunch a protagonist of logical and precise planning such an admission had a deep and lasting effect.

At the end of May the spring battle for Kharkov came to a close. The final result was a great victory for the Germans, who surrounded and captured or destroyed a very considerable portion of the enemy armies that had participated in the Soviet offensive. After the battle, Bock was full of praise for Paulus' leadership.[1]

Paulus himself, however, was far from being puffed up with pride. After the battle, talking to his son Ernst Alexander, who as a Panzer officer had taken part in the engagement and had been wounded in it, he gave his views in more or less the following words: 'The Russians, of course, suffered the most frightful losses at the hands of your Panzer troops. The whole battlefield was strewn with hordes of destroyed Russian tanks. A Russian officer who fell into our hands told us that Timoshenko himself became involved in one of the tank engagements and that when he saw with his own eyes how his forward troops, and particularly his tanks, were being literally shot to pieces by the attacking German forces, he exclaimed: "this is frightful!" and then, without another word, turned and left the battlefield.' His son, however, had a feeling that his father was not expressing satisfaction but was rather asking himself how many more tanks and reserves could this hydra-like foe produce in the future?

For his part in the battle of Kharkov Paulus was awarded the Knights' Cross, a decoration which at that time had not fallen victim to the general inflation of the later war years. The name Paulus started to appear in the Press. For a brief and fugitive period, Paulus became a show-piece of the National Socialist propaganda in much the same way as Rommel. Congratulations poured in from other Generals, from former officers on his staff, from half-forgotten relatives, old comrades of the First World War, girl friends of his sister and Rumanian relatives of his wife. His photograph began to appear in all the illustrated papers. And, as is only natural, many officers who had previously served under him, now wrote to remind him of their existence in the hope that Paulus might get them promotion, some job they were after or, perhaps, a transfer to the General Staff.

The advance on Stalingrad

On the Aidar, the Chir, the Don and the Volga summer began to stride across the Steppes. After a period of heavy rains and rumbling

[1] Bock's letter of appreciation is in possession of the Paulus family.

thunder storms, new offensive enterprises were set afoot. The Sixth Army straightened out the Volchansk bulge, north east of Kharkov. Then came the new major offensive, Operation 'Blau'. Had the enemy suffered decisively crippling losses at Kharkov? Was he gathering reserves (as seemed to be the case), or was he planning an evasive withdrawal into the depths of his limitless eastern territories? These were the main questions that were being asked.

It seemed almost as though fate decided to hint at the answers. On 19 June 1942, Major Reichel, GSO I of 23 Panzer Division, XXXX Panzer Corps, paid a visit by Storch helicopter to the front. Quite unnecessarily and wholly irresponsibly he took with him the operation orders and maps for phase one of Operation 'Blau'. The pilot lost his way, and the machine was shot down between the lines; and before a German patrol could recover the bodies of the GI and his pilot, these documents were already in Russian hands. The Soviet High Command was thus presented with the detailed intentions of Operation 'Blau', Phase I – to attack and capture Voronezh on the Don in order to secure the German north flank. Though this, of itself, might well have had far-reaching and very adverse effects, since by then it was too late to make any alterations in the plan, in fact it produced a quite grotesque reaction which was all to the Germans' advantage. From the documents he had captured, the enemy jumped to the conclusion that, having taken Voronezh, the Germans intended to press on northwards to Moscow! He therefore massed his troops north of the Don and left but thinly held the Don elbow in the south-east, at which the German main thrust was directed.

Hitler now intervened. In spite of Field-Marshal v. Bock's representations, he called for disciplinary action against the two officers who, in his opinion, were primarily responsible, General Georg Stumme, GOC XXXX Panzer Corps, and Lieut-General Freiherr v. Boineburg, GOC 23 Panzer Division. Order No. 1, which laid down that no individual was to know more than was essential for the execution of his immediate task, was to be strictly obeyed, Hitler directed, and any further breach would be severely punished.

To summarize briefly the salient features of the events in Army Group South's sector since the end of June: Victory followed upon victory, but the Supreme Command, ignoring the ever-increasing losses in men and material, the unending crises as regards the supply of fuel so vital to the armoured and motorized formations, the backbone of the armies in this war of movement over vast distances, never for one moment considered giving the armies concerned – and particularly the Fourth Panzer and the Sixth Armies – a respite or of organizing any system of relief for the exhausted and battle-weary formations.

And even though victory followed upon victory, the final ultimate victory seemed to be as far off as ever. Brilliantly though Paulus was able, under these conditions, to exercise all his consummate skill as a commander in the field, the decisive victory, the ultimate aim of the art of leadership, eluded him.

From 28 June 1942 the new German summer offensive rolled steadily forward. On 3 July the Sixth Army, together with the now dreaded XXXX Panzer Corps and the Second Hungarian Army, annihilated an enemy force at Stary Oksol, on the Sixth Army front. 40,000 prisoners fell into German hands. Would the spring of enemy manpower never run dry? It seemed to be inexhaustible.

All these, however, were secondary operations. The major objectives were the operations envisaged in Phases III and IV – the pincer move on, and the capture of, Stalingrad, the great industrial metropolis of South Russia, with its armament factories and its important river docks on the Volga, and the conquest of the Caucasian oilfields.

Greatly to the dissatisfaction of Field-Marshal v. Bock, Hitler had split the old Army Group South into two, Army Groups B and A. Bock, the Prussian cavalier, Guardsman and General Staff Officer of the old school, who had initially been given command of Army Group B, now found himself summarily dismissed. He had become *persona non grata* because he had so strongly opposed the splitting up of the original command. He was replaced by General Maximilian Freiherr v. Weichs zur Glon.

Step by step, the Sixth Army pressed eastwards over the river Chir to the great sluices on the Don opposite the kneebend of the Volga, with Stalingrad before it.

On 23 July, Hitler issued his Directive No. 45 – and now the last vestige of commonsense was truly flung to the winds! In Hitler's view, the enemy was now really down and out. The Seventeenth

Army, the Third Rumanian Army, the First and Fourth German Panzer Armies, concentrated under the command of Army Group A (Field-Marshal List), was ordered to advance to the conquest of the Caucasus via Rostov, where Hitler proposed to surround and defeat the enemy! Sixth Army (Army Group B) was ordered to capture Stalingrad and throw a cordon between the Don and the Volga. Almost at once, yet another re-grouping was ordered; for the attack on Stalingrad the Fourth Panzer Army, Colonel General Hoth, was placed under the command of Army Group B. On the east of the Don it advanced in a north-easterly direction on Stalingrad, while the Sixth Army from west of the Don prepared to attack the Soviet bridge-head at Kalach, on the right bank of the Don.

In these operations there were two factors, the importance of which cannot be overemphasized: Throughout the whole course of the operations, the Army Group was faced with an uninterrupted series of supply crises; and it had no reserves of any kind. Very soon Air Fleet 4, which, under the command of Colonel General Freiherr v. Richthofen, was co-operating with both Army Groups B and A, was forced to come to their assistance with lorry convoys to save the situation, at least as far as the supply of fuel was concerned.

After having had two of its Panzer Corps detached from it, the Fourth Panzer Army had under its command the XXXXVII Panzer Corps, consisting of one Panzer division and one motorized infantry division, the IV Corps with two infantry divisions, while the VI Rumanian Army Corps, consisting of four divisions, was on its way to join it. Sixth Army, organized in two attack groups, 'North' and 'South', now had under its command the XIV and XXIV Panzer Corps, the VIII and LI Army Corps and, for a while, the XVII Army Corps.

At the end of July the enemy attempted, with some initial success, to broaden his bridge-head to the west of Kalach. Here the enemy strength was twelve infantry divisions and five armoured brigades. It was not until 7 August that Paulus was able to make any real impression on the position. But then, in a battle that lasted for three days, the enemy forces in the bridge-head were completely destroyed.

The battle of Kalach was yet another of those – to use Schlieffen's terminology – 'humdrum' victories, in which the eastern campaign was so rich. His exceptionally stubborn resistance, however, helped the enemy to gain time. And beyond the burning summer of the Steppes another winter lay in wait.

As a result of the three-day battle of Kalach, with its extremely important bridge over the Don, it was not until a fortnight later, on 21 July, that Sixth Army was able to launch its attack across the Don and advance on Stalingrad, the objective it had been ordered to capture. General Hollidt, who at that time was covering Sixth Army's northern flank on the Don with his XVII Corps, saw his old friend of Reichswehr days several times (and also for the last time) during this August. He found him often tired out and listless when he returned to his command post, covered with dust after a visit to the front. He was, too, full of anxiety about his troops and the series of fresh and heavy demands that he was forced to make of them, with no hope of being able to relieve any of his exhausted formations.

At Army Headquarters Halder watched closely over the manner in which Sixth Army was being led and came to the conclusion, quite rightly, that as an Army Commander Paulus had proved himself. During the second half of August, immediately before the fresh advance on Stalingrad, Paulus' successor as OQuI, Lieut-General Blumentritt, who had previously been Chief of Staff, Fourth Army in the central sector, was sent by Halder to visit the Sixth Army. At that time the Army Staff were living in their command vehicles in the steppes to the east of Millerovo, at the knee of the Don.

In his talks with Blumentritt Paulus made no secret of his grave concern with regard to his inadequately protected northern flank, which, he said, would have to be extended further eastwards if, as was hoped, he succeeded in occupying the area between the Don bend and the Volga elbow. On the left of Hollidt's XVII Corps was the Eighth Italian Army, which had been formed out of the Italian Expeditionary Force that had been sent to the Russian theatre the year before. Apart from the fact that they failed, not unnaturally, to grasp the essentials of this whole struggle in the vast expanse of Russia, the Italians were neither armed nor equipped for warfare on this grand scale.

It so happened that on the night of 20 August the Russians launched an attack with weak forces across the Don, southwards against the Italians at Serafimovich. The Italian Sforcesca Division broke. Paulus, gravely concerned about conditions on his flank, asked Blumentritt to go personally and find out what the situation was like with his Italian neighbours.

Blumentritt found that the very good and courageous cavalry group Barbó, which consisted of the famous cavalry regiments Savoia and Novara, though inadequately armed, had been doing its best to plug the gaps in the line; and, thanks to Blumentritt's intervention, the retreating Sforcesca Division was halted and sent forward again.

This, however, did not alter the fact that the northern flank of the German thrust on Stalingrad was inadequately protected. Nor did Blumentritt's very detailed report to Generals v. Weichs and Halder alter the situation in any way.

The new Verdun

On 21 August, in the face of violent but unsuccessful enemy resistance, the Sixth Army crossed the Don on both sides of Vertyachi. On 23 August tanks of the XIV Panzer Corps reached the Volga at Rynok, to the north of the great city of Stalingrad, sprawling along the banks of the mighty river. The remaining elements of the Sixth Army advanced much more slowly, and for a while an extremely critical situation arose at Rynok. General v. Wietersheim, Commander of the XIV Corps, asked permission to withdraw his tanks. Paulus, very properly, refused. General v. Wietersheim was relieved of his command and was replaced by General Hube, the Commander of 16 Panzer Division, which had been the first to reach the Volga and had held on to its position at Rynok. At the end of August units of the Fourth Panzer Army advancing from the south reached the Basargino area near Stalingrad, and on 2 September they made contact with the Sixth Army.

The enemy now withdrew to the outskirts of the city itself. And there then began a struggle reminiscent of Verdun for the possession of the crumbling metropolis which was to continue for five months and which the Germans could not bring to a victorious conclusion, in spite of numerous local successes.

As the troops fought their way into the outskirts of the city, the higher command once more became of little or no account. The spearhead, thrust far into the east, now found itself involved in static warfare, a soldiers' battle and war of attrition. Far away to the south, in the West Caucasus and on the Terek in the North Caucasus, the same thing was happening to Army Group A. The dual-pronged, diverging attacks of the two Army Groups, with forces inadequate for the vast areas in which they had to operate, juggling eternally with their own formations in an attempt to compensate for the complete lack of reserves at their disposal, had been brought to a standstill.

Paulus' main task now was to occupy that part of the city which stretched for five miles along the right bank of the Volga, to surround the whole circumference, some twenty miles in length, and to push the Soviet forces back into the heart of the town itself, and thus to bring the banks of the Volga under the effective control of the two attacking armies. This involved long weeks of exhausting and costly street and house-to-house fighting, during the course of which it was the enemy formations and not the German armies that increased in strength; and foremost among them were the 62 and 64 Infantry Divisions, operating in Stalingrad itself and on the Volga respectively.

The pattern of the operations prior to the capture of the outskirts of the city had given the impression that the enemy was trying to avoid becoming committed to battle in order to tie down German forces (and, incidentally, to gain time, with his eye on a winter campaign to follow); but during October it became patently clear that what in September had been no more than a fear – namely, that the Soviet High Command might be massing completely fresh and formidable forces north of the Don and east of the Volga – did, in fact, materialize. The stepping-up of the Soviet war industry in the trans-Ural areas of Siberia to full productive capacity – a great feat of organization – was now beginning to make itself felt. And in addition there was the material aid being given to Russia by her Anglo-Saxon allies.

During his frequent visits to the front, the Commander-in-Chief of Air Fleet 4, Col-General Freiherr v. Richthofen, a man of dynamic though perhaps over-optimistic temperament, rather inclined to jump to conclusions, repeatedly voiced his conviction that it only required just one more mighty effort to 'settle Stalingrad once and for all'; but in this he was overlooking the fact that it was lack of adequate forces that prevented the Army Commanders from doing just what he advocated. The Fourth Panzer Army had failed to capture the commanding high ground at Krasnoarmeysk to the south of Stalingrad, and the Sixth Army had been unable to reach those positions in the north, between the Don at Kotluban and the Volga, which were essential to the protection of its flank.

Paulus himself was compelled to make great demands on his own physical stamina during these late autumn days. To judge from a letter written to him on 20 August from Dresden by Dr Flade (who was still in hospital recovering from injuries received when v. Reichenau's plane crashed), the dysentery, the 'Russian sickness', had not hesitated to attack both the Army Staff and its Commander. Flade in friendly concern asked Paulus whether he had yet been able to instil the dysentery with 'a proper respect for his person'? 'Militarily,' he added, 'everything is going marvellously, though the hardships endured must, of course, be terrific.'

While the latter half of the good doctor's military comment was apposite, the former part was euphemistic in the extreme. To be honest, nothing, militarily, was 'going' even well. The German front was stretched in a long, thinly held line of over 1,000 miles from Anapa and Tuapse in the mountains of the West Caucasus and the Terek area (Seventeenth and First Panzer Armies), over a gap in the Kalmuck Steppes, screened by one, solitary motorized division, to the Volga and the Don. On the Sixth Army's left flank were the Eighth Italian, the Second Hungarian and the Second German Armies. In the Italian sector, Soviet forces were maintaining their bridge-heads at Kletskaya and Serafimovich on the south bank of the Don.

The quite abnormal length of this thinly-held,)-shaped German front line, with the concentrated masses attacking Stalingrad at the apex of the), must inevitably have been an invitation even to a strategically completely untutored adversary to initiate operations with the object of cutting off either the forces attacking Stalingrad or those of Army Group A, stuck fast in the mountains of the Caucasus. General Halder repeatedly and emphatically drew attention to the dangers of this strategically quite impossible situation. Nor could it be claimed that the Soviet High Command were exactly amateurs at the game. Hitler, it is true, still adhered to his conviction that the enemy was at the end of his tether. He found what he chose to describe as Halder's 'schoolmarmy outlook' increasingly irksome. Initially, of course, his wrath fell upon Field-Marshal List of Army Group A, who advocated a calling-off of the offensive in the West Caucasus, and on General Jodl, who, after one of the rare visits he was allowed to pay to the front, had said that List was right.

List was relieved of his command, and Jodl for the time being fell into disfavour. Hitler decided that he would himself direct Army Group A's operations from his forward Headquarters, 'Werewolf', in Vinnitsa in Western Ukraine. In the midst of this command crisis, on 12 September 1942, Generals Weichs and Paulus, both men of calm and deliberate temperament, arrived in Vinnitsa. Both drew attention to the hazardous position of the Sixth Army and to the fact that the northern flank on the Don was quite inadequately protected, while the southern flank had no protection worth mentioning at all. The one consolation was that the whole of this eastern campaign had been based on such seemingly impossible improvisations and that, somehow, the impossible had always been achieved. And Hitler knew only too well how to make this consoling thought sound plausible and, with his uncanny power of influencing men's minds, he was an adept at instilling confidence. Even so, Paulus was by no means completely satisfied when he left Vinnitsa.

Twelve days later he received a piece of information which, to judge from the brief correspondence between Halder and himself on the subject, affected him deeply. On 24 September Hitler abruptly dismissed Halder from his post of Chief of the General Staff. His successor was General Kurt Zeitzler, who until then had been Chief of Staff to the Commander-in-Chief, West. This was the final act in the long drawn-out transformation of the General Staff. From now onwards, as far as the eastern campaign was concerned, the General Staff was no more than a rubber stamp. Independent planning by General Staff Officers ceased. The post of Chief of the Army Personnel Branch was given to Lieut-General Schmundt, the Adjutant-General of the Armed Forces, a new Principal Staff Officer of whom it can be truly said that he was 'filled with the glow of enthusiasm for the National Socialist idea' – a virtue in which Hitler had found Halder to be distressingly lacking.

Halder's dismissal was an even harder blow to Paulus' career and destiny than had been the death of Reichenau. That is not meant to imply that when the crisis came General Zeitzler did not do all he could on Paulus' behalf. But to Halder, Paulus was something more than an Army Commander in a vital post and an unfortunate situation. He was his master-pupil, a man in whom Halder, not given to fulsomeness in the expression of his feelings, recognized a kindred spirit and a soldierly character of his own kind.[1] Whether Halder, had he remained in office, could have done more for Paulus than Zeitzler is a question which, frankly, cannot be answered. It was just during these autumn days that there occurred another case which showed the cold-blooded manner in which Hitler dealt with those who opposed him. General v. Schwedler, commanding IV Corps of the Fourth Panzer Army, was summarily dismissed because he protested in no uncertain terms against leaving the Sixth Army where it was, in its impossible situation in Stalingrad.

Paulus, who was an old friend of Schmundt from the manoeuvres and courses they had attended together in the innocuous days of the old Reichswehr, felt that he ought to send Schmundt his congratulations. During this general re-shuffle, he himself, though he did not know very much about it, was also being considered for a different post. In the Paulus family the belief is tenaciously held, particularly by Elena Constance, that eventually, had Paulus brought the Stalingrad operations to a successful conclusion, he would have been appointed Chief of Staff, Supreme Headquarters, in place of Field-Marshal Keitel. Elena Constance herself derived considerable satisfaction from the thought that in that case he would at least have been able to reorganize those Headquarters on a sounder basis. Another rumour had it that Paulus was earmarked to replace Jodl as Chief of the Armed Forces Directing Staff.[2] Paulus himself states that, while on a visit to the front in October, Schmundt had told him that he had been earmarked for other employment and that then command of the Sixth Army would be given to General v. Seydlitz-Kurzbach (Commander LI Corps), who enjoyed Hitler's confidence.

It has, however, been definitely established that, because of his

---

[1] In his letter to Paulus dated 13.7.42, General Halder refers to 'that inner friendship which has for so long bound us old soldiers together'.

[2] Questioned at the Nuremberg trial on the subject, Paulus replied that he had heard nothing official, but that a rumour to this effect had reached him.

Rumanian contacts, Paulus was selected for the post of Deputy Commander-in-Chief of the Rumanian-German Army Group, Don, which was to be formed and placed under the command of the Conducatorul, the Rumanian Head of State, Marshal Antonescu. Early in the autumn, the Fourth and Third Rumanian Armies were brought up to protect the left and right flanks respectively of the Sixth Army. Both these formations, from the fighting point of view, were, frankly, very inadequately armed, having neither heavy artillery nor anti-tank weapons. Under the command of Marshal Antonescu all the Rumanian and German forces – the Third and Fourth Rumanian Armies, Sixth German Army and Fourth Panzer Army – were to be concentrated between the Don and the Volga. To make the preliminary arrangements for the formation of this coalition Army Group, a 'mobile group', under Major-General Hauffe, Head of the German Military Mission in Rumania, had already arrived in Rostov, where later it became the caucus of the new Army Group's General Staff.

In the meanwhile that process which Halder, shortly before his dismissal, had described as the 'cauterization' of the German attacking forces in Stalingrad was steadily continuing.

Bit by bit, step by step, the German troops, suffering heavy losses, gnawed their way deeper and deeper into the giant, crumbling city. Paulus begged for reinforcements, for the strengthening of the protection of his flanks, for better arms for his Rumanian neighbours. He had urgent need of fresh infantry divisions, but all he got were five Pioneer battalions, which arrived by air. He lost no opportunity of sounding the alarm whenever senior officers like Schmundt, his old friend, Fellgiebel, and Ochsner, visited his front. He tried his utmost to enlist the co-operation of General Dumitrescu, the G O C-in-C Third Rumanian Army, in the hope that, via Antonescu, of whom Hitler held quite a high opinion, help might be extended to the Rumanians and to his own Army. And from the faithful former Medical Officer of the Sixth Army, Dr Flade, he received repeated warnings that he must give heed to his shattered health. Flade thought it was essential that Paulus should obtain leave and have a complete rest in Bad Kissingen, Bad Elster or Bad Brambach.

Any such thing, however, was quite out of the question. On the other side of the Don and the Volga, it was becoming ever plainer that very strong hostile forces were massing preparatory to an advance. At a meeting at the Sportspalast in Berlin, Goering, posing heroically, assured his audience that this time nothing untoward could happen. What a Russian winter looked like, he said, we now all knew. Touching lightly on the command crisis, he declared that the General Staff was now no more than a tool in the hands of the Fuehrer, that there were, God be praised, plenty of first-class Generals, and that those who proved not good enough would be thrown out.

Hitler – in theory perfectly aware of what could happen under the peculiar front-line conditions in winter, namely, a Soviet break-through on Sixth Army's northern flank over the Don in a deep thrust to Rostov, launched forth, at one of his 'situation conferences' in Vinnitsa—on the subject of what had to be done to strengthen the flanks – reinforcement of the Rumanians by German forces, erection of obstacles, minefields and so on and so forth; but he never asked which of these measures were feasible and how long it would take to implement them, or what, if anything, had already been done to put his directives into practice. It seemed as though he were trying to salve his own conscience by showing that he, Hitler, the Fuehrer, had foreseen and prepared for every eventuality.

Conversely he ordered the continuation of the attack on Stalingrad. And again conversely, Hitler the People's Tribune did the greatest possible wrong to Hitler the War Lord, Supreme Commander of the Armed Forces and Commander-in-Chief of the Army. On 8 November 1942, in his Munich speech in commemoration of the 1923 Putsch, he condemned himself out of his own mouth. In his hoarse, throaty voice he told his audience that we had wanted Stalingrad and, well, we'd have it. The tenor of his speech was: Where the German soldier stands, no one shall pass! And as far as the actual fighting at Stalingrad was concerned, well, he said, he was conducting that in his own way, with just small raiding parties, in order to prevent unnecessary bloodshed . . . The applause, as may be imagined, was frenetic. But one thing had now become abundantly clear: Any elastic and orderly withdrawal from Stalingrad had been ruled out by Hitler – because the Fuehrer must, on all occasions, be right.

In the late autumn, when Hitler moved from Vinnitsa to Obersalzberg, the reports of disaster began to flow in – the African Panzer

Army had been defeated in Egypt and was in retreat, the Allies had landed in North Africa . . . In the middle of November Hitler sent Paulus a signal saying that of the gallant Sixth Army he now expected one final, supreme effort to wipe out the Russian forces in Stalingrad.

Surrounded – to obey or disobey?

Then on 19 and 20 November reports of further disasters began, gradually, confusedly and in driblets, to reach Army Headquarters in Golubinskaya on the Don. The Russians had broken through on the front of the Fourth Rumanian Army, on the Third Rumanian Army front, and on the front of the Fourth Panzer Army, which had been split in two; there was a grave danger of encirclement, and from all sides came the question: What is to be done? That was the question posed to an Army Commander and his Chief of Staff who, in spite of marked differences in their characters, understood each other well. And the answering of it demanded robust obstinacy from a man who had always found it difficult to make great and crucial decisions.

Details of these events will be found in Part II of this volume. Here, in this biographical sketch of Paulus, primary concern is centred on two fundamental questions: When an Army Commander finds himself faced with a critical situation and confronted with overwhelmingly superior hostile forces, what should be the guiding principles, as far as his own decisions and the reconciling of his own views with those of his superiors are concerned, which should govern the manner in which he exercises his command? Should his primary concern be the preservation and salvation of his Army – but within the framework of the situation as a whole? Or should it be purely and simply the safety of his own Army, regardless of extraneous circumstances? Or, again, was this solely a military problem demanding a soldierly solution, or was the crucial issue one of whether or not he should, now and at the front, raise the standard of rebellion against Adolf Hitler?

After the war we in Germany tried initially to scrutinize the history of the war solely from the angle of the conflict between the traditional military caste on the one side and Hitler and the protagonists of National Socialism on the other. Now, however, we must draw a line of demarcation between resistance activities and the prosecution of war. Opposition to one's own régime on moral grounds is just as much a part of this dreadful 'cosmic civil war' as is the resistance of partisans against enemy occupying forces. But as a guiding principle, it is not universally applicable and certainly not universally admissible!

On 21 November and the days following, the Commander-in-Chief, Sixth Army realized that his forces, together with elements of the Fourth Panzer Army, stood in danger of being hemmed in between the Volga and the Don. The formations involved were four Army Corps, one Panzer Corps, fourteen Infantry, three Armoured, and three Motorized Divisions, one Rumanian Infantry and one Rumanian Cavalry Division and innumerable Army Troops – a total, according to the ration strength, of approximately 260,000 men.

Later the feeling grew in Germany that Paulus should have acted at once and on his own responsibility, like Yorck in bygone days, and broken through the closing ring, thus giving the signal for the rebellion of the Generals against Hitler. . . .

Such ideas may perhaps have been expressed in the circle round General Beck, who retired as Chief of Staff in 1938. They were certainly ideas with which ex-Ambassador Ulrich v. Hassell, executed after the 20 July plot, toyed. But it was only after the collapse that Paulus himself learnt that thoughts of this kind had been exercising the minds of people at home. When the German forces were completely surrounded, General v. Seydlitz, it is said, reminded Paulus of Yorck and what he had done. But Paulus, with every justification, could have retorted that the position of General Yorck at the end of December 1812 was very different to that in which the Sixth Army and its Commander found themselves during the crucial period 21 to 24 November in Stalingrad.

Yorck, without any reliable means of communication with his King, acted, admittedly, on his own responsibility, but always, nevertheless, in the name of the King. Paulus, at the crucial moment in the battle and with a swift, reliable and perfectly functioning communication link with his superiors, would have had to raise the standard for a rebellion which could not even count on a solid core of *frondeurs* in the homeland. Furthermore, by so doing he would have been gambling with the fate of the whole vast front, locked in desperate combat, without himself possessing any detailed knowledge of the military situation as a whole. Yorck, on the other hand, was in the happy position of being able to act when the situation at the front was quiet and with, at least, the certain knowledge that the Napoleonic Army had been utterly defeated and that the time had come for Prussia to change sides and fight against the despot of Europe.

Paulus and his Chief of Staff, the Commander-in-Chief of Army Group B and his Chief of Staff, and Field-Marshal v. Manstein, the Commander-in-Chief Army Group Don, were all unanimously convinced that – in theory – Sixth Army's correct action was to attempt to break out in a south-westerly direction from the encirclement that was threatening it. But in war, the theoretically correct solution is not always correct, or even feasible, in practice. And none of the officers primarily concerned felt that, in the extremely delicate military situation, they could accept the responsibility of acting without orders or against the orders of the Higher Command, and particularly of Army Headquarters and the Chief of the General Staff, General Zeitzler, since they themselves had no full knowledge of the situation as a whole. And in those days, of what account, after all, was a mere Army Commander, restricted to the control of a limited sector of a well defined front? Therein, perhaps, lies the major difference between the positions of Paulus and Yorck, the independent Commander-in-Chief of the Prussian Corps and Governor of East Prussia, at the time of Tauroggen in 1812.

The situation at Army Headquarters was very different, however. Here they must have realized – and, indeed, did realize – that the Stalingrad position could in any case not be maintained, any more than could the position on the western and northern fringes of the Caucasus. General Zeitzler, in an open and bitter argument with Hitler, insisted that the Sixth Army should be given orders to break its way out; but he had to give way when the Commander-in-Chief of the Air Force, Marshal Goering, announced through his Chief of Staff, General Jeschonneck, that the Air Force would guarantee to supply the encircled Sixth Army until such a time as it was relieved. And it must be borne in mind that the strength of the Sixth Army, plus attached formations, was estimated by the Directing Staff, Supreme Headquarters, to be approximately 400,000 men. That the giving of such a guarantee was an act of frivolous irresponsibility is incontestable, and it can be presumed that General Jeschonneck did have some grounds for shooting himself some nine months later....

In any case, it can today be asserted that no reproach can be levelled at Paulus for his handling of the situation in November 1942. In any case, too, if he were to prevent the enemy from rolling up his army from the rear, he had no option but to direct those formations which were cut off to organize themselves for all-round defence, regardless of whether the final decision would be in favour of an attempt to break out or of awaiting the arrival of relieving forces. Relief had been promised to him. Supplies had been guaranteed by the Air Force. The degree in which both these promises were utopian he was not in a position to judge. That relief, given a sound concentration of adequate forces at the right place, would have been possible – in spite of the new theatre of war in North Africa and the creation of an Italo-German bridge-head in Tunis and the occupation of the whole of France – can today be clearly demonstrated. As regards supplies by air, it is true that all the responsible senior Air Force officers in the southern sector, both inside the ring with Sixth Army and outside it, left Paulus and Schmidt in no doubt that, owing to lack of transport aircraft, it could not be done. But since relief had been promised by the beginning of December, Schmidt's oft repeated assertion that 'somehow or other we'll manage' was, for a limited period of time, completely justified.

In the event, a certain volume of supplies was flown in, but nowhere approaching enough to satisfy Sixth Army's requirements. The crucial question, however, was not one of supply by air, but of the efforts to be made to relieve the surrounded army. And the fact that the conduct of these operations had been entrusted to Field-Marshal v. Manstein, strategically quite the ablest of all the Generals, was, in Paulus' eyes, the best possible guarantee of success.

Typical of the way in which Paulus, having moved his battle headquarters forward from Golubinskaya to Gumrak railway station, nearer to Stalingrad, exercised his command was the regular manner in which he visited his subordinate commanders and obtained their views, the calm detachment with which he listened to Seydlitz's passionate advocacy of an independent break-out, and the all but unnatural self-control with which he received the information that on the evening of 23 November General v. Seydlitz on his own responsibility had ordered a partial withdrawal of his own LI Corps on the northern front, with the unfortunate result that the pursuing enemy had caught and destroyed the 94 Infantry Division. But once Paulus had made his decision, he adhered to it with rock-like imperturbability, and the gist of his retort to all subsequent appeals was: 'I'm sorry – those are the Fuehrer's orders, and I must obey.'

Colonel Selle, the Engineer-in-Chief of the Sixth Army, recounts in his memoirs how, in reply to his own suggestion that the time had now come to follow Yorck's example, Paulus had said: 'I know that history has already passed its verdict on me.' Later Paulus himself, in conversation with his son, gave a different version. Selle, he said, had asked him what history would have to say about Stalingrad. To which he had replied that history had already given its verdict. In this context he was referring not to the actual conduct of the Stalingrad operations but to the faulty premises and actions which had placed the army in so precarious a position.

By then, however, there was no point in dwelling on past mistakes. His immediate concern was to rescue his army and to prevent a catastrophe on this sector of the front. Some idea of the physical strain under which the Army Staff worked can be gathered from the fact that both Colonel Arnold, the Chief Signal Officer, and Selle, the Engineer-in-Chief, suffered serious breakdowns. Paulus himself, in by no means robust health, showed great stamina.

In one of the few letters, dated 7 December, which he wrote to his wife during the siege, he said: 'At the moment I've got a really difficult problem on my hands, but I hope to solve it soon. Then I shall be able to write more frequently. You may rest assured that, as soon as it is humanly possible, I shall ask for as long leave as they will grant me. . . .'

On 18 December he wrote: 'Just now we are having a very hard time indeed. But we'll survive. And after the winter, there is another May to follow . . .' Yet all the time he well knew how critical the situation was and what demands he would be compelled to make of the troops under his command. Without fail, on alternate days he or his Chief of Staff went forward to see for themselves the situation as it was on each sector of the front. All this was very unobtrusively done; in his eyes the solitary private soldier, stuck in the snow and ice, was doing much more than he was. In taking an interest in the welfare of his troops, a Commander, after all, was doing no more than his duty, and he saw no reason why the fact that he was doing his duty should be rammed down the troops' throats. In this respect he was, perhaps, underestimating the psychological effects of these visits, which showed the troops that their General was there, sharing everything with them; in the same way, Field-Marshal v. Manstein, too, perhaps underestimated the psychological effect which his own personal appearance in their midst – perfectly feasible by aircraft – would have had on the beleaguered garrison. A man like Reichenau would have acted otherwise. But Paulus, like v. Manstein, still subscribed to the old adage, unfamiliar to the new mass era, '*Mehr sein als scheinen*'.[1]

Decision before Christmas

The second of Paulus' letters quoted above was written in the crucial period between 12 and 24 December. Details will be found in Part II of this book.

But now, great though the imponderables attached to it were, the question of independent action had to be decided one way or the other. On 12 December Operation 'Wintergewitter', the relief of Stalingrad, was launched. The Fourth Panzer Army, under General Hoth, advanced from the south against the encircling enemy ring round Stalingrad. Initially, Hoth had under command the completely rested and fully equipped 6 Panzer Division from France and the battle-scarred 23 Panzer Division, withdrawn from the Caucasus; subsequently, and too late, the 17 Panzer Division was also placed at his disposal.

By 19 December, after severe fighting against the stubborn resistance of strong Soviet armoured forces, the leading elements of Hoth's force had established a bridge-head over the Myshkova river, some twenty-five miles from the main besieging Soviet forces. Operation 'Wintergewitter' envisaged that the armoured forces of the Sixth Army would now break out in support of Hoth. It further envisaged that a convoy of lorries carrying supplies, particularly of the fuel so urgently required, would crash its way through to the

[1] Be more present than apparent.

besieged Sixth Army. As Hitler saw it, the sole object of Operation 'Wintergewitter' was to re-establish contact with the Sixth Army and thus keep open a winter supply 'pipe-line'. Stalingrad, the cornerstone of the summer offensive of 1943, was to be held at all costs.

As Paulus and Manstein saw things, however, Operation 'Wintergewitter' made sense only if it were the preliminary to a second operation, namely, Operation 'Donnerschlag', the break-out of the whole Sixth Army. It is beyond dispute that, if the Army were to be rescued at all, the last chance was now at hand. It is equally beyond dispute that bulk supply by air over a long period had proved to be impracticable. The average daily load flown into Stalingrad was about 100 tons, while the minimum daily requirements of Sixth Army amounted to some 500 tons. Through his Chief of Staff, Major-General Schulz, his GSO I (Operations), Colonel Busse, and his Intelligence Officer, Major Eismann, Manstein did his utmost to remain in close and constant contact with Paulus. All three officers visited the beseiged garrison. In addition, a telephone line between Sixth Army and Army Group Headquarters in Novocherkask had, in some remarkable way, survived; and when this was torn up at the beginning of December, the technicians succeeded in establishing communication by means of radio telephone and teleprinter, using an ultra-short wavelength.[1] In this way direct, personal liaison was maintained.

And it was for this very reason that Paulus himself, without any first-hand knowledge of the general situation as a whole in the sectors of Army Groups Don, B and A, felt that he was bound to act solely in accordance with the orders that Manstein issued to him. During these December days, however, Manstein had many other problems to contend with apart from the relief of the Sixth Army, surrounded at the time by strong enemy forces amounting to some ninety major formations with strong artillery support and a very powerful tank

---

[1] In Russia it was found that the effective range of these 'decimetre' sets was far greater than normal. In Stalingrad, thanks to the clear winter air and the absence of any hills, the sets functioned at a range of nearly forty miles. From mid-December, as the distance between stations increased, contact could be maintained only by teleprinter; and at the end of December, with the loss of the air bases at Morozovsk and Tatsinskaya, whence the sets were operated, teleprinter contact also ceased and there remained only communication by ordinary wireless.

force. In the far south in the Caucasus, Army Group A, on Hitler's orders, was still standing fast, and on the Don in the north the enemy might at any moment succeed in breaking through the Eighth Italian Army; to the west, the German defensive dispositions on the Don and the Chir, protecting the great air bases at Tatsinskaya and Morozovsk, from which supplies were being flown into Stalingrad, were being held only with great difficulty. And the second relieving operation, envisaged from this area, never materialized at all.

Manstein, as is revealed in his own memoirs, did not feel justified in acting in any way independently or contrary to the directives of Supreme and Army Headquarters; but according to his own account, he would have accepted the responsibility had Paulus played his part in the initial Operation 'Wintergewitter' and followed that with the initiation of Operation 'Donnerschlag'. But to achieve absolute clarity and agreement on this issue would presumably have entailed a personal conference between himself and Paulus in the beseiged city, rather than merely the despatch of a Staff Officer in the person of Major Eismann. But Manstein hesitated to make the necessary trip because he felt that the possibility of a catastrophe elsewhere, in some other sector, made it impossible for him to leave his own Head-quarters even for a single day.

From the orders issued to him on 19 December – firstly, to proceed as soon as possible with his part in Operation 'Wintergewitter' but not to initiate Operation 'Donnerschlag' without further specific orders to do so, and then, secondly, the order that 'everything was to remain as it was' – Paulus could get no clear picture of what Manstein had in mind, to what extent he regarded as justifiable a whole-hearted attempt at a break-out *en masse*, or the limits beyond which he regarded independent action as inadmissible. Nor was the confusion completely cleared up in the days that followed, though it did become clear that Manstein did not consider that the time had yet come for the unleashing of Operation 'Donnerschlag'. These issues, too, are dealt with in Part II.

General Hoth, whose views on independent action had coincided, in November, with those of Paulus, now felt that the time had come for the swift execution of the whole of Operation 'Wintergewitter', to be followed at once by the implementation of Operation 'Donner-schlag', even though permission had not been given specifically either by Manstein or by Army Headquarters. Time was pressing, and Hoth was itching for action.

In preparation for his part in Operation 'Wintergewitter', Paulus had concentrated what armour he had left in the southern sector of his position under General Hube. Of exactly how many tanks this force consisted cannot be ascertained.[1] But it can safely be assumed that there were not more than about sixty. The force had enough fuel for a thrust of about twelve miles, after taking the wise precaution of allowing for a possible return journey if these last 'fireworks' failed to achieve their purpose, and the tanks had to return to base. Paulus therefore found that his liberty of action would be strictly limited unless Hoth, as he was urged to do, succeeded in pressing further forward northwards, or unless fuel were flown in for his own armour. And as far as the latter alternative is concerned, the airlift once more failed to meet its obligations.

At Army Headquarters, where Zeitzler was demanding permission for the Sixth Army to break its way out, Hitler took advantage of Paulus' report on the fuel situation and replied: 'But what, exactly, do you wish me to do? Paulus can't break out, and you know it!' To him, the ready-to-hand solution seemed obvious. The Army must stay where it was until the major relieving operation took effect. In this connection, it should be remarked that preparations for such an operation, to be executed by a new SS Panzer Corps with three fully equipped divisions, were in active progress; but unfortunately Hitler asked neither himself nor anyone else how long the Sixth Army, with insufficient rations and inadequate supplies, could still hold out in the snow and ice!

So, with the advent of Christmas the chance of a last-minute reprieve slipped away. Just before New Year's Eve, the long-expected catastrophe on the Eighth Italian Army front occurred. The Russians crossed the Don and advanced southwards. For a time there was a real danger that a Super-Stalingrad, the cutting off and encirclement

---

[1] *Die 14. Panzer Division, 1940–45* by Rolf Grams put the tank strength of the division on 17.12.42 as twenty-six tanks. *Geschichte der 16. Panzer Division, 1939–45* by Wolfgang Werthen contains no detailed figures, but places the total number of tanks in Stalingrad in December at 'about one hundred'. For 24 Panzer Division, the third armoured division in Stalingrad, no figures are available.

of the whole of Army Group A, might well occur. And now Manstein found himself in what must certainly have been the bitterest dilemma in his life. He had no option but to withdraw armour from Hoth, initially 6 Panzer Division, in an endeavour at least to plug the holes in depth. And of the Sixth Army he had to demand that it should hold on – not 'for as long as seemed expedient', but for as long as it could in the impossible and fatal position in which it found itself and for which neither Manstein nor Paulus was responsible.

The only alternative open to Paulus and his Chief of Staff was to act independently and order a break-out, without the slightest regard for the situation as a whole. But even this, with formations which had become virtually immobile and were encircled in an area measuring some thirty miles by twenty-five, would take time – four to five days at least. And it would have meant the sacrifice of the sick, the wounded and the physically unfit and the abandonment of most of the guns and vehicles. But on this Army, whose fighting spirit was wholly unimpaired, such an order would have had a tremendous moral effect and set free forces like those of a dam bursting its banks. Field-Marshal v. Reichenau would probably have done just this. But Paulus and Schmidt had other views on the exercise of command; they were accustomed to meticulous, precise and minute calculation; and they knew very well that Manstein could hardly approve of so desperate a stroke, for the simple reason that its success was in any case problematical, and Manstein would fear that independent action of this nature might well make the general confusion on the Don front worse even than it now was.

Nevertheless, there were at Army Headquarters certain circles which saw in such an attempt the salvation of the Army and which perhaps wished to give Paulus a sign, without betraying that for them there was more to it than a question merely of saving the Sixth Army – the political aspect, the chance to curtail the unlimited powers that Hitler had bestowed upon himself. It would, in any case, be difficult to find any other motive behind the sending of the van Hooven mission, arranged by Paulus' friend, General Fellgiebel.

On New Year's Eve, General Fellgiebel at the Fuehrer's Wolfs-schanze Headquarters in East Prussia sent for Colonel Hans-Gunther v Hooven, the Commander of the Headquarters Communications Regiment, who was well known to him both as a Major on the Staff of the erstwhile Signals Inspectorate and later as the successful Commander of the Signals Section of XXXX Panzer Corps, under General Stumme. He asked him whether he knew Paulus personally. Van Hooven replied that he did not, whereupon Fellgiebel said in more or less these words 'In Paulus you will meet a man of honour and a *chevalier* in the truest sense of the word, and in addition a very wise, able and warm-hearted man, but one who has always been rather more of a theoretician than a man of action. He is a great friend of mine. Give him my warmest regards and tell him I hope very much to greet him personally before very long. About the actual position in which Sixth Army finds itself I needn't say anything – you know it all as well as I do.'

By Colonel Hahn, Fellgiebel's Chief of Staff, van Hooven was then told that he was to take over direct control of all signal units in the Sixth Army and reorganize them into a signal entity capable of dealing with all communications as soon as the Sixth Army had broken out southwards or south-westwards. When he had done so, he was told, he could fly out again. (This last van Hooven did not do.)

At Army Headquarters, van Hooven recalls, on 24 December they were still expecting that Hoth's group would thrust further forward in the direction of Voroponovo on the southern edge of the besieging forces. Fellgiebel, apparently, had not heard that on 23 December v. Manstein had withdrawn 6 Panzer Division from Hoth's command.

On 26 December van Hooven arrived at Army Group Don Headquarters in Novocherkask, where preparations for a move to Taganrog were already in progress. The interpretation that van Hooven had put on his mission was that he was to try to persuade Paulus to break out, regardless of what orders, if any, he had received. He realized that Fellgiebel could not, of course, have expressed himself as bluntly as that.

In Novocherkask he obtained a true picture of the situation. Hoth was already incapable of making any further advance. He would, indeed, be lucky if he succeeded in holding on to the line he had fought so hard to reach. He met General v. Greiffenberg, Chief of Staff, Seventeenth Army, who remarked dryly: 'Help for Sixth Army? We could do with a bit of help ourselves!'

Three days later, Colonel van Hooven found himself with Paulus in the latter's dug-out near Gumrak railway station. He gave the

General an unvarnished description of the situation, conveyed the message and greetings from Fellgiebel and Hahn and then said that, taking everything into consideration, he had come to the conclusion that there was only one way in which the Sixth Army could save itself and that was to act independently and break its way out. That, he added, would of course entail heavy sacrifices, but at least part of the Army would get through to safety.

Van Hooven did not feel that Paulus was in any way conscious that he was being urged to action at the behest of some politically actuated group. Politics were miles removed from his thoughts, and even more hazardous would have appeared to him the idea that the situation here in Stalingrad should be exploited to serve political purposes. In reply he said quite simply that he was not *au fait* with the situation as a whole and that he must obey orders. If things were as van Hooven had described them, and he did not wish to cast any doubt on the accuracy of van Hooven's picture, then the conclusions that van Hooven had reached were obviously correct; but he, as the Commander-in-Chief of an Army, could not, unfortunately, act as van Hooven suggested.

It was about this time that General Hube, the best of Paulus' subordinate Generals, was summoned to Fuehrer Headquarters to report on the situation. He described in detail the position as regards Sixth Army – and he, too, independent and greatly experienced soldier though he was, was convinced by Hitler that all could still be saved, that the great operation for the relief of Stalingrad was being prepared for 23 February and that the possibility of putting the actual date further forward was at that very moment being examined.

In reality, the period of martyrdom had already begun. In the situation as it was, the continued resistance of the Sixth Army was now as essential and as logical as the plan for the approach march in July 1942 had been bad and senseless. Now Sixth Army's primary task was to tie down the very strong enemy forces concentrated in the Stalingrad area and thus to give v. Manstein time to reorganize the whole southern front, and, equally, to cover the withdrawal of Army Group A from the Caucasus, which Hitler had at long last sanctioned. It was in this light that Paulus saw the task before him; and it was for this reason that, on 8 January 1943, as the Commander of an Army that was still capable of fighting and defending itself, he rejected the Soviet demand that he should lay down his arms.

Two extracts from letters written to his wife are apposite at this point. On 28 December he wrote: 'Christmas, naturally, was not very happy. In times like these, it is better to avoid celebrations. One must not, I think, ask too much of one's luck.' Two days later, in the last letter received from him: 'I must, of course, be ever on the alert.'

The sacrifice

In the second part of this book Paulus himself gives for the first time an account of the struggles and the hardships, the sacrifices and the final fall of the Sixth Army between Christmas 1942 and the capitulation on 31 January and 2 February 1943. To this account nothing need be added beyond two statements of fact which concern reproaches levelled at him after the war: It is not true that any Sixth Army Order was given to open fire on Russians sent to discuss the surrender; and it is not true that during the last and worst weeks a Sixth Army Order was issued that henceforth rations would not be issued to the sick and wounded, but would be reserved for the effective fighting troops.[1]

On the fundamental question of how long the Governor of a fortress or the Commander of a force surrounded in the field should continue to resist, there occurs the following passage in Napoleon's account of the campaign of Frederick the Great, dictated to Count v. Montholon by Napoleon himself:

'Do the rules of warfare and the principles of war authorize a General to order his troops to lay down their arms or to surrender himself and the force under his command? As far as the garrison of a fortress is concerned, there are no doubts on the subject. But the Governor of a fortress is in a special category. The laws of all nations authorize him to lay down his arms when his food supplies

[1] General Roske, the last Commander of 71 Division, who was in charge of the distribution of rations, admits in a letter to the Field-Marshal's widow that at the very end he had, on his own authority, said: 'From now on, rations will only be issued to men in the front line.' He insists, however, that this was not done and that in the distribution of what remained of the food supplies priority was given to the 17,000 odd sick and wounded.

come to an end, when the defences of his fortress have been battered to pieces and when he has already met and repulsed a number of assaults.

'Since the law and usage among all nations authorizes a Commander of a fortress to surrender under certain specified conditions, but has never authorized a General to do so in any circumstances, it can be asserted that no Prince, no Republic and no rule of warfare authorizes him to do so.

'There has been hardly a battle in which a few companies, sometimes a few battalions, have not found themselves hemmed in, in houses, in graveyards or in wooded country. The Commander who, when he realizes that he is surrounded in this way, prepares to capitulate is betraying his Prince and his honour . . . Now a Lieut-General is to an Army what a Battalion Commander is to a Division. The capitulations made by forces surrounded, whether in actual combat or in the course of a campaign, result in a contract which is advantageous to both contracting parties, but detrimental to the interests of the Prince and the Army of those who surrender. Thus to evade danger and by so doing to make more dangerous still the position of one's comrades in arms is obviously the act of a coward. . . .'

Napoleon, War Lord and Head of the State in one, dictated this passage with reference to the capitulation of Finck's Corps at Maxen during the Seven Years War.[1] It could well be applied to the fate which overtook the Sixth Army, surrounded in the open country, except that, later, when everything had collapsed and the fallacies of Hitler's maxims of leadership and moral principles had become apparent, the Germans came to the conclusion that any and every soldierly sacrifice was a crime and that judgment on the history of this war could be passed solely from the angle of what each individual

---

[1] In the autumn of 1759 Lieut-General Finck was ordered by Frederick the Great to advance with his Corps and threaten the rear of the Austrian Army under Field-Marshal Daun – a bold diversion, aiming at compelling Daun to withdraw from Saxony and Bohemia. Finck protested against the order, but obeyed it. On 20/21 November 1759, surrounded with his 11,000 men by overwhelmingly superior Austrian forces, he saw no option but to surrender. After the peace of Hubertusberg by command of the King he was court martialled, sentenced to one year's fortress detention and dismissed the Service.

had contributed towards ending it. Such a hypothesis entails a cessation of the writing of military history and its replacement by an unhistorical Inquisition. The Russians were not backward in charging German Generals with war crimes and hanging them or sending them to Siberia. But Paulus was never even charged!

Capitulation

The rest is swiftly told. With the collapse of the outer ring of Sixth Army's defences under the pressure of the Soviet offensive in January 1943, the fighting became confined to the ruins of the great metropolis itself. In view of the increasing signs of disintegration, Major-General Schmidt advised Paulus on 23 January to sanction the surrender of such units as were no longer capable of fighting, of the hospitals and of the various supply installations that had now become useless, in order, as he put it, 'to regulate the death-roll'. About this time, Manstein came to the conclusion that he could not count on any further resistance by the Sixth Army.[1] After the Hube mission, Paulus had sent yet another officer to Fuehrer Headquarters, Captain Behr, his Chief Ordnance Officer. Behr was brutally frank in his report on the situation. But it was all of no avail. Paulus then came to the conclusion that he must carry on to the end. At Schmidt's insistence he once more got in touch with Hitler's Headquarters. Hitler refused to sanction capitulation. This was sheer madness on his part, and it absolved Paulus of any further obligation to obey.

On 25 or 26 January, Paulus and his GSO II (Ops), Colonel Adam, sheltering in a cellar during an air raid, were slightly wounded in the head. The besieged army had now been split into two parts. Paulus retained command of the southern half, while command of the northern half was assumed by General Strecker of the XI Corps. The last Army Battle Headquarters was set up in a ruin in Stalingrad's Red Square. It was here, on 30 January 1943, the tenth anniversary of Hitler's assumption of power, that Paulus received the news that he had been promoted to Field-Marshal. The very next day, 31 January, Soviet troops appeared in Red Square. The

[1] Vide: *Lost Victories* by Field-Marshal v. Manstein, p. 340 (Methuen & Co, London).

guard over Army Headquarters voluntarily laid down their arms. The end had come . . . Paulus had to give in.

At the end of January, the Army Headquarters Liaison Officer with Sixth Army, Major v. Zitzewitz, who had been flown out on 20 January, submitted his report in the presence of Hitler and Generals Zeitzler and Schmundt. 'Mein Fuehrer,' said Zitzewitz quite bluntly, 'I feel bound to tell you that there is no point in your appealing to the troops to fight to the last round, firstly, because they are no longer physically capable of doing so, and secondly, because they haven't got a last round to fight with!'

Just before this remark, Hitler had been speaking about his plan of bursting across the steppes with a force armed with the new Panther tank, Mark V, of which deliveries to the Army had just begun. Now he seemed taken aback. Then: 'Man is a resilient animal', he muttered – a remark which seemed meaningless to Behr.

Was Hitler still thinking in terms of the relief enterprise he had been planning with the new SS Panzer Corps? Or about the airlift, to reorganize which he had appointed – too late – Field-Marshal Milch and General Hube? Whatever may have been his thoughts, he never paused to consider how much men could accomplish or what lay beyond their power to do.

On 1 February Fuehrer Headquarters learnt that the new Field-Marshal, together with Generals Schmidt and v. Seydlitz and other senior officers of the Sixth Army, had surrendered. The northern half of the beleaguered garrison held out until the next day. The following passage from the transcript of the Fuehrer's 'situation conference', headed 1217 hours, 1 February 1943, requires no comment:

THE FUEHRER: They've just simply thrown their hands in! If they hadn't, they'd have got together, fought on and kept the last round for themselves.

ZEITZLER: I just don't understand it, either. I can't help thinking there's been a mistake somewhere, that perhaps he's lying there, seriously wounded . . . (This latter refers to the Russian report that Paulus had been wounded.)

THE FUEHRER: No – it's true, all right. The Russians will now . . . (text mutilated). They'll be taken straight to Moscow and handed over to the GPU; and then they'll start issuing orders to the rest of the garrison to surrender. Schmidt will sign anything put before him. A man who hasn't the guts, at a time like that, to tread the path that all men must sooner or later tread, won't have the courage to stand up to them. The trouble with us is that we pay too much attention to the development of the intellect and too little to the formation of character.

The shattering of mutual confidence and esteem

The lack, in the above-quoted passage, of any vestige of human sympathy, of consideration for their brothers-in-arms, of respectful admiration for the deeds of the Sixth Army and its leaders heralded the beginning of the debasement of the concept of soldierly devotion to duty, and the extent to which the *esprit de corps* of the German Corps of Officers had been shattered became at once apparent; and this, perhaps, is the most baleful heritage left to us by the Stalingrad catastrophe. With the fall of Stalingrad, not only did the superstitious belief in the exceptional abilities of Hitler, the layman who had usurped full control of the Armed Forces, melt away, but, with the indecent haste with which the unfortunate Commander-in-Chief of the Sixth Army was reviled and maligned, mutual distrust began to spread among the senior ranks of the Corps of Officers. And this is the most significantly fateful feature which this battle contributed to the history of the German Army in the Second World War.

PART II

1. Hitler and England – Operation 'Sea Lion'

(*Vide* Sketch Map 1)

....

Introduction

After the victories over the Netherlands, Belgium and France in May and June 1940, Hitler was master of most of Central, Northern and Western Europe. Since the Polish campaign in September 1939, he had won victory after victory in swift succession, he had completely torn up the map of the States of Europe, but he had not yet won the war. Britain had not been defeated, nor did she evince any readiness to make peace, as Hitler undoubtedly hoped she would during the weeks immediately following the capitulation of France.

The question then was – what happens now? Would it be possible, by combined land, sea and air operations against her, to make Britain willing to conclude peace or even, perhaps, to defeat her completely? Among the papers of Field-Marshal Paulus is a memorandum, written in his own handwriting between 26 April and 3 May 1946, while a prisoner of war in Russia, on this first turning point in the course of the war. The memorandum is one of the first of a series of studies written by the Field-Marshal and is undoubtedly based on a questionnaire in German and Russian put before him by the Soviet authorities. It is quite obvious that the Russians were at that time most interested in every detail of the projected German invasion of England.

The future Field-Marshal had played an active part in the preparation of Operation 'Sea Lion', firstly as Chief of Staff, Sixth Army, under Field-Marshal v. Reichenau in France, and then, from 3 September 1940, as Oberquartiermeister I, General Staff.

Walter Goerlitz.

Memorandum by Field-Marshal Paulus on Operation 'England'

In the summer of 1940, after the victorious conclusion of the campaign in France, Germany, it seemed, stood at the zenith of her might. The economic resources of Central and Western Europe and North West Scandinavia were all at her disposal. But there was still one difficult problem that had not yet been solved. The outcome of the war with Britain was uncertain. All Hitler's peace-feelers had been rejected. The attitude of the United States was still not clear, though it was known that under Roosevelt's leadership the American Government was hostile to the concept of National Socialism.

At this juncture the German Air Force was preparing for its massive assault on the British Isles, the General Staff of the Army and Naval High Command, working in close unison, were making the first complicated preparations for the invasion of England and were concentrating and training the invasion forces of the Army and the naval personnel and ships required to carry them and to protect them in transit.

The question, of such vital consequence to the subsequent prosecution of the war, of why the German Supreme Command decided not to proceed with the invasion of England is one which, quite rightly, will occupy a conspicuous place in all discussions on the history of the war. I do not propose to examine here in any detail all the decisions taken at that time and the reasons that lay behind them; but in view of their obvious connection with later events in the East, I propose to tabulate the salient features, as I now see them in retrospect, as I saw them while playing my part in them and as I heard them discussed at Army Headquarters and Supreme Headquarters of the Armed Forces.

The reasons why Operation 'England' was abandoned

Before seeking the reasons which caused Hitler to abandon his plans for the invasion, it is necessary to take a look at the situation as it was in the summer of 1940.

At the end of May, in one single eastward thrust, the German forces reached the Channel coasts of Holland, Belgium and northern

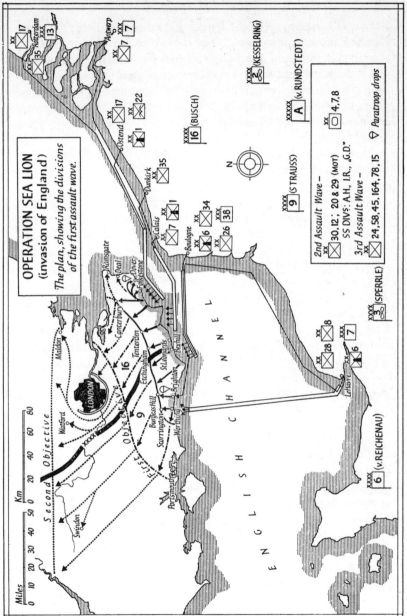

OPERATION SEA LION
(invasion of England)

The plan, showing the divisions
of the first assault wave.

MAP I

France. The remnants of the British Expeditionary Force fled from Dunkirk in sea-going vessels, coastal craft and small boats of every conceivable type and size. The German forces halted at the coast and did not attempt to pursue them; nor, indeed had any preparations for a possible pursuit of this nature been made. Hitler wished first and foremost to effect the swift and complete defeat of France, and for this he considered he required the whole of the German armed forces.

After a re-grouping of the forces available, the attack on the rest of France was launched on 5 June, and on 20 June France capitulated.

Thereupon the forces were again re-grouped on the Channel coasts, in preparation for the invasion of England. The relevant orders were issued at the beginning of July. For the actual landing three Armies – Sixth, Ninth and Sixteenth – were detailed. The orders were couched in positive terms, which left no doubt that the invasion would be launched, and they were regarded by both the Army Commands and the troops concerned as definite orders to that effect. This did not apply to Army, Norway, to which, from the very beginning, tasks for deceiving and confusing the enemy were ascribed. The Navy was directed to obtain and prepare the requisite landing-craft, and the Army Commands were ordered to collect all the coastal and river craft to be found in their respective areas. An immediate start was made with the necessary modification of these craft and with the training of the troops in the loading and unloading of them. Naval officers were attached to the various Headquarters as advisers.

No one for a moment doubted that the Supreme Command intended to go ahead with the undertaking. On the other hand misgivings, both at Army Commands and among the troops themselves, at the inadequate numbers and for the most part unsuitable types of craft being provided very quickly became apparent; and these misgivings were reflected in the representations made by the various Armies to Supreme Headquarters. The answer given was to the effect that preparations and training were to proceed with all possible despatch with the means available, that new types of landing craft were being evolved and would be delivered to the Army by the Navy in due course. Plans of these new types were issued to the

Armies concerned, with the recommendation that the Pioneer Battalions should re-model available craft, as far as was possible, according to the sketches provided.

One of the training exercises of the Sixth Army, held at St Malo in the middle of August 1940, was attended by the Chief of the General Staff, General Halder. The Sixth Army had been exceptionally badly treated as regards the provision of landing-craft and equipment, and the subsequent protests and requests were proportionately vehement and comprehensive.

Towards the end of August, the Sixth Army – the left flank of the proposed invasion – was informed that it had been decided that Sixth Army's part in the operations would be confined to the delivery of a feint attack, but that this decision was not to be made known outside the Army General Staff. The actual invasion would be carried out by Ninth and Sixteenth Armies, and the concentration of all available means of transport in these two armies, it was added, would ensure the feasibility of the operation. The Navy calculated that 4,000 craft of all types would be required.

At this time the situation in the air was regarded as being very favourable – as, indeed, it was. The two air fleets, under Field-Marshals Sperrle and Kesselring, were concentrated in France and Belgium and were held to be more than a match for the British Air Force.[1]

Our sole anxiety concerned the relative strength of the two sides at sea. The main question was – would the very considerable inferiority of the German Fleet be counter-balanced, having due regard for the frequent periods of bad weather in the Channel, by the possession of superior forces in the air? At the time, I heard it said at Army Headquarters that the Navy were fairly confident that, given certain specific conditions, a landing could successfully be accomplished, but had grave doubts whether, in conjunction with the Air Force, the Navy would be able for any length of time to keep the way across the Channel open for the passage of reinforcements and supplies. Strong reaction by the Royal Navy from $X+1$ day onwards was, in any case, taken for granted.

Meanwhile all the preparations for the invasion were going ahead

[1] A very optimistic assumption by Field-Marshal Paulus, which was not shared by Kesselring and other authorities.

at great speed. Staff conferences were also held to discuss the subsequent operations for the capture of London, and all the arrangements for the carrying of supplies and the administration of the occupied territories were, in fact, completed.

When I was transferred to Army Headquarters in Fontainebleau on 3 September, the General Staff (Brauchitsch and Halder) still believed that Hitler was in earnest in his determination to invade England. To my own knowledge the Commander-in-Chief (Brauchitsch) attended several of the exercises carried out by the Ninth and Sixteenth Armies in the autumn, and the Chief of the General Staff was present at war games held by Ninth and Sixteenth Armies' General Staffs at the end of September and the beginning of October respectively; and orders, based on the results of these games, were issued to both armies.

Hitler, however, kept on postponing the operation until, in October and in view of the unfavourable weather to be expected in the late autumn and winter, any invasion in 1940 was out of the question. Even so, no orders cancelling the operation were issued.[1] In the late autumn, Hitler directed that preparations were to be continued and that all the experience gained during the winter was to be evaluated with a view to its being used as soon as the next opportunity for carrying out the invasion occurred in the spring of 1941.

In the spring, a major re-grouping took place as the result of the projected Operation 'Barbarossa'. Ninth, Sixteenth and Sixth Armies were replaced by Fifteenth, Seventh and First Armies. Some time in the second half of October a new Army Group, Army Group D, was created at Melun under the command of Field-Marshal v. Witzleben, with Lieut-General Hilpert as his Chief of Staff. The Commander of this Army Group was later given the title of Commander-in-Chief, West.

From now onwards, preparations for the invasion were carried on simply as a means of deceiving and confusing the enemy, with the object of tying down British forces in the island, of preventing any major reinforcement of the Mediterranean theatre of war and also of distracting attention from the East.

[1] On 17 September Hitler decided to postpone the issue of orders for the launching of the invasion 'indefinitely'.

If, after a survey of the historical sequence of events, the question is asked whether Hitler ever really intended to invade England and, if so, why he abandoned the project, I would say that, in my opinion, these events cannot, of themselves, be said to furnish conclusive proof either way. Nor does the fact that the Commander-in-Chief of the Army and his Chief of Staff both firmly believed until late into the autumn that the operation would take place prove anything, for Hitler was not in the habit of disclosing his most secret intentions to these two officers.

I must confess that I myself have no reliable information regarding Hitler's intentions at the time. I think, however, that the idea of Operation 'Sea Lion' must have originated with Hitler, for Field-Marshal Keitel himself had no creative ideas of his own and confined himself, in unison with General Jodl, to accepting Hitler's ideas and intentions and passing them on to the Armed Forces Directing Staff with orders to work out the details and prepare a plan. Nor could Goering be regarded, strategically or operationally, in any way as a man of creative vision. He carried out the orders issued to him by Supreme Headquarters, though he often created difficulties if he thought that the prestige of his Air Force was concerned. Against all this must be set the fact that, from the comments they made, the officers on Field-Marshal v. Rundstedt's Staff from the very beginning doubted whether the operation would ever take place.[1] For what it is worth, I am myself inclined to think that, under the influence of the swift and decisive victories in Norway and France and of his own exaggerated ideas of the technical potentialities of his forces, Hitler really did, originally, intend to invade England.

It is perhaps also of interest to note that, immediately after the capitulation of France, orders were issued for the staging of a Victory Parade in Paris. The parade was first postponed for three or four weeks by Hitler and was then suddenly cancelled altogether. It may well be that Hitler was hoping that Britain would sue for

[1] This exposé of the views held by Field-Marshal v. Rundstedt's Staff, made by General Paulus in response to the Russian questionnaire on Operation 'Sea Lion', was based, presumably, on information given to Paulus by Lieut-General Vincent Mueller – though whether in 1940 or later in Soviet captivity is not clear.

peace and was postponing the parade until that happened. For the
same reason, probably, he held his hand for the time being as regards the major air offensive against England. This latter was not
launched until a considerable period had elapsed and all hope of
peace with Britain had disappeared. Goering is said to have then
expressed the view that his air offensive would force Britain to
sue for peace. These facts seem to support my own view that
Hitler hoped very much to be able to put an end to the war with
Britain without incurring the risks of an invasion.

For the subsequent abandonment of the enterprise there would
appear to be four reasons:

(1) The risk and the feared loss of prestige in the event of failure.

(2) The hope that the mere threat of invasion, coupled with the
U-boat successes and the air raids, would make Britain ready to
conclude peace.

(3) The wish to avoid doing Britain too great an injury, for it had
always been Hitler's cherished ambition to come to an understanding with Britain.

(4) The envisaged campaign against Russia, which had already been
decided upon in the summer of 1940.

Additional comments by the Field-Marshal

(1) In any case, land operations in England entailed a . . . (crossed
out in the original) risk. Although at the moment of her greatest
weakness after the defeat at Dunkirk Britain disposed of only some
eleven divisions fit for service,[1] she nevertheless had in the Home
Army, the so-called Territorial Army, a great reservoir of manpower. On the other hand, owing to the shortage of sea transport
facilities, the German Armed Forces would have been able to land –
swiftly – only a strictly limited number of divisions.

Although the Naval High Command had told Hitler that it considered an invasion feasible (given certain ancillary support), this
was by no manner of means an opinion universally held in naval
circles. I myself repeatedly heard naval officers express doubts as

---

[1] According to German calculations Britain at the time had thirty-four
divisions available, of which it was considered that eleven infantry and one
armoured division were fit for service. Paulus, writing here from memory, was,
therefore, pretty accurate.

to the Navy's ability, in view of the superiority of the British Fleet, to maintain lines of communication and supply across the Channel for any considerable length of time.

On the other hand, due consideration must be given to the superiority, at that time, of the German Air Force over the Royal Air Force[1] and the potential threat that the former constituted to the British Fleet at the narrowest part of the Channel between Dover and Calais – a threat that was increased by the fact that, as soon as a landing in England had been effected, German Air Force units would be transferred to air bases on the coast of England itself.

Taking into consideration all the factors enumerated above, therefore, it is not possible to give an unequivocal 'no' in answer to the question: Was invasion at that time possible? And when one remembers the hazardous nature of the previous enterprises undertaken by Hitler – Norway, the break through the Eifel via Sedan to the Channel coast – one is, I think, justified in assuming that Hitler would have accepted the risks entailed in an invasion, had the defeat of Britain been his sole concern – particularly as he would have had the whole might of the German Armed Forces at his disposal for the operation. So there must, I think, have been other considerations which contributed to the decision to abandon Operation 'Sea Lion'.

(2) Hitler certainly hoped that after the collapse of France and the defeat at Dunkirk – the effects of which he grossly overestimated – Britain would be ready to make peace and that it would require only the threat of invasion, coupled with the U-boat successes and the air raids, to bring this readiness to fruition.

(3) To this must be added a measure of wishful thinking on his part. Hitler's political attitude towards Britain and his desire to woo her favour are sufficiently brought out in his book *Mein Kampf* and in many subsequent speeches and statements, and no elaboration of the fact is required here. Considered in retrospect, it seems certain that he remained true to these ideas. It can, then, be safely assumed, I think, that his hesitation to commit himself to the invasion was influenced by this old desire to come to an agreement with Britain, and that therefore he must not do her too great an

[1] A superiority which, in fact, did not exist!

injury. To sum up, one is justified in assuming that the defeat of
Britain was not Hitler's primary war objective.

(4) There remains one final question to be examined: Was it his
intention to attack Russia that caused Hitler to abandon the projected invasion of England?

Apart from the risks involved in the actual attempt to effect a
landing, he could not foresee how long the subsequent operations,
the capture of London and the occupation of the whole island, would
take and the extent of the inroads that these operations would make
on the strength of the German armed forces. But he must have realized that his ability to concentrate adequate forces for the subsequent attack on Russia would thereby have been jeopardized.
Furthermore, had the attempt to invade ended in failure, so great,
inevitably, would have been the loss of prestige, that Hitler must
have feared that the German people would then no longer give him
whole-hearted support for so major an enterprise as an attack on
Soviet Russia.

When it is further remembered that Hitler's intention to attack
Russia dates from the beginning of July, immediately after the
collapse of France (as is proved by General Halder's diary[1]) it
becomes increasingly clear that there must have been a connection
between this intention and the abandonment of Operation 'Sea Lion'.

---

[1] Halder's diary, 3 July 1940: 'The strategic question of the moment is:
England or Russia?'

2. Russia's Strength – 'The Great Unknown'; 'Barbarossa': the strategic war game and the concentration of forces in the East

Introduction by Field-Marshal Paulus

At the end of July 1940, Hitler informed the Directing Staff, Armed Forces and the Commanders-in-Chief of the three Services that a campaign against Russia was not out of the question, and he directed them to make the necessary preliminary studies. While the war in the West had still not ended and its outcome was still not certain, Hitler, then, voluntarily abandoned the great advantage of fighting on one front and accepted the risk of war on two fronts.

That, however, is the purely military aspect of the ideas with which he was toying. From the ethical point of view his decision to attack Russia meant the breaking of a ten-year pact, which had only recently been signed and which ensured for him very considerable economic advantages and the supply in massive quantities of materials essential for the prosecution of the war.[1]

The General Staff of the Army viewed Hitler's offensive plans with mixed feelings. It viewed with some apprehension the opening of a second front. It regarded, even then, the entry of the United States into the war against Germany as certain; and it believed that Germany would be able to resist so formidable an array of power against her only if Russia were swiftly and totally defeated.

Russia's strength was the great unknown.

Operations against her were held to be feasible only in the good seasons of the year. But these were of short duration.

The General Staff regarded it as its duty to set down the operational, material and manpower possibilities and limitations. For the rest, it felt that it must obey the behests of the political leaders of the State.

[1] The German-Russian Non-Aggression Pact of 23 August 1939, which provided for very considerable deliveries of grain and iron ore from Russia.

Plan 'Barbarossa' and Directive No. 21
of 18 December 1940

The transition from the theoretical consideration to the practical preparation of the attack on Russia was initiated by the momentous Directive No. 21 of 18 December 1940. In view of its significance, the text of this directive is given below:

SECRET

The Fuehrer & Supreme Commander
OKW/WFST/Sec L(1)
No. 33 408/40
Fuehrer Headquarters
18 December 1940

DIRECTIVE NO. 21
OPERATION 'BARBAROSSA'

The German Armed Forces must be prepared, even before the end of the war with Britain, for a swift campaign for the overthrow of Soviet Russia. (Operation 'Barbarossa'.)

Except for such forces as are required as safeguards against surprise in the occupied territories, the Army will make available the whole of its forces for this operation.

In support of the Army, the Air Force will make available forces in sufficient strength to ensure that the land operations will be swiftly completed and that damage in East German territory by enemy air attack will be reduced to the minimum possible. A limitation is imposed upon this concentration of air power for the eastern theatre by the necessity of ensuring that the whole area of operations and the armament industrial areas under our control remain protected against enemy air attack and that our air offensive against Britain, and in particular against her imports, is not brought to a standstill.

The activities of the Navy will remain concentrated against Britain.

I shall issue the order for the concentration of the requisite forces for the attack on Russia, if this is finally decided upon, eight weeks before the date fixed for the start of the operation.

Preparations that demand a considerable period of time – in so far as they have not already been made – will be taken in hand at once and will be completed by 15 May 1941.

Primary importance will be attached to ensuring that our offensive preparations do not become apparent.

The preparations to be made by the various High Commands will be based on the following considerations:

I. General Intention
The mass of the Russian Army now concentrated in Western Russia will be destroyed, bold thrusts by columns of armoured formations will be made deep into enemy territory, and the withdrawal of major enemy forces into the depths of Russia will be prevented. A swift pursuit will then be executed to a line from which the Russian air arm will no longer be able to deliver attacks against Germany proper. The ultimate objective is the cordoning off of Asiatic Russia along the general line Volga – Archangel.
Etc, etc.[1]

(signed) Adolf Hitler.

In the middle of December a preliminary war game on the planning of Operation 'Barbarossa', which lasted for two days, was held under my direction at Army Headquarters in Zossen. It coincided more or less with the issue of the above directive.

Aids available

We had at our disposal the 'Consolidated Files, Russia', from the Foreign Armies, East, Branch (statistics regarding the Russian Army, armament industry and so on), parts of a new Military Geography of Russia, which was in process of compilation by Foreign Armies, East, Branch and the Military Geography Branch, and 1:1,000,000 maps and 1:300,000 map of the railway systems.[2]

[1] The remainder of the directive is not reproduced here, as it has already been published *in toto* many times before.

[2] What follows is based on a memorandum, dated 13 August 1946 and written by the Field-Marshal, in which he emphasizes that his reconstruction of this war game had been written from memory. His son, Captain Ernst Alexander Paulus, has taken this original memorandum and the numerous addenda and amendments made to it by the Field-Marshal himself, and has produced this revised account.

Participants: The Heads of the Branches concerned, plus certain Senior General Staff Officers specifically detailed. Those present were: The Chief of the General Staff, the OQuIV (Foreign Armies Branch), the Quartermaster-General, the Director General of Transport, the Director General of Communications and the Air Force General attached to Army Headquarters.

The object of the exercise was the formulation of the basic idea and an exchange of views regarding the plan of the campaign, to serve as a basis for the working out of the real plan for the concentration of forces by the Operations Branch. The conference was purely academic in character and was therefore organized in the form of a planning exercise, in which the Director of the exercise played the parts of both Army Headquarters and Commander-in-Chief, Red Force (enemy).

For this purpose, the Head of the Foreign Armies, East, Branch and two assistants were attached to the Director's staff. He attended the 'Blue' (German) side's conferences, and his job was from time to time to draw the attention of Blue Command to such courses open to the enemy as would have an adverse effect upon Blue Force's intentions.

During the exercise, the exchange of views was confined purely to questions of strategy, all other such aspects as the disguising of offensive preparations, the occupation of enemy territory and so on were ignored.

The following issues were discussed:

(1) The first phase of the offensive, with particular reference to co-operation between the armies and the Panzer Armies, and a ruling on the system of command to be adopted. This, at the time, was the subject of sharp controversy. Supreme Headquarters and the Commanders of the Panzer arm, citing the experience gained during the second phase of the campaign in France, stressed the necessity of accepting the principle that the Panzer arm was an independent entity, to be used in independent operations at long-range, and rejected the idea that Panzer formations should be placed under the command of the GOC an Army. The Army General Staff, on the other hand, regarded this as an extreme solution and preferred to see the question left open, to be decided according to the circumstances of each individual case.

(2) a. In Army Group, South, the co-operation between the Armies debouching from Rumania (Armies A and B) and those debouching from South Poland (Armies C and D and First Panzer Army).

b. In Army Groups, Centre and North, the dividing line between the two sectors, having due regard to the threat to the flank of the Army Group from the North.

c. The re-grouping after the first strategic objective had been reached (the line Dnieper – upper Dvina – Chudskoye Ozero).

In this connection, consideration to be given to the effect of the supply situation on the timetable.

(4) The question of reserves.

(5) a. Definition, in general terms, of the demands to be made by the Army on the Air Force.

b. Co-operation with the Navy was not discussed.

Now that the actual course of the campaign has become part of history, it may perhaps be of both use and interest to the military student to compare what actually happened with the ideas formulated and the intentions laid down during this war game – and particularly with the broad appreciation of the situation made at that time.

In the following description of the premises upon which the planning exercise was based, it is, of course, not possible to go into all the details, practically all of which, nevertheless, were discussed at considerable length.

Initial Situation - Blue (German) Army

(1) The exercise started with a re-statement of the broad strategic objectives, in accordance with instructions issued in July 1940 by Supreme Headquarters:[1] by means of a series of swift operations, including thrusts by armoured columns deep into enemy territory, to destroy the Russian forces concentrated in Western Russia and to prevent the withdrawal of organized major formations into the distant interior of Russia.

First Objective: Ukraine (inclusive Don basin) – Moscow – Leningrad.

---

[1] Not quite correct. No formal directive was issued by Supreme Headquarters before 18 December 1940. It is true, however, that on 5 December Halder and Brauchitsch submitted a report on the subject to Hitler, on the basis of the exercise carried out by Paulus.

Main Thrust: Moscow.
Final Objective: Volga – Archangel.

Based upon the directives from Supreme Headquarters, the deliberations of the General Staff of the Army came to the following conclusions:

Moscow, as the political capital and the armament and communications centre, the Don basin and Leningrad as armament centres, and the Ukraine, as the country's principal granary, were all of crucial importance to Russia's prosecution of the war. It was therefore anticipated that the Russians, even if initially they exploited the vast extent of their territories and withdrew, would be compelled to stand and fight to retain the abovementioned areas.

The Army's task, therefore, was:

(a) With air support to destroy, at the latest in the decisive battle for these important localities which was to be forced upon the enemy at all cost, the finest cadres of the Russian Army and thus to preclude the possibility of a subsequent planned and full exploitation of the vast manpower at the Russians' disposal.

(b) To achieve the above swiftly, before the Russians had time to develop their defensive powers to the full.

(c) Having made the initial break-through, to strive with every possible means to isolate and destroy in detail Russian formations before the enemy was able to form a new, corporate front.

Although the war would not be brought to a conclusion by the attainment of the above objectives, it was assumed that Russia would then not be in any position, either as regards material or trained personnel, even to hold out for very long, let alone to bring about any radical change in the general situation.

(2) In the assessment of Russian reaction to the offensive, it was assumed that the Russians would probably offer stubborn resistance all the way from the frontier onwards:

(a) for political reasons, because they would presumably not willingly surrender territories which had so recently been incorporated into the Soviet Union, and

(b) from the military point of view, with the dual objects firstly of weakening the German onslaught from the very outset and thus of preventing them from obtaining that swift decision, which their situation compelled them to seek, before the Russians were able to mobilize their full defensive strength; and secondly, by means of evasive tactics to compel the Germans to fight the ultimate, decisive action in a battle-weary and weakened state, far away from their bases.

(3) The task allotted to the Army therefore demanded:

(a) The concentration of as strong a force as possible, echeloned in depth, for the advance on Moscow (Army Group Centre).

(b) The co-ordination on the two flanks – Army Groups South and North – of the diverging objectives allotted to them, namely, the occupation of Leningrad and the Ukraine and the protection of Army Group Centre's flank.

While contact between Army Groups North and Centre would be both close and direct, Army Group South, for the first part of the attack as far as the Dnieper, would be separated from the rest of the force by the Pripiet Marshes.

(c) The first objective of the offensive, selected as being well within the capacity of the Army to attain, was the general line: area between the Upper Dnieper and the Dvina – Lake Peipus. This line was selected partly for reasons of the terrain and partly because it was recognized that the troops would require both a breathing space and the opportunity to organize a defensive line, before embarking on the presumably imminent and decisive battle before them.

Initial Situation – Red (Russian) Army

The initial situation as far as the Russians were concerned was worked out solely on assumptions. The general considerations enumerated in paragraph 2 above were taken as representing the basis of the Russian High Command's plan of campaign. It was assumed that the Russian forces would amount to: 185 infantry divisions, 50 tank and motorized brigades, of which some 20 infantry divisions would be tied down on the Finnish frontier, some 25 would be in the Far East and approximately 15 in the Caucasus and Middle East. On the Russo-German front, therefore, there would be in all about 175 formations, made up of 125 infantry divisions and 50 tank and motorized brigades. (These figures are quoted from memory.)[1] It was assumed that the Russian forces would be organized in three Army Groups, deployed roughly in the same way as the German Army Groups, with Army Staffs about one third stronger than on the German side.

Of the 125 infantry divisions it was thought that roughly two-thirds would be in the front line on the frontier or in tactical reserve and that one third, organized partly in Armies, would be held in strategic reserve at the disposal of Army Groups or Supreme Head-quarters. The tank and motorized brigades were presumed to have been allotted to Armies, both at the front and in reserve.

It was calculated that by three months after the beginning of the war these forces would be augmented by some thirty or forty divisions, partly newly raised and partly transferred from other Russian frontiers, and that after six months these would be aug-mented by a further 100 divisions.

These calculations of enemy strength did not affect the planning exercise itself, which was concerned solely with the opening weeks of the campaign; but they were of primary importance when it came to determining the objectives and the timetable of the German offensive.

In an appendix to this memorandum, those interested will find a detailed account, written from memory, of the step by step

[1] Cf these figures quoted by the Field-Marshal from memory with the report submitted to German Supreme Headquarters by Foreign Armies, East, Branch on 29 January 1941:

Peace strength of the Russian Army: 100 infantry, thirty-two cavalry divisions, twenty-four motorized and mechanized brigades. Approximately two million men. War strength of Russian Field Army: twenty Armies, 150 infantry divisions (fifteen of them motorized), thirty-two cavalry divisions, thirty-six motorized and mechanized brigades. Approximately four million men.

Of these it is assumed that twenty-nine infantry and seven cavalry divisions, five motorized and mechanized brigades will be stationed in Soviet Central Asia. In Europe, Russia's strength can be taken as 121 infantry and twenty-five cavalry divisions, and thirty-one motorized brigades. Of these fifteen infantry divisions will be on the Finnish frontier and six mountain divisions in the Caucasus.

No reliable figures have, unfortunately, been published by the Russians. According to General Shaposhnikov, the Soviet CGS, the Russians had avail-able for an advance into western Europe 120 infantry, sixteen cavalry divisions, with 5,000 guns, 9,000 to 10,000 tanks and 5,000 to 5,500 aircraft. These figures refer to the summer of 1939.

progress of this war game. The main point, however, is that the Russian Army was assumed to be inferior in armour, artillery and, particularly, in the air.[1]

Of the assumptions made and the situations envisaged during the course of the exercise, quite a number of the former proved to be correct, and of the latter actually arose, when the campaign took place. Here, however, I do not propose to detail the hypothetical movements of the various Army Groups.

The various points which emerged as the exercise progressed were discussed in detail. No final summing-up conference was held. The Chief of the General Staff's primary object in holding the exercise was the hope that from it would emerge a series of data and suggestions, which would be of value to him and the Chief of the Operations Branch in framing the orders for the first strategic concentration and approach march.

Air Force

Co-operation with the Air Force was discussed in detail for each phase of the operations and along lines which ensured that the ground forces would receive the maximum possible support from the air. Without going into details, the main demands made of the Air Force were:

(1) First and foremost – apart from the neutralization of the enemy air arm – continuous and close fighter support for the troops in action and the effective engagement of enemy formations on the move towards the battle area, and the creation of a comprehensive system of communications between the Air Force and the Army.

(2) Continuous air attack on road and rail junctions and on troop movements by road and rail.

(3) In order that the maximum force of all arms should be available to ensure a swift decision, the Air Force to postpone the initiation of

---

[1] This assumption was wrong – at least as far as armour was concerned – and not only in the estimate of relative strengths. In his memoirs Guderian states (p. 129) that when a Russian Military Mission visited the German Tank School and Tank factories in the spring of 1941 and were shown the latest model (Panzer Mk. IV), they refused to believe that this was the heaviest tank the Germans had. Apparently they knew all about the Mk. T.34, which was then in process of delivery to the Army!

independent and essentially air operations, such as the bombing of industrial areas and so on.

A further point that was discussed was the necessity of training Staff Officers in the proper allocation of tasks to the air arm and in the correct distribution of tasks as between reconnaissance and fighter formations.

The Question of Forces Available

The general conclusion reached as the result of the exercise was that the German forces were barely sufficient for the purpose. Even at this stage it was obvious that the Army Groups would have at their disposal only such reserves as they themselves were able to create from their own front-line formations. A general reserve of some eleven divisions for a front of something over 1,200 miles was in any case far too small – particularly in view of the inadequate means of lateral communication behind the front line.

It was agreed that as early as the second phase of the operations the General Reserve (Army G) would have to be committed, and this meant that for the final and, it was hoped, decisive blow in the Moscow area the only reserves available would be the few odd divisions which the attacking forces themselves could spare and hold back for that purpose.

The order of battle on both sides, as calculated during the exercise, is given in the appendix.[1]

The final objective, Volga – Archangel, was, in any case, far beyond anything that the German forces available could hope to achieve; but it is a typical example of the megalomaniac extravagance of National Socialist political thinking. Nevertheless it was on the basis of these orders that the plans for the concentration of forces and the approach march were framed.

From the very outset there was a sharp divergence of opinion between Supreme Headquarters (Hitler) and the Army General Staff regarding both the manner in which the operations should be conducted and the intermediate objectives that should be set. Both

---

[1] The paragraphs which follow, inclusive of the tabulated strength of each side, are based on notes made by the Field-Marshal for the lectures he delivered in Dresden. They are therefore a much later addition to the original memorandum.

the Commander-in-Chief of the Army and the General Staff regarded the destruction of the enemy forces in the field and the
prevention of the escape of any significant portion of them into the
depths of Russia as the primary objective of the campaign. In their
opinion the main objective of the offensive should be the capture of
the capital, Moscow. Should this objective not be attained, they
foresaw a long drawn-out war beyond the capacity of the German
Armed Forces to wage.

Hitler held completely different views. His interest was concentrated on the flanks. He had the quite astounding idea that by
capturing Leningrad he would be able to neutralize and render
impotent the political centre of the Soviet system and with it the
power of its world-wide aspirations; and his primary objective was
the occupation of the Ukraine and the Caucasus, economically the
most important areas and the producers of grain, iron ore, coal and
oil.

With these in his possession, Hitler believed he would be able to
maintain and eventually stabilize his domination of Europe.
Coupled with this was his hope, already mentioned, that Britain
would then realize the futility of continuing to fight against Germany
and would be ready to make peace. This concept he enunciated in an
address which he delivered to the Commanders-in-Chief of the
three services in Berlin in June 1941, shortly before the opening of
the campaign.[1] In other words, in order to put an end to the old war
he was launching forth on a new one. The man who in the past had
consistently criticized German policy for its failure to avoid war on
two fronts was now creating a second front of his own free will.

---

[1] Address delivered in the Chancellery, Berlin, on 14 June 1941 in the presence
of the Commanders-in-Chief of the three Services, their Chiefs of Staff and
the Army and Panzer Army Commanders. On 17 June Hitler gave the order:
Operation 'Barbarossa' will begin on 22 June.

Appendix:

War Game 'Barbarossa', December 1940;
calculation of respective strengths

GERMAN			RUSSIAN		
In all	210 divs.		In all 185 infantry		
of which Norway			divisions, fifty tank		
and Denmark ..	11 ,,		and motorized brig-		
France	41 ,,		ades, of which		
Africa	4 ,,		Finnish Frontier	20 divs.	
	———		Caucasus	15 ,,	
	56 divs.		Far East	25 ,,	
				———	
				60 divs.	

Available for
Russo-German front: 154 divs.
consisting of

Infantry ..	107 divs.
Cavalry ..	1 ,,
Panzer	18 ,,
Motorized Infantry	18 ,,
Security (behind the front)	10 ,,
Final total for striking force:	144 divs.
Plus Rumanian (initially)	10 ,,
	———
	154 divs.

Available for Russo-German front: 125 infantry divisions, fifty tank and motorized brigades.

Subsequent build-up:
(a) within three months, by withdrawals from other areas and newly raised formations: 30–40 divs.

(b) Within six months (newly raised) about 100 divs.

The German Infantry Division was taken to be approximately one third stronger in armament (heavy weapons) than the Russian Infantry Division. Marked German superiority was held to exist in:

(a) Artillery, including Artillery Observation units.
(b) Tanks.
(c) Signals and Communications.
(d) Air Force (very marked superiority).

As regards the raising of new formations, it was considered that lack of training cadres and equipment would prevent full use being made of the vast reserves of manpower available.

The existence of the armament industrial areas in the Urals was known, but no information was available regarding their productive capacity.[1]

War Game 'Barbarossa' : the operations of the Army Groups

The tasks allotted to the Army Groups were roughly as follows: *Army Group South.* Attack from Rumania and South Poland with main thrust on Kiev, to be captured by Panzer forces as soon as possible. The forces debouching from Rumania will (a) engage and pin down as strong forces of the enemy as possible, with a view to preventing them from intervening against the forces debouching from South Poland, and (b) at the same time establish a bridgehead over the Dniester in preparation for their own advance eastwards in unison with the Group, South Poland.

Army Group Centre. Will deliver an encircling attack from the area Brest Litovsk and Southern East Prussia with the object of destroying the Russian forces located in the Bielystok arc. Tank columns will advance as rapidly as possible on Orsha and Vitebsk and establish bridge-heads across the Dnieper and seize the area between the Upper Dnieper and the Dvina east of a line Orsha – Vitebsk.

Army Group North. Debouching from East Prussia will advance on Leningrad and at the same time protect the northern flank of Army Group Centre. First objective: the line Veliki Luki – Staraya Russa – Lake Peipus.

[1] Notes found later among the Field-Marshal's papers contained the following statistics:

Initial Strengths			
Blue Force		Red Force	
Men	3,098,000	Men	2,611,000
Artillery all calibres, inclusive			
AA	8,616 guns		
Tanks	3,600		
Armoured Recce			
Vehicles	1,188		

Method of execution

Army Group South. As regards the forces debouching from Rumania the Army Group Commander ordered the two Armies concerned to advance eccentrically, Army A to establish a bridge-head on the east bank of the Dniester on both sides of Sorochi and to the south, Army B to establish a bridge-head in the area Mogilev-Podolskiy – Kamenets-Podolskiy.

The Commander of Army A, in spite of the wide dispersion of his forces, allowed himself to be misled into pursuing the retreating Russians beyond his bridge-head. Army B succeeded in establishing a broad bridge-head across the Dniester at Kamenets-Podolskiy and a smaller one further to the east, but used up all his reserves in the process. Of the forces debouching from South Poland, Army C was ordered to direct its main attack from the area north and north-west of Rava Ruska on Lemberg. In Army D's area, as soon as Army D had crossed the Bug, First Panzer Army was ordered to thrust towards Kiev, regardless of the neighbouring sectors on the Stokhod and the Styr and the strong Russian reserves that were known to be concentrated to the east of them.

Situation on X+8 Day

(1) ARMY GROUP SOUTH

(a) *Rumania Group.* Army A, after fierce fighting on the frontier, was pursuing the enemy retreating eastwards between the Dniester and the Bug. Its northern wing and flank was mauled by a strong enemy counter-attack delivered by some six divisions.

At the same time, Army B, on A's left, was heavily engaged in defending its bridge-heads to the north of Mogilev and Kamenets against heavy enemy counter-attacks and was unable to afford any assistance to Army A.

As a result, the northern wing of Army A was thrown back across the Dniester, and the Army was then compelled to withdraw its centre and right wing as well.

This made it impossible for the Rumania Group to give any effective support in the engagement in progress south of the Pripiet Marshes. The conclusion drawn from this situation was that the Rumania Group, echeloned forward as it was over a great distance, was too weak. This group could have carried out its mission – to tie down as strong enemy forces as possible and be prepared to advance in unison with South Poland Group – only by keeping its forces closely concentrated. In addition it had been forced to commit most of its reserves for the establishment of the Mogilev – Kamenets bridge-heads. The decision to advance on a broad front, it was held, would deceive and tie down the enemy only for a short while.

The Rumanian forces participating in the operations were given the task firstly of linking up with Army A and protecting the lower Prut and later, deeply echeloned to the right, to follow Army A.

The question was raised whether it would not have been preferable to launch Army Group South's main attack from Rumania rather than from South Poland? The conclusion arrived at was: Road and rail facilities were inadequate to cope with the assembly and concentration of large forces in Rumania. Concentration would have taken too long, and secrecy would thus have been jeopardized. The road network in the Ukraine runs west – east and south-east. The main attack therefore had to be delivered from South Poland (Armies C and D and First Panzer Army) in the direction of Kiev and to the south of it.

(b) *South Poland Group*. The position resultant upon the orders given by the German Command and the counter-measures taken by the enemy was as follows: Army C was fighting for the possession of Lemberg. Immediately after Army D's break-through across the Bug, First Panzer Army was directed to press on beyond Army D's area to Rovno and from there to thrust towards Kiev. The First Panzer Army was held up at the Styr, where it was now fighting in conjunction with advancing elements of Army D in an attempt to cross the river in the face of increasing enemy resistance. At the same time, air reconnaissance reported strong enemy concentrations, including large tank forces, in the Rovno area.

Scrutiny of this situation led to the following conclusions: The presence of strong Russian reserves in the back areas was known. It could therefore be assumed that stubborn enemy opposition would be continuous even after the break-through on the frontier had been achieved. As a first measure, therefore, Army D would have to fight its way through a number of defended localities between the frontier and the Styr and then fight its way across the river. Before this, however, it was felt that some formations of First Panzer Army should have been placed under the command of Army D, to help in the swift clearing of the area up to and over the Styr.

In view of the primary task allotted to First Panzer Army – the thrust on Kiev – to have sent it forward independently from the Bug and allow it thus to become heavily engaged in a costly battle was regarded as a mistake.

(c) As the method of the initial commitment of the forces debouching from Rumania and South Poland was judged to have been unsound, Army Group was unable to co-ordinate the operations of these two forces. The establishment of a strong bridge-head in the Mogilev–Kamenets–Podolskiy area by the Rumania Group, had it remained concentrated and with adequate reserves, might have made possible the launching of an attack in the direction of Proskurov and have led, in conjunction with the South Poland Group, to the encirclement of strong Russian forces.

In the event of an unexpectedly swift retreat by the Russians to behind the Dnieper, the Rumania Group would have been able to take advantage of its forward distribution in depth to make a thrust towards Cherkassy and beyond and, in conjunction with First Panzer Army, to have prevented the escape of major Russian forces across the Dnieper.

The above considerations led to the conclusion that both Armies debouching from Rumania must be placed under the command of the senior Army Commander for as long as they were called upon to fight independently of, and separated from, the forces debouching from South Poland.

(d) As regards the dividing line between Army Groups South and Centre, there remained the question of the Pripiet Marshes. According to the information available, these marshes constituted an impassable obstacle for any large-scale movement of troops. Opinion was divided, however, as regards the scope and importance of the harassing operations that the enemy might be able to launch from this area against the long flanks of Army Groups South and Centre.

The measures advocated to guard against such harassing operations ranged from the employment of a complete but weak Army to the mere establishment of flank guards by the Army Groups concerned. On this question no final conclusion was reached during the exercise.

2. ARMY GROUP CENTRE

The main problem facing Army Group Centre was how to carry out the order '. . . bold thrusts by columns of armoured formations will be made deep into enemy territory and the withdrawal of major enemy forces into the depths of Russia will be prevented.' Protruding westwards on the Army Group front was the Bielystok salient. The two Army Commanders concerned agreed that the salient should be attacked from the south-west and south by Army E and from the north-west and north by Army F.

Accordingly, Second Panzer Army was ordered to advance from Brest Litovsk via Slonim, Baranovichi on Minsk, and Third Panzer Army from the apex east of Suvalki on Vilna and Molodechno.

These dispositions were assumed to have led to the following situation: After heavy fighting on the frontier, Armies E and F were still striving to capture the Bielystok salient, which had been constricted, but which the enemy was still defending stubbornly. Enemy withdrawals eastwards had nevertheless been observed. The two Panzer Armies, ignoring this situation, had set out on the tasks allotted to them.

The forward elements of Second Panzer Army were in action in front of Baranovichi with newly arrived enemy forces. Its rear elements were engaging enemy withdrawing eastwards from the Bielystok area in a battle in which the main body of the Army, wheeling north, would soon be called upon to intervene.

The forward elements of Third Panzer Army had reached the area to the east of Lida and the west of Olkeniki, when they were heavily attacked by strong enemy forces advancing from the direction of Vilna in the north. This compelled Third Panzer Army to form a front facing north and to withdraw its forward elements which had thrust further eastwards. At the same time, it was compelled to allot some of its units to form another front facing south and south-west against the enemy retreating from Bielystok.

From these moves and counter-moves Headquarters, Army Group B deduced that the intention of the enemy was to counter-attack and destroy the forward elements of Blue Force and then to advance from the Vilna area in strength in a south-westerly direction, in order to enable the Red forces still in the Bielystok area to withdraw eastwards, with the ultimate object of establishing a line Vilna-Baranovichi and a new front further to the south. The conclusions drawn from the above appreciation of the situation were as follows:

Full advantage of the chance to encircle the Red forces in the Bielystok salient could be taken only if the two Panzer Armies operating on the outer flanks, having broken through the Russian front, were kept more closely concentrated – e.g. on the Shara and the Niemen with a screen facing east, in order swiftly to complete the encirclement of the Red forces in the Bielystok area, before major portions of them could escape or strong reinforcements could come up to their assistance.

For this purpose, it was felt that from the outset infantry corps should have been allotted to the Panzer Armies with the task of delivering the initial attack and of then advancing in rear of the Panzer Armies, thus enabling the mobile elements of the latter to disengage as swiftly as possible from the encircling operation and press on eastwards.

3. ARMY GROUP NORTH

The Army Group Commander selected as his first objective the capture of Daugapils and Riga. With this in view, he placed Fourth Panzer Army in the centre, with orders to advance in the general direction of Panevishis and to support either the right Army (Army J) or the left Army (K) as circumstances and opportunity dictated.

As the Red forces retired very rapidly on Riga, however, the Army Group Commander, by a mistaken application of the principle of exploitation of success, committed the error of concentrating the bulk of his armour with the left Army (K). As a result right Army (J), with Kovno and beyond as its objective, advanced but slowly against strong enemy opposition, the northern flank of the Army Group (Third Panzer Army) was badly mauled by a powerful enemy counter-attack from Vilna, the attempt to surround the enemy in the Bielystok area failed, and the envisaged rapid thrust on Vitebsk by Third Panzer Army had to be postponed.

Conclusions

(a) The course of the operations had clearly shown the importance of close co-operation between the inner wings of Army Groups Centre and North. In this connection, the desirability of altering the dividing line between the two Army Groups was discussed, but it was decided to leave things as they were.

Reasons: Throughout its whole course the main attack of Army Group Centre would, presumably, be under constant threat from the north. On Army Group North, therefore, devolved the task – in addition to the capture of its objective, Leningrad – of providing continuous flank protection for Army Group Centre. The town of Vilna, however, with its network of roads, was of primary importance to Army Group North. Consequently it was felt that the co-operation between the inner wings of the two Army Groups would have to be ensured by calling upon the Higher Command to co-ordinate a precise distribution of tasks as between the two Army Groups concerned.

(b) The capture of Leningrad and the Russian naval bases was an important strategic objective. The threat against them would therefore certainly tie down considerable Russian forces for their defence, and eventually a large-scale Russian counter-attack in this area could be regarded as certain. Nevertheless, in accordance with the basic concept of the campaign as a whole and in view of the limited German forces available, the attack on Leningrad would have to be regarded as secondary to the main task – the protection of the northern flank of Army Group Centre.

War Game, Phase 2. The situation on X+20 Day

(1) After severe fighting on the frontier, the German Army had succeeded in gaining ground swiftly in West Ukraine, White Russia and the Baltic and in reaching the general line: Dnieper to the south of Kiev, with a westward bend round the salient formed by the bridge-head still held by the Russians on the west bank of the Dnieper, and then, to the north of this salient, the line east of Mozeir – Rogachev – Orsha – Vitebsk – Veliki Luki – south of Pernau – south of Pleskau.

Thus, both in extent and according to the timetable, the general line had been reached which had been laid down in the plan of campaign as the first objective and the springboard for the decisive advance on Moscow.

Before the general offensive could be resumed, a pause of some three weeks would be required for:

(a) The concentration and reorganization of formations and the partial replacement of casualties and deficiences,

(b) the technical overhaul of the Panzer and motorized formations, and

(c) above all, the establishment of new supply bases.

(2) In the appreciation of the situation as regards the Russian side, it was assumed:

(a) The Russian Army, in view of its stubborn resistance in the frontier battles, particularly in White Russia and North Ukraine, had suffered severe losses in both men and equipment (up to 50 per cent).

(b) The retirement to the line Dnieper – Upper Dvina and to the north had nevertheless proceeded according to plan, and a new, continuous front had been established, though in places it was thinly held.

(c) As regards the further steps being taken by the Russian High Command, the following picture (based on air reconnaissance and intelligence reports) was given to the Blue Commanders:

The general pattern of road and rail movement – apart from large-scale replacements at the front – indicates the transfer of divisions from the Caucasus and the Far East. It is further antici-pated that a number of new divisions are in process of formation, but would not be ready to take the field for three months.

(d) On the basis of the above information the final appreciation of Russian intentions was as follows:

(i) It was unlikely that in the present situation the Russian High Command would elect to stand and fight a decisive battle, since, for the protection of Moscow, it still had plenty of room in which to manoeuvre and fight defensive, delaying actions, and in the time thus gained it would be able to add materially to the strength of its forces.

(ii) In view of the current relative strengths of the two sides, no counter-offensive on a strategic scale was anticipated.

From a conference with the officers detailed as Army Group and Army Commanders, based on the above assumptions, there emerged the following: The need to resume the offensive before the Red side was able to concentrate additional forces was generally recognized. It was also agreed that the ultimate decision should be sought in an advance on Moscow. With regard to the method in which subsequent operations should be conducted, the following divergent views were expressed:

(a) The forces of Army Group South were held up before Kiev on the one side and were widely dispersed as far as the mouth of the Dnieper on the other. The Army Group Commander, with the ultimate objective in view, put forward a plan to cut off the Russian forces in the Kiev area. He proposed to launch one attack from his bridge-head south of Kiev and another from the area south-west of Gomel across the Dnieper and the Desna and on, via Chernikov, to Neshin. For this operation he asked for the temporary loan of supporting armour from Army Group Centre and of a portion of the General Reserve located in the Gomel area.[1]

(b) The Commander of Army Group North expressed the view that the occupation by the right wing of his Army Group of a line north of Veliki Luki – Lake Ilmen was an essential preliminary to the resumption of its offensive by Army Group Centre. For this operation he, too, asked for the temporary loan of armour and portions of the General Reserve.

(c) The Commander of Army Group Centre and his Army Commanders also agreed that the operations envisaged in (a) and (b) above were necessary preliminaries to the resumption of their own offensive. But in view of the paramount importance of preserving their own resources at maximum possible strength for the final, ultimate onslaught on Moscow, they felt that the other two Army

---

[1] It is interesting to compare this project with the critical situation that occurred in July-August 1941, which, referred to later by the Russians as a 'second miracle of the Marne', was accentuated by the fact that Hitler in his own mind had never accepted the General Staff's concept of Moscow as the primary objective of the campaign and that neither the C-in-C nor the CGS ever succeeded in persuading him to do so. The result was that the whole of August was wasted in debate; then, on Hitler's orders, forces were diverted from A-G Centre to A-G South, the great battle of Kiev was fought, but did not end until 2 October – far too late to launch an attack on Moscow.

Groups should carry out these operations with their own forces, even if this necessitated a slight postponement of Army Group Centre's own attack.

Taking all the above into consideration, it was agreed that the guiding principle governing the resumption of the general offensive should be as follows:

Granted the necessity for the pause for technical overhaul, accumulation of supplies etc. (paragraph (1) sub-paragraphs (a) (b) (c) above), the offensive should be resumed as soon as possible on the whole front. This, however, was not to be interpreted as meaning that the whole front would advance simultaneously. On the other hand due weight should be given to the fact that every day's delay was a day gained by the Russians for the strengthening of their defensive measures.

It was regarded as of primary importance that the two flank Army Groups should draw enemy forces against themselves as soon as possible. For the rest, it was felt that the attack should be delivered on as wide a front as possible, in order to prevent massive Russian counter-attacks on individual and perhaps isolated formations.

The broad outline of the tasks allotted to Army Groups was therefore roughly as follows:

The main task of all three Army Groups will be to ensure that the operations of all three of them are conducted in a manner that will result in the co-ordinated concentration of all available forces for the ultimate and decisive advance on Moscow.

Particular emphasis was laid on the observance by Army Group South of this guiding principle. After capturing Kiev and advancing across the Dnieper on a broad front, the Army Group's immediate main object will not be the occupation of the Don basin. Rather, it will concentrate the mass of its forces on its left flank and centre, with the object of protecting the southern flank of Army Group Centre throughout the whole of the subsequent operations. If while so doing it should succeed in defeating whatever enemy forces it encountered on its front, the occupation of the Don basin would follow as a matter of course.

The following orders were then issued to the three Army Groups:

Army Group South

With its main strength concentrated in its northern wing and echeloned in depth to the right, the Army Group will attack via Kharkov – Kursk in the general direction of Yelets. Its first objective will be the establishment of a bridge-head on the east bank of the Dnieper, approximately on the line Kremenchug – Lubni – Priluki – Chernikov. The echeloning of its left wing and centre, imposed by the course of the Dnieper, will be exploited to cut off the enemy forces in the area west of a line Kharkov – Kursk.

Various methods of carrying out this task were discussed. The final solution accepted was:

Army C, First Panzer Army and certain elements of Army D will attack from the bridge-head south-east of Kiev and surround the enemy forces located in the Kiev area. In this operation the primary task of Army C will be to form a screen on the approximate line Lubni – Priluki, while First Panzer Army, reinforced by elements of Army D, will attack in the direction of Chernikov, at the same time putting out a protective screen to the east of Neshin.

This solution had the dual advantage that it ensured a swift encirclement of Kiev and that on the completion of the battle of encirclement the First Panzer Army would be on the northern flank of the Army Group – in position, that is, for the main thrust of the subsequent offensive operations.

Army B was directed to co-ordinate its movements with the advance of Army C and to force a crossing of the Dnieper on both sides of Kremenchug, preparatory to an advance on Poltava.

These operations, it was considered, would result in the establishment of an excellent springboard east of the Dnieper for the launching of the major offensive along the whole front.

The orders issued to Army A and the Rumanian forces were that later, when the Army Group attack in the direction Saporozhe – Dnepropetrovsk was well under way, they would establish a protective screen facing the Crimea and then, echeloned in depth to the right, would advance into the Donets area.

Army Group Centre

1. The Army Group was ordered to be ready to advance at the

latest on X+40 day. The earliest possible date for the advance would be notified later.

2. Army Group Centre will break through the Russian positions east of Gomel and north-west of Smolensk. The Panzer Armies will operate on the outer flanks of the break-through in such a manner as will ensure the surrounding of the maximum enemy forces in the area west of Briansk – Kaluga.[1]

Army G (General Reserve) will move forward and will be placed under the command of Army Group Centre.

With the object of protecting the northern flank and maintaining contact with the southern wing of Army Group North, subsidiary attacks will be launched via Demidov – Toropez in the direction of Rshev.

Army Group North

Army Group North still found itself faced with the two conflicting tasks of protecting the northern flank of Army Group Centre and of capturing Leningrad and destroying the enemy forces in the Baltic States. The Chief of the General Staff (i.e. Halder) decided that the first of these was to be regarded as the primary task.

Army Group North was accordingly given the following instructions:

(a) To concentrate its forces on its centre and right wing and to occupy, as soon as possible, the line Veliki Luki – southern tip of Lake Ilmen – Lake Peipus.

(b) Then, in conjunction with Army Group Centre's attack, to advance its right wing via Ostashkov and seize the area in the vicinity of Bologol.

(c) To tie down enemy forces in the Leningrad and Baltic areas and repulse any attacks launched from Leningrad.

(d) The date of the attack on Leningrad itself would depend on the progress of the general offensive against Moscow.

[1] The battle of encirclement in the Viasma—Briansk area envisaged in the war game was actually fought at the beginning of October 1941. On 9 October Dr Dietrich, the Chief of the Press, announced that the eastern campaign was over and that Russia was 'down and out'. But in the war game calculations the second offensive was due to be launched by X+40 day. Taking 22 June as X day, the second offensive should have been launched on 2 August In actual fact it was not launched until eight weeks later, on 2 October!

3. Deputy Chief of the General Staff, 1941: memoranda and letters

···

Preface by Field-Marshal Paulus[1]

After the decision to attack Russia had been taken, the transit of troops to their strategic assembly areas was not carried out in one short, concentrated movement, but was spread over a considerable period. Transfer of troops to East Prussia and Poland commenced in July 1940, as soon as the campaign in France ended, when the following formations moved from France:

Army Group B (Later 'Centre')
    Army Group Headquarters to Posen
    Twelfth Army to Cracow (relieved in December by the newly raised Seventeenth Army in Zakopane)
    Fourth Army to Warsaw
    Eighteenth Army to Königsberg.

In addition there were about eight or nine independent commands, with a total strength of some twenty-five to thirty divisions. In the second half of September about forty new infantry and Panzer divisions were raised in Germany. To direct the training of these new divisions, Headquarters, Army Group C and Second Army moved from France to Dresden and Munich respectively, and Eleventh Army was formed in Leipzig.

From April 1941 onwards the eastward movement of troops increased in volume, and the following formations were transferred from France and Germany to their strategic assembly areas:

Headquarters, Army Group C (later Army Group North)
    Sixteenth Army   ⎱
    Fourth Panzer Army ⎰ To Army Group North.

---

[1] Most of this preface was written as it stands by the Field-Marshal. One or two paragraphs, however, based on notes left by the Field-Marshal, have been re-drafted and inserted by his son, Captain Ernst Alexander Paulus.

Ninth Army
Second Panzer Army } To Army Group Centre.
Third Panzer Army

Headquarters Army Group A (later Army Group South).
Sixth Army
Eleventh Army (to Rumania) } To Army Group South.
First Panzer Army (from Jugoslavia)

The Allies

Steps to ensure the co-operation and, it was hoped, the active participation of allied countries in the fight against Soviet Russia were taken in hand as part of the general preparations. From a well-informed Finnish source I learnt that both the Finnish political attitude towards the Soviet Union and the military situation were such as would permit an early opening of negotiations on the subject of Finland's participation in the war against Russia.

In December 1940 General Heinrichs, the Chief of the Finnish General Staff, was received by General Halder at Army Headquarters in Zossen. There he was told about Operation 'Barbarossa', and himself delivered a lecture on the Russo-Finnish winter campaign of 1939–40. A reception was given by the Finnish Ambassador in Berlin, and General Heinrichs also conferred with Generals Jodl, Warlimont and Buschenhagen, of Supreme Headquarters, to discuss the plan for an attack on Murmansk.

In February 1941, Supreme Headquarters directed that contact be established with the Finnish General Staff to discuss the conduct of joint operations against the Soviet Union. In addition Headquarters, Army Norway discussed with the appropriate branches of the Finnish General Staff the details of the attack on Murmansk and the White Sea. After a joint reconnaissance tour, lasting eight or ten days, the final details of this operation were settled in Oslo on 3 March.

At the end of April, after Supreme Headquarters had approved the plan, Major General Buschenhagen was again sent to Helsinki to discuss with General Heinrichs the mobilization timetable, the measures to be taken to camouflage it (Reservists' training, etc.) and the concentration of the German and Finnish forces. Army Headquarters was then directed to work out a detailed plan for joint operations by the Finnish Army and Army Group North against Leningrad. Before he left Helsinki, Buschenhagen was received by Marshal Mannerheim, and when he returned to Berlin he submitted a detailed report on the results of his mission.

In May 1941 General Heinrichs took up residence at a hotel in Salzburg and started negotiations with Supreme Headquarters. He was not received by Hitler, and the negotiations were conducted by Heinrichs and the Finnish Military Attaché, Colonel Tapola, on one side and Generals Keitel, Jodl, Buerkner and Buschenhagen on the other.

Movement of German troops into Finland began on 12 or 15 June. Major-General Buschenhagen and General Erfurth (Liaison Officer Army Group, North – Finland), with his senior Staff Officer, went to Helsinki for further conferences with General Heinrichs.

In conclusion I should like to make it clear that no pressure whatever was brought to bear by Germany on Finland – not that there was, in any case, any need to exert pressure. Finland voluntarily accepted the German proposal that she should participate in the war against Russia and, mindful of the Soviet Union's attack on the Finnish frontier in 1939, she aligned herself without hesitation on Germany's side.

The only light I can shed, from personal observation, upon the preparatory steps initiated by Supreme Headquarters concerns the measures taken to ensure Hungary's participation in the war against Russia. Having myself taken part in the conferences and the subsequent planning, I would describe the sequence of events, as I saw them, in the following terms.

It was only natural that Hitler should do his utmost to secure the co-operation of Hungary in the implementation of his policy as regards east and south-east Europe. What were his prospects of succeeding in so doing? Hitler counted on Hungary's readiness actively to participate in the war for two main reasons. Firstly, she would be eager, with Germany's help, to regain and extend the territories she had lost in 1918, and secondly, with a Rumania which was growing stronger every day and was aligning herself politically with Germany, Hungary feared that she would be left out in the cold if she held aloof.

Even so, Hitler was at first very reticent *vis à vis* Hungary with regard to his real intentions. In view of Hungary's close contacts with countries hostile to Germany, and with Britain in particular, he felt that the Hungarians could not be relied upon to preserve secrecy with regard to his plans, and in any case he did not wish to tie himself down prematurely with any promises of territorial readjustments. Hungary, therefore, was treated as a special case in these general preparations.

At the end of 1940 the Hungarian Army, from the viewpoint of arms, equipment, organization and stock-piles, cannot be said to have been fit to engage in a modern war. Hitler and Supreme Headquarters were therefore faced with the problem of persuading Hungary to modernize her Army, without prematurely disclosing that their real object was to fit her for participation in a war against Soviet Russia. Since the autumn of 1940, it had been known in Hungary that the Rumanian Army had been modernized with German assistance. Trains carrying German instructors, arms and equipment of all kinds had travelled over the Hungarian railways. This fact alone must have sufficed to awaken a desire in Hungary not to lag behind her neighbour, a desire that must have been strengthened by the tension between the two countries as the result of the wretched bone of contention between them.[1] The possibility that she might become involved politically in the Balkans as the result of the Italian attack on Greece may also have influenced her strongly.

As far as I myself am concerned, the first signs of Hungary's intention to modernize her Army became apparent to me in December 1940. At about that time, Colonel Laszló, Chief of the Operations Branch of the Hungarian General Staff, arrived at Army Headquarters, whither he had been sent by Supreme Headquarters. The primary object of his visit was to discuss questions of organization – the conversion of brigades into divisions, the organization of motorized and armoured units and so on. (At that time, no

---

[1] On 30 August 1940, an Italo-German Arbitration Commission had tried to impose upon Hungary and Rumania a readjustment of territory in Siebenburgen, which was not welcomed either in Bucharest or Budapest.

divisions existed in the Hungarian Army, which was organized on a basis of infantry, mountain and motorized brigades.) Between us, the Chief of the Organization Branch and I were able to give him all the information he wanted. At the same time various other Hungarian Military Missions were in Berlin, among them one headed by the Hungarian War Minister, General v. Bartha, who was negotiating for the supply by Germany of arms, tanks, aircraft and other war material to Hungary.

In view of the political developments in Jugoslavia at the end of March 1941,[1] Hitler decided to attack Jugoslavia, in order to protect the flank of the offensive about to be launched from Bulgaria against Greece, to gain possession of the railway line from Belgrade via Nish to the south and to ensure that his right shoulder would be free when he set Operation 'Barbarossa' in motion. For this attack the concentration of German forces in Hungary was regarded as essential.

With a team of specialists I was sent to Budapest as the representative of Army Headquarters to conduct the negotiations for this concentration and to discuss the question of the participation of Hungarian troops in the campaign. The way had been paved for me through diplomatic channels. My task was to co-ordinate with the Hungarian General Staff the concrete military measures for a joint offensive. The conference, held on March 30 with General Werth, the Chief of the Hungarian General Staff and his senior Staff Officers, was brief and objective, and agreement was quickly reached.

In addition to the troops detailed to take part in the attack on Jugoslavia – one mobile corps (cavalry and motorized formations) and two infantry corps – the Hungarian General Staff decided to place a protective screen in the vicinity of the Russo-Hungarian frontier, a decision which shows that the Hungarians were well aware of the significance of their participation in the Jugoslav operations and its possible effect on the attitude of the Soviet Union.

---

[1] The *coup d'état*, which overthrew the Government of the Prince Regent two days before Jugoslavia was to have joined Hitler's Three-Power Pact. On same day Hitler informed the Commanders-in-Chief of the Army and the Air Force that he was going to smash the corporate State of Jugoslavia.

Supreme Headquarters, however, had forbidden me to make any reference whatever to Operation 'Barbarossa' during these negotiations, and this prohibition remained in force even after the conclusion of the campaign against Jugoslavia.

By thus securing Hungary's participation in the Jugoslav campaign Hitler had at any rate achieved one of his objects. Should Hungary later refuse to take part in the campaign against Russia, there would always be at least the possibility that, by occupying Jugoslavia and mopping up such pockets of resistance as remained, the Hungarian Army would free German troops for Operation 'Barbarossa'.

The question of Hungarian participation in the campaign against Russia was not decided until much later. Hungary, as far as I know, was given no indication regarding our intentions until very shortly before or just after Operation 'Barbarossa' began. Several days then elapsed, before Hungarian troops went into action against the Russians, and even then the élite of the Hungarian Army remained concentrated on the Hungarian-Rumanian frontier.

All these events seem to indicate that Hitler counted on Hungary's entry into the war against Russia, in spite of all the complications which might ensue. On the other hand, they also show that he was determined to time Hungary's entry according to his own ideas.

The beginning of Operation 'Barbarossa' – I need not here go into any detail about the offensives against Jugoslavia and Greece, which had such unfortunate repercussions on German plans – was fixed for 22 June. . . . Yet even at this stage, when it was so vital that the whole strength of the German High Command should have been concentrated on the settlement of an agreed and accepted objective, the differences of opinion between Supreme Headquarters and Army Headquarters on the conduct of the military operations had not yet been finally resolved; throughout the campaigns of 1941 and 1942 they continued to be a cause of friction between senior Commanders in the field . . . and they manifested themselves in even more acute form whenever questions regarding the general conduct of the war arose, and most particularly in the case of those questions which were connected with the great battle of Stalingrad.

General intentions and objectives of the German High Command at the beginning of the 1941 Campaign

The strategic objectives selected were in accordance with the general intentions described above.

The primary objective was Moscow. To protect the advance on the capital from any threat from the north, the Russian forces in the Baltic States were to be destroyed and Leningrad and Kronstadt captured (thus at the same time depriving the Red Fleet of its bases). In the south the first objective was the occupation of the Ukraine and the Don basin, to be followed by operations in the Caucasus and the capture of the oil fields.

In the Army Headquarters' plan the capture of Moscow was regarded as the principal objective. Its capture, however, was to be preceeded by the capture of Leningrad, the fall of which would deprive the Baltic Fleet of its main base, the Russian war effort of the armament production of the city and, above all, the Russian Army of a strategic assembly area for a counter-offensive against the flank and rear of the German forces advancing on Moscow. For this last reason alone it was essential that Leningrad should be the first objective.

Proposed method of execution

The operations were to be conducted in a series of phases. Army Headquarters' first operational directive went no further than the laying down of the objective for phase one, which was the general line Kiev, with a major bridge-head east of the Dnieper – Roslavl – Smolensk – area south and west of Lake Ilmen. After that it was considered that a pause would be necessary to rest the troops, re-group formations and replenish supplies, before phase two could be defined in detail.

For Army Group North this pause would be of brief duration. In co-operation with the Eighteenth Army and Fourth Panzer Army on one side and the Finnish Army on the other, Army Group North was to capture Leningrad as quickly as possible.

The motorized formations of Army Group Centre (Third Panzer Army) were directed to afford strong support to Army Group North's operations. On reaching the Smolensk area, these armoured forces were to wheel north and, advancing to the east of Lake Ilmen, were to assist in surrounding the Russian forces fighting in the vicinity of Leningrad and the area south-east of the city.

The main body of the Finnish Army was instructed to advance to the old frontier, beyond which it was not to advance until Army Group North launched the final attack on Leningrad. Supreme Headquarters was anxious to avoid exposing the Finnish Army to the risk of isolated action and defeat.

In the defining of all operational objectives, it was emphasized that the primary object was to destroy the Russian forces and to prevent any major portions of them from withdrawing into the distant interior of Russia; and to achieve this purpose, full and bold use was to be made of armoured columns, thrusting forward deeply into enemy territory. It was calculated that it would take three to four weeks to reach the general line Dnieper (and Kiev) – Smolensk area – area on both sides of Lake Ilmen. Moscow, it was hoped, would be reached during the autumn, before the bad weather set in.

The question of whether it would be possible to reach the Caucasus was left open. In any case, however, in order to open the way for an advance in this direction as soon as the opportunity occurred, it was decided that a bridge-head to the south of Rostov should be established at an early date.

The fact that we had no option but to accept this appreciation and formulate our plans accordingly does not, of course, mean that the Army Commanders and Staff Officers responsible were unanimous in their approval thereof. There was, indeed, no dearth of warning voices, both as regards the feasibility of the undertaking as a whole and as regards the degree of difficulty of the individual tasks allotted. On the other hand, there were many who felt – though this possibility was not taken into consideration in the official conferences – that there was always a chance that Russian resistance might collapse swiftly, as the result of the internal political dissensions which it was anticipated (or hoped) would ensue and of the organizational and material weaknesses of the 'colossus with the feet of clay'.

Any review in retrospect is always handicapped by the fact that its author already knows what actually happened, and his objectivity is often confused by fading memory and the inability of his imagination to re-capture the mood and temper of the time under review. In these circumstances, it is easy to overlook the tremendous vigour of the National Socialist policy, which was then at its zenith, the complete confidence born of the victorious issue of the western campaign and last but not least the great psychological effect, on politicians and soldiers alike, of the lightning victories over Poland, over Norway and, above all, over France. And it was on the soldiers themselves that the speed and ease of these victories – previously declared by so many experts to be beyond our ability to achieve – made their greatest impression.

Operation 'Barbarossa' – Phase One : a brief survey

The objective laid down for phase one – the general line Dnieper – Smolensk – Lake Ilmen – was reached by the advanced elements of the German forces in the middle of July – within, that is, the time calculated. From the operational point of view, however, the campaign had not gone quite as we had hoped. The great blow – the bringing to action and destruction of the mass of the Russian forces in the frontier areas – had not come off. The results of the Bielystok cauldron had been over-estimated by Supreme Head-quarters; in actual fact very considerable Russian forces had es-caped from it. The battle for Lemberg had not yielded any great number of prisoners – far less, indeed, than had the battle of Uman.[1] In the face of strong enemy opposition the fighting to secure a crossing of the Dnieper and the capture of Kiev proved to be very prolonged and costly.

The situation was much the same on Army Group Centre's front in the Smolensk area. Not only did Russian resistance stiffen, but very soon strong Russian counter-attacks were also launched, par-ticularly at Yelnaya, Dorogobush and to the north, which inflicted severe casualties on our forces.

Then, in August 1941 there followed a series of Russian counter-attacks from Staraya Russa on Dno, which exposed the weakness of the German Sixteenth Army and constituted a threat to the northern

[1] In the Uman cauldron, the first battle of this type to be fought by Army Group South, the Russians lost 100,000 prisoners, 450 guns and about 100 tanks.

flank of Army Group Centre. And further still to the north, the operations of Army Group North had not proceeded with the smoothness we had anticipated.

The initial reason for the halting of Army Group Centre's advance in the Smolensk area was the pause, the necessity for which had been realized from the outset, to give the troops a rest and to replenish supplies. It soon became obvious, however, that for the latter purpose much more time would be required than the three weeks originally envisaged. As they retreated, the Soviet forces had all but completely destroyed the railway network. Considerable time and massive labour forces had beeen required to repair the damage; and no sooner were some portions of the line restored, than they were again torn up in many places by partisans. The fighting in the Smolensk area had entailed a very great expenditure of ammunition, and replenishment had made great inroads on the supplies that had been accumulated for the continuation of the offensive.

Furthermore, the actions which were developing in the Briansk and Smolensk areas, coupled with the general situation on the front as a whole at the end of July, caused Supreme Headquarters to make a number of alterations in the original dispositions.

The envisaged wheel northwards of strong elements of the Third Panzer Army had to be abandoned. Army Group Centre considered that, in view of the operations in the Briansk and Smolensk areas, these armoured formations could not be spared. Eventually, in August, only XXXIX Panzer Corps, consisting of twelve Panzer and twenty Motorized Infantry Divisions, was sent north behind the front line via Vitebsk and Pskov and attached to Army Group North.

In the meanwhile, Supreme Headquarters had changed its mind about the attack on Leningrad. The attack by Eighteenth Army and Fourth Panzer Army was halted immediately to the south of the city. As a result, the advance of the main Finnish Army was cancelled. Supreme Headquarters was anxious to avoid the very costly losses in men and material which inevitably accompany the capture of a big city, and decided to be content with sealing it off instead. The link-up with the Finnish Army on the Svir was to be postponed to a later date.

As Army Group North had proved to be too weak for the task allotted to it, it was reinforced, as has been mentioned, by the transfer to it of CXXIX Panzer Corps from Army Group Centre.

Apart from the local operations in the Briansk-Smolensk areas, the situation at the southern end of the front also had a marked effect on the position of Army Group Centre at the end of July. In its own sector, Kiev was still holding out. Army Group South's attack east of the Dnieper, where it was confronted by powerful Russian forces, had made no progress.

As long as Army Group South hung so far behind Army Group Centre, any advance by the latter in the direction of Moscow was regarded, with its southern flank thus exposed, as too hazardous an operation. Something like one third of Army Group Centre's whole strength – Second Panzer Army under General Guderian to the west of Briansk and Second Army south and south-west of Mogilev – was already being used to protect the flanks. Supreme Headquarters' primary object, then, was to set Army Group South's advance in motion again as soon as possible, in order to provide that protection for the southern flank of Army Group Centre as would enable it to accelerate its advance on Moscow. It was therefore decided that, as a temporary measure, Second Panzer Army and Second Army should wheel south and attack the Russian forces east of the Dnieper. By this means it was hoped at the same time to surround and destroy very considerable Russian forces and thus swing the balance of relative strengths in Germany's favour.

It was not until 10 September that Kiev fell. The northern wing of Army Group Centre, thanks to the atrocious going caused by bad weather, was able to advance only very slowly on Kharkov and Bielgorod. In the Smolensk area, bitter fighting continued from the middle of July until the end of September.

Meanwhile, in the north XXXIX Panzer Corps had been launched in an attack on Tikhvin and the Volkhov. Supreme Headquarters' reasons for ordering this attack were:

(a) the economic object – to seize the bauxite mines at Tikhvin;

(b) the military object – to establish an eastern screen to the sealing-off of Leningrad;

(c) the ultimate objective – to establish contact with the Finnish Army on the Svir.

Under the command of General Rudolf Schmidt, the Panzer Corps succeeded in thrusting a weak column forward as far as Schlüsselberg on Lake Ladoga, but in the wooded swamps on the middle Volkhov the attack came to a standstill. Once again it was made obvious that Army Group North was too weak to carry out the tasks allotted to it. The Finnish Army, it will be remembered, had been directed to advance to the old frontier and wait there, until Army Group North was in a position to launch, with good prospect of success, its final assault on Leningrad. But in view of Supreme Headquarters decision not to capture Leningrad, but to seal it off instead, any further advance by the Finnish Army was now out of the question. All that could be expected of it was, at the most, a counter-thrust on the Svir front. But as a result of the German reverses at Tikhvin and on the Volkhov, this counter-thrust, too, never materialized.

The bad weather season had already started in the southern sector of the front and was about to break in the central and northern sectors.

It had to be admitted, then, that the original objects of the 1941 campaign had not been attained. Now, at about the beginning of October, the question which Supreme Headquarters had to answer was whether, with the exception of local adjustments of the line, the whole front should go on the defensive, with the object of consolidating its position, building up anew the requisite supplies and making thorough preparations for a resumption of the offensive in the spring of 1942, or whether the original objectives set for 1941 could still be attained by continuing the offensive throughout the late autumn and the winter immediately ahead? How, then, did the German High Command appreciate the situation on the eastern front, as it was at the end of September 1941?

The view taken by Supreme Headquarters was:

Although we had not succeeded, in the frontier areas, in destroying the Russian forces to the extent that we had hoped, and a very considerable portion of them had made good their escape into the interior of Russia, we had nevertheless weakened the Russians to a fatal degree. The Russian Army was now split in three – in the south one group east and south-east of Kiev, in the centre one group in the area east of Smolensk, and in the north one group in the

Leningrad area and to the south-east of it. It was felt therefore that it was still possible, with one more final effort, to achieve our 1941 objectives, albeit somewhat later than was originally envisaged.

Tasks and objectives of the Army Groups

Supreme Headquarters decided to continue the offensive, the main objective of which was the capture of Moscow by Army Group Centre. The first step, to be initiated in October, was to be an attack to destroy the Russian forces in the Briansk and Viasma areas.

In the north, the sealing-off of Leningrad was to be completed and contact established with the Finns on the Svir. The right wing of Army Group North (Sixteenth Army) was ordered to advance with its right flank directed at Bologoye and capture the Valdai Heights and thus ensure the protection of Army Group Centre's northern flank.

In the south, Army Group South was ordered to occupy the whole of the Don basin and establish a bridge-head south of Rostov, in anticipation of the subsequent advance into the Caucasus. The northern wing of Army Group South (Sixth Army) was to capture Kharkov and advance to the Oksol, where it was to link up with Army Group Centre, whose Second Army was directed to attack and occupy the line Kastovnoye – Yelets – Yefremov.

The carrying out of these orders proved, as was only to be expected, difficult in the extreme. Sixth Army, for example, in its advance from the Dnieper towards the line Kharkov – Bielgorod – Oboyan, lost so great a number of horses and mechanical transport vehicles that most of its heavy weapons (artillery, heavy machine guns and the like) were rendered immobile and its supply system was in grave danger of breaking down. On its northern flank, the 239 Division had to be disbanded and its personnel distributed among other divisions, because it was impossible to replace the great number of horses that the division had lost. Furthermore, in the operations in which it was engaged and as a result of climatic conditions, the Army lost so many men, that its fighting powers were seriously diminished. In these circumstances, the Army Commander, Field-Marshal v. Reichenau, refused to advance any further. To do so, he asserted, would place his Army in an impossible situation.

Results of the October – November 1941 offensive and the German High Command's appreciation of the situation

At the end of the October operations, the appreciations of the situation made by Army Headquarters and Supreme Headquarters revealed a sharp divergence of view. The operations in the Briansk-Viasma area (2 October to 7 October) had proved successful but costly. In the middle of October the weather broke.

In the south, Kharkov did not fall until the end of October. Bad weather and the state of the ground prevented Sixth Army from advancing any further. In the opinion of Army Headquarters it had therefore to be conceded that the operational objectives for 1941 had not been attained and that any further endeavour would have to be postponed until 1942. The offensive against Moscow, it was considered, could not be continued during the winter, and new and thorough preparations would have to be made for its resumption in the spring. With this appreciation Army Group Centre agreed.

Supreme Headquarters held other views. The Russians, it was asserted, were at the end of their tether, and only one last effort was required to bring about their complete and final collapse. Orders were accordingly issued that the offensive would be continued as soon as the frost came and hardened the ground.

This occurred in the middle of November, and the result of the subsequent operations was, of course, negative. . . . The attack on Moscow failed, and the subsequent withdrawal resulted in heavy casualties in men and even more serious losses in material, and had to be continued a long way, before it could be halted.

Supreme Headquarters attributed the Moscow reverse to inefficient leadership on the part of Army Group Headquarters and the Army Commanders, and a number of changes were made in the higher command.[1]

Supreme Headquarters were of the opinion that the Russians had

---

[1] Between October and December 1941 the following were either dismissed or relieved: v. Brauchitsch, C-in-C, Army, v. Rundstedt, GOC A-G South (at his own request), v. Bock, GOC A-G Centre, and the following Army Commanders: Guderian (Second Panzer), v. Weichs (Second Army), v. Stuelpnagel (Seventeenth Army).

concentrated the whole of their available forces for the defence of Moscow. Nevertheless they came to the further conclusion that the German forces available for operations on a major scale in 1942 would suffice for the prosecution of only *one* of the offensives originally planned.

That none of the objectives set for the 1941 campaign had been reached is undeniable. Leningrad had not been captured, Moscow had not fallen and contact with the Finns on the Svir had not been established.

The retreat from Moscow had been brought to a halt with difficulty. It had made heavy inroads on the strength and resources of the Army and it had left its mark on the morale of Commanders and troops alike. The operations during the summer and autumn in the south had been held up partly by enemy action and partly by the weather, and the winter months of 1941-2 brought further reverses at Rostov, Isium and Kharkov.

Having admitted that the forces available in 1942 would not suffice for all the operations envisaged in 1941, Supreme Headquarters now had to decide which of them it would pursue. And in this connection they were acutely conscious of the time factor and the vital necessity of forcing a decision in the east before the expected establishment of a second front in the west.

Extracts from the correspondence of Lieut-General Paulus, Oberquartiermeister I of the Army, 1941

Foreword

Mention has already been made of the fact that General Paulus was no great letter writer and that he had always refused to keep a diary. The few letters, written in 1942, which have survived, suffice nevertheless to show the brief and terse manner in which he was wont to express himself. He obviously felt no need to disclose his anxieties, his feelings or his views in letters written from the front. It is quite possible, too, that he would not have considered such disclosures to be in keeping with security regulations. Among his papers, however, were two files with letters he had received and, on a few rare occasions, with copies of the replies he had written.

All these letters are from the years 1941 and 1942.

From the time that the Sixth Army was besieged in Stalingrad, his wife received very few letters from him. His last, farewell letter, written when the end seemed inevitable and with which he enclosed his wedding ring, his decorations and his signet ring, did not arrive. As far as his son knows, its contents were purely personal.

The correspondence of the years 1941–2 contains many letters of a more or less trivial character – telegrams and letters of congratulation, of thanks from people who had visited him, of requests for help or employment and so on. But it also contains a number of letters, written to him as Deputy Chief of the General Staff, on the situation on the eastern front, on questions of armament and on subjects of general or politico-strategic importance, which bear testimony both to the esteem in which he was held and to the confidence which his correspondents, frequently sharp critics of Hitler and his Supreme Headquarters, reposed in him as a friend and an officer and gentleman.

The most important of these letters are therefore reproduced here, in strict chronological order, as appendices to Chapters 3 and 4, partly in précis form and partly in the form of extracts from the actual text. They complete the picture of the Field-Marshal's personality, for they are all from people who knew him well and with whom he had worked or was still working.

Walter Goerlitz

Letters to Paulus - 1941

From Captain Count Muenster(?)

(Original signature illegible)

Field Post Office No. 15941   10 February 1941

(The writer announces that he has been given a Staff appointment with effect from 30 January. He recalls the happy days he spent with the Sixth Army and says that at the moment he is Ib (GSO II) in a Panzer division which has been in Rumania since October 1940 as an instructional unit.) He continues:

'. . . Here we see and hear all sorts of things. Whether our activities in the instructional field are bearing any real fruit, I very much doubt. With but few exceptions, which won't affect the efficiency of the Rumanian Army one way or the other, the Rumanians have shown great skill in swopping round the people sent to us for training in a haphazard way which gives us no chance of teaching them anything. Incidentally, what with earthquakes and putsches, we have plenty of fun. . . .'

From General v. Manstein

HQ LVI Corps (Mot).   5 June 1941

Dear Paulus,

I enclose herewith a copy of a request which I have sent to you through the Official channels. Whether and when the latter reaches you remains to be seen. But please don't forget that the fact that the Army has any assault artillery at all is thanks solely to my efforts as Head of Branch I OQuI. So the least they can do is to let me have some.

With best wishes,
v. Manstein.

From Major U. Buerker
Directorate of Military Training

Army Headquarters   24 July 1941

(After some preliminary remarks on the current situation, with particular reference to the Panzer formations and their tactical handling in the southern sector, the writer compares the situation as it had been envisaged in the winter war game and as it now actually was, and makes a number of operational suggestions.)

From Major U. Buerker

On Field Service   4 August 1941

(The writer gives a general review of the situation and says that half the division – 10 Panzer Division, of which he was then GSO I – is fighting at Yelnaya and half is out of the line, resting.) He continues:

'. . . The hold up on this front has not been brought about by the enemy, but by the fuel, transport and ammunition situation. . . . The morale of the troops is excellent. They still feel that, provided they have the wherewithal with which to move and fight, they are better than the enemy in every respect. They are itching to attack again, because they know that only by attacking can they force a decision. . . .

Buerker.'

From Colonel Burmeister[1]

12 August 1941

(The writer, who had paid frequent visits to Paulus at Fuehrer Headquarters, reports on the situation regarding tank replacements from 12 June onwards for Second and Third Panzer Armies and on the position in the tank workshops in Minsk. He thinks that by 21 August both Armies will have got 70 per cent of their 'full authorized establishment', but anticipates that swift losses up to about 25 per cent must be expected when operations start again. He then outlines a plan for the amalgamation of the two branches which deal with tank reinforcements and tank training and suggests that the Panzer General, Army Headquarters, should, in addition, be appointed Inspector of the Panzer Arm, with everything connected with it under his direct control – reinforcements, training, schools, courses, testing establishments and tank replacements. The Inspector, he adds, should be given wide powers and full authority, to enable him 'to get his own way both politically and with the industrialists'.) He concludes:

'. . . I hope, Sir, you will forgive me for thus unburdening my armoured heart to you.

Burmeister.'

From GOC-in-C Sixth Army

On Field Service   17 September 1941
My dear Paulus,
    (The writer reminds Paulus of the campaigns of two years ago,

---

[1] Colonel Burmeister, Branch In.6 (Pz), Army Headquarters, and a tank expert. His suggestions, which were pre-eminently sound, were implemented – but only after the Stalingrad disaster, when Guderian was appointed Inspector of the Panzer Arm on 28 February 1943 – by which time it was too late.

'easily the best campaigns of the whole war', sends him birthday greetings and asks whether he knows what has happened to his [Reichenau's] son.) He concludes:

'. . . All goes well with me – and with the battle. And what more can one ask than that?

With best wishes,

Yours,

v. Reichenau.'

From Field-Marshal v. Reichenau

On Field Service   27 September 1941

(The writer thanks Paulus for his congratulations on the capture of Kiev.) He adds:

'. . . I was right up in front every day of the battle. The vast cauldron kept on splitting up into isolated dog-fights. The situation kept on changing more swiftly than ever it did in any of Napoleon's battles, and I found that I often had to intervene personally in the actual fighting. For instance, on 22 September, to plug a gap, I put speed into 44 Infantry Division's attack by personally leading the assault by 5 Infantry Regiment. I led the assault for three kilometres, quite literally not only with the first wave, but as the leading man in it. Enemy resistance was very stubborn, their mortar fire being particularly severe, and the only way we could avoid it was to advance just as fast as we could. We repeatedly passed through disintegrated groups of the enemy, until I spotted some high ground some three hundred metres away and made for it. I myself brought the fire of three machine-guns to bear on it, knocked out a dug-in-tank in the process, and in no time the position was captured. The fighting has been really fierce, literally to the last drop of blood. . . .

'I did not lead this assault out of any lust for adventure, but because I have continually been finding myself compelled to call upon my subordinate commanders to lead the way, in order to bring these fierce actions to a swifter conclusion. . . .

Yours,

v. Reichenau.'

From Lieut-General Himer
(GOC 46 Infantry Division)

Divisional Headquarters
Field Post Office No. 38621   5 October 1941

(The writer reports on Operation 'Perekop', the advance into the Crimea . . . he states that his battalions are reduced to about 180 to 200 men each.)

' . . . The Russians are resisting with unparalleled tenacity. Strong point after strong point has to be captured individually. As often as not, we cannot get them out even with flame-throwers, and we have to blow the whole thing to bits. . . . As soon as we get some reinforcements, we'll push through the last inch on the map and we'll be in the Crimea.

With best wishes.

Heil Hitler!

Himer.'

From Field-Marshal v. Reichenau

On Field Service   6 October 1941

(Thanks Paulus for his 'good letter' of 1 October and says he feels that 'the worst part of this great struggle is now behind us'.)

' . . . I am sincerely very touched at your having once again taken up the cudgels on my behalf. To put you in the picture, I should like you to know that Army Group's proposals were put forward in detail and every detail was justified. Meanwhile, exactly nothing has happened, and I've won my bet with Schuler (his ADC) on the subject. I should be interested to know whether they even bothered to submit the proposals to the Fuehrer. . . .

'As has happened frequently in the past, I've now been given a new task – Kharkov and beyond. I only hope we shall succeed in the not too distant future.

With best wishes, my dear fellow,

Your old friend,

v. Reichenau.'

From Field-Marshal v. Reichenau

On Field Service   11 October 1941

'. . . What great satisfaction it must give you, to see your plans maturing in this splendid way![1]

'We are pressing on gaily towards Kharkov, and we all have the feeling that the Russian is not nearly so cocksure as he was in June and July. Our own troops are in excellent fettle.

Yours,

v. Reichenau.

PS—Thank you for your friendly lecture on the value of reticence! You're quite right, of course!'

From General Rudolf Schmidt
(Commanding XXXIX Panzer Corps)

13 November 1941

Dear Paulus,

Very many thanks for your letter. Please don't let my heartfelt outburst worry you in any way. I just had to have someone to whom I could unburden by mind freely, and you were the only one I felt I could trust. So – please don't be angry.

(The writer goes on to say that he has been put in command of Second Army during the absence of General v.Weichs, who is ill. . . . He complains bitterly about 'P-A Keitel' (General Keitel, brother of the Field-Marshal and head of Army Personnel Branch) who, he says, is 'about as much use as a sick headache', because Keitel has left him without any precise orders as temporary commander of the Second Army. . . . He feels that he should not have left his own corps in its 'present abominable situation' and complains about the 'highly-coloured' intelligence reports, about battalion strengths dropping to as low as sixty men, and the increasing number of frost-bite cases and the lack of winter clothing.)

'. . . Boots are torn to shreds and are a disgrace. Many of the men are going about with their feet wrapped in paper, and there is a

---

[1] v. Reichenau is referring here to the December 1940 war game, directed by Paulus, in which the position before Moscow (the Briansk-Viasma cauldron) was accurately predicted.

great dearth of gloves. As far as winter clothing is concerned, the Quartermaster-General deserves every curse that can be hurled at him. . . . This total lack of foresight and care makes even these splendid fellows of ours dispirited and rebellious. . . . Then in the newspapers they read wonderful speeches – "come what may, this winter our brave soldiers need not fear the cold"! . . .'

(Schmidt then describes the 'quite new offensive spirit' of the enemy and his complete domination of the air. If his corps is to hold on to the main position at Tikhvin, he says, he will need a reinforcement of ten thousand men. He wishes very much that he could pull his corps out for a rest, and he emphasizes that he is writing frankly and without 'pulling his punches'.)

From General Himer

Divisional Headquarters
near Kerch   14 November 1941

(The writer describes the battles in the Crimea and on the Kerch peninsula . . . serious difficulties over supplies, continuous rain, insufficient ammunition for the artillery, snow storms, bitter cold and strong winds. . . . All three of his Regimental Commanders, he says, are temporarily out of action, either wounded or sick; six battalions are being commanded by Lieutenants, and for two weeks two of his artillery companies have had only five and seven guns apiece.)

'The troops have fought splendidly and I take off my hat to them. . . . To the very end there has been nothing that we haven't had to put up with. But we've done the job and we're proud of it!

Best wishes and Heil Hitler!

Yours, Himer.'

From Dr Walter Flade (ADMS Sixth Army)

16 November 1941

(A personal note on Field-Marshal Reichenau's state of health, which had been causing him anxiety throughout the summer. Thanks to his sound constitution, however, the Field-Marshal has got over all the attacks.)

'But I find it difficult to make him understand that even his robust constitution in not indestructible.'

From Buerker, GSO I, 10 Panzer Division
17 November 1941

(The writer gives a picture of the situation and confesses that he had written several times direct to Major Count Stauffenberg, Organization Branch, Army Headquarters, on the subject of the Division's strength. He had done this, he explains, because, although Panzer Army Headquarters had been repeatedly addressed on the subject of the Division's strength and general state, nothing seemed to have been done. While realizing the vital importance of capturing Moscow, he rather questioned the wisdom of the present manner in which the Division was being used in broken, wooded and marshy country.)

'. . . I am worried about this aspect, simply because I realize how hard put to it we shall be in the spring to muster a sufficient number of good Panzer divisions, ready for the next offensive.'

(He goes on to say that on 2 October he had firmly believed that the offensive being launched would give Russia the *coup de grâce*, but that now he had to admit that the objectives set had not been attained. He also begged leave to doubt whether the attack to be launched on 18 November would 'go smoothly forward' (as Paulus, apparently, must have asserted). He finished by saying that he was despatching this letter on 11 December only after very careful reflection.)

From Dr Flade
27 December 1941

(He sends his best wishes for 1942 and goes on to talk about v. Reichenau.)

'. . . During the last six months I have been very anxious about the Field-Marshal, and I still am. What a pity that the "marriage" with his old Chief of Staff of pre-war days could not have been a lasting one.' (This refers to the time when Paulus was Chief of Staff to v. Reichenau.)

4. The advance on Stalingrad

(*Vide* Sketch Maps 2 and 3)

• •

Introduction

The Stalingrad cauldron (19 November 1942 – 2 February 1943) may well be described as the second and final act in the drama of the Sixth Army and its Commander, Field-Marshal Paulus; but without a preliminary study of Act I, the advance to the Volga and the Caucasus, to understand how it came to be fought at all is as difficult as is any proper appreciation of the events of 1942 on the southern sector of the eastern front, without a prior scrutiny of the campaign of 1941.

It is for this reason that Field-Marshal Paulus' memoranda on the events of 1942–3, his reports on Operation 'Sea Lion' and the 'Barbarossa' war game, and his summing up of the 1941 campaign are of importance – even though they contain no facts that were not already known and even though the Field-Marshal has not indulged in any personal comment in these recollections, but has confined himself strictly to the sequence of operational events.

Why he adopted this attitude can only be surmised. But, in the first place, he died before he was able to carry out his intention of writing a comprehensive work on the eastern campaign and the battle of Stalingrad; and secondly, he may well have been influenced by the fact that all the memoranda he wrote and all the notes he made for his lectures in Dresden were written either in Soviet captivity or in Dresden, where he was still living in a communist zone. And under the Communists frank and sincerely written individual memoirs of the pattern accepted in the west are rare indeed!

On the other hand, the Field-Marshal's memorandum on the war game, 'Barbarossa', which has never before been described in such great detail, shows clearly that, by and large, the German High Command's appreciation was both realistic and correct and

Conference at Poltava before the summer offensive, 1942. l to r: Heusinger, Paulus, Hitler, v. Weichs

Above: l Field-Marshal v. Reichenau, r Field-Marshal v. Manstein.
Below: l Lt-Gen Heim, r Maj-Gen Schmidt

paid due attention to Clausewitz's famous 'frictions'. The General Staff's one failure was their failure ever to persuade Hitler to accept the General Staff view regarding the main strategic objective of the campaign; and it is for that reason that the whole timetable went awry.

Then, after the defeat before Moscow in December 1941, there at once arose the question: In what way is it proposed to conduct the 1942 campaign? Should the German Army adopt a purely defensive attitude and content itself with holding the great territorial gains it had acquired, or should it once again take the offensive? And if the latter, should the offensive against Moscow be renewed, or were there other objectives deemed to be of more importance?

This was the situation when, on 5 January 1942, Paulus handed over the duties of OQuI to General Blumentritt (till then Chief of Staff, Fourth Army, on the eastern front) and assumed command of the Sixth Army. And once he was an Army Commander he became a cog in the highly functionalized system of command, completely centralized, and controlled by Hitler, without being in a position to exercise any influence whatever either on the planning or on the conduct of the operations as a whole.

In this connection, it must be constantly borne in mind that for Hitler, Supreme Commander of the Armed Forces and Commander-in-Chief of the Army, the main objective of the 1942 campaign was the capture of the Caucasian oil fields. This it was that caused the Chief of the General Staff, General Halder, to declare, at a conference of Army Group and Army Commanders held in Orsha two days after the issue of Hitler's directive of 11 November 1941, that 'when weather conditions permit, we shall feel justified in making an all-out thrust in the south towards Stalingrad in order to occupy the Maykop – Groznyy area at an early date and thus improve the situation as regards our limited supplies of oil'.

The main objective set for 1942 was the occupation of the Caucasus and its oil fields, of which the Maykop and Groznyy areas were of only secondary importance, the most valuable fields being those at Baku in Azerbaijan, far away on the Caspian. The emergence of Stalingrad and the land-bridge between the great Don bend and the Volga elbow as the second main objective did not occur until the summer campaign was well under way. In this way, the German campaign as a whole, with its twin-pronged, diverging offensive, the main objectives of which, Stalingrad and the Caucasus, were originally unrelated, assumed a pattern that was, frankly, quite impossible.

Let the Field-Marshal himself continue the story. It should, however, be mentioned that the following exposition of his views is a summary, based on his drafts and the notes he made for the Dresden lectures, which has been compiled by his son, Captain Ernst Alexander Paulus.

Walter Goerlitz

The Soviet Forces and the spring 1942 plans of the Soviet High Command : an appreciation of the situation by German Supreme Headquarters

. . . Supreme Headquarters were of the opinion that in the winter of 1941 all available Russian forces had been thrown into the battle for Moscow and were now concentrated in the area to the east of Smolensk.

The Soviet successes during the winter in the area Kharkov – Isium – Barvenkovo were attributed less to the employment of significantly strong Russian forces than to the numerical inferiority of the German formations in that area and their lack of adequate, prepared positions. Supreme Headquarters believed that with the advent of German reinforcements in the spring of 1942 this crisis could be overcome.

Nevertheless, the determined will to resist shown by the Russian High Command, the almost reckless commitment of fresh troops brought to the front via Moscow and the immediately apparent strength of their material resources should have warned German Supreme Headquarters that the time had come to make a reappraisal of an enemy whom they had hitherto underestimated. They should have realized that the temporary advantage in both material and personnel which aggression always confers on the aggressor no longer existed. But such very relevant factors as these were not taken into consideration by Supreme Headquarters.

The general conclusion reached was that the Russians would not have sufficient forces to undertake several major operations simultaneously, and that their most likely course of action would be:

(1) A continuation of the Russian offensive westwards and southwestwards from the Smolensk area. This, if successful, would prevent the development of any new threat to Moscow and would at the same time place the southern sector of the German front in an awkward situation.

(2) A possible continuation of the offensive in exploitation of the break-through on the Lozovaya – Barvenkovo front. The object of this offensive would be to cut off and destroy the German southern wing (Seventeenth Army and First Panzer Army) and thus very materially weaken the strength of the German forces. If this succeeded, it would deprive the Germans of any prospect of further successful offensive operations.

The general objectives of the German summer offensive, 1942; the tasks allotted to the Army Groups and the phases of the envisaged operations

Before attempting to give any details of Supreme Headquarters' intentions for 1942, I must point out that, from January 1942 onwards, when I handed over my duties as OQuI and assumed command of the Sixth Army, I had no personal insight into the planning. Nevertheless, thanks to the general information that I had acquired as OQuI and the more detailed information I gained as Commander-in-Chief of the Sixth Army, I had formed a picture in my own mind of Supreme Headquarters' intentions, the salient features of which I reproduce here. I would further point out that, in assessing the value of these comments of mine, the fact must be borne in mind that Hitler's strict orders on security forbade the passing of any information on the general situation even to the high Commanders and their Staffs – a prohibition which in practice frequently added greatly to our difficulties.

Intentions of Supreme Headquarters for the summer 1942

Army Groups Centre and North – apart from local readjustments to their fronts – were to remain in their old positions. The defences of the centre of Army Group Centre's sector opposite Moscow (Smolensk area) were to be strengthened by every possible means (artillery, anti-tank weapons, reserves) against possible Russian attack.[1]

The German defences in the central sector were regarded as adequate, but at the same time it was hoped that, if the offensive in the southern sector (with which I deal below) proved successful, the Russian High Command would be compelled to withdraw troops from the central sector.

A resumption of the offensive against Moscow in 1942 was not contemplated.

The main operations were to be conducted in Army Group South's sector. Strategic objective: The oil fields of the North Caucasus. The capture of these oil fields was described as being vital to the further prosecution of the war by Germany and her allies.

To cover the flank and rear of the Caucasian operations, an advance to the Volga at Stalingrad was to be made. This would at the same time neutralize the great Volga channel of communications and deprive the Red Army of the Stalingrad armament factories.

Headquarters, Army Group Sout'ı and the Armies concerned were not given Stalingrad itself as an objective until the end of July 1942. Until then the objective given had been an arc on the general line mouth of the Don – Nizhne Astakhov – Vishenskaya.

Tactically, the object of these operations was to deal a crippling blow to the southern wing of the Russian forces, thus eliminating them from any further participation in the war and restoring the balance of strength in Germany's favour.

This switching of the main operations to the southern sector of the front constituted a complete departure from the plan upon which the whole of the Russian campaign had been built. The latter had envisaged the capture of Moscow, the political, economic, armament and communications centre of the Soviet war effort, as the main objective. If the economic objectives mentioned earlier really were vital

---

[1] The Field-Marshal overlooks the fact that Army Group North had been ordered to capture Leningrad and that to assist it, Eleventh Army was withdrawn from the southern sector in July 1942, contrary to every principle of concentration of force.

to Germany's war effort, as Hitler asserted, then, apart from anything else, it is obvious that he had embarked upon a war without
having first assured for himself the supplies essential for its prosecution.

The plan of operations and the phases of the summer campaign, 1942

In order to be able to launch a decisive offensive in the southern
sector, we had first of all to create suitable assembly areas for the
participating forces. The carrying out of these preliminary preparations was entrusted to Army Group South Headquarters (Field-
Marshal v. Bock) in Poltava.

Assembly areas for this Army Group (from north to south)

Second Army (and Second Hungarian Army)	Kursk area
Fourth Panzer Army	Kharkov area
Sixth Army	Area south east of Kharkov

First Panzer Army ⎫
Seventeenth Army ⎭   Stalino area

In the second line, behind Seventeenth and First Panzer Armies:
Eighth Italian Army
Third Rumanian Army.

Order of Battle, Sixth Army
     XXIX Corps (General Obstfelder)
        336 Infantry Division
         75 Infantry Division
     XVII Corps (General Hollidt)
        384 Infantry Division
         79 Infantry Division
      VII Corps (General Heitz)
        376 Infantry Division
        389 Infantry Division
        113 Infantry Division

XXXX Panzer Corps (General Stumme)
   3 Panzer Division
  23 Panzer Division
  29 Motorized Division
   LI Corps (General v. Seydlitz)
  44 Infantry Division
  79 Infantry Division
 294 Infantry Division (?)
 305 Infantry Division (?)

It was intended that during the course of the operations this Army Group would be split into two – Army Group 'A' (Field-Marshal List) and Army Group 'B' (Field-Marshal v. Bock).

Army Group South's first task, as a preliminary to the main attack, was to initiate local operations in the Don bend with the object of securing a suitable starting line for the summer offensive.

The time that must elapse before the troops detailed for the main offensive were in position and ready was to be used to destroy as strong forces of the enemy as possible and to occupy, before the summer offensive began, those sectors to the north of the Donets and Oksol which were close to the front and in the line of the intended advance.

The time between these preliminary operations was to be utilized in re-grouping the Panzer formations to the best advantage.

Accordingly, the following operations were carried out in the spring of 1942:

(a) 8 – 20 *May. Attack by Eleventh Army on the Kerch peninsula.* This attack was designed to create a springboard for a subsequent attack from the west in the direction of Temriuk and Krasnodar, the object of which was, in co-operation with the forces advancing southwards from Rostov, to surround the Russian forces situated south of that town.[1]

---

[1] Cf. v. Manstein: *Lost Victories*, pp. 230 et seq., and 260 et seq. (Methuen.) Logically, this operation should have been co-ordinated with the operation for the capture of Sevastopol. It was only on 12 August that v. Manstein announced that the plan was not to link Eleventh Army via Kerch with the operations of the southern wing, but to transfer it to A-G North for the attack on Leningrad.

(b) *Operation 'Fridericus I'*, *17–28 May*, attack by First Panzer Army and Sixth Army on the Barvenkovo salient. The immediate objects of this attack were to remove the direct threat to the German lines of communication running from Dnepropetrovsk to the southern flank and at the same time to ensure that Kharkov, Sixth Army's main supply base, could be held.

As a result of the great Russian break-through in January 1942 in the Kharkov – Isium – Barvenkovo area and the severe and costly fighting which continued into the spring, a critical situation had arisen, which had been further aggravated very considerably by the Russian attacks east and north-east of Kharkov at the beginning of May.[1]

It therefore did not seem feasible to Army Group South to postpone the attack on the Barvenkovo salient (Operation 'Fridericus I') until all the troops detailed for the attack had duly assembled. The original intention – to begin Operation 'Fridericus' towards the end of May and to allow the phases 'Fridericus I' and 'Fridericus II' to overlap with the major offensive on the Don bend – was therefore abandoned. 'Fridericus I' was, in fact, launched on 17 April. Its object was to wipe out the Russian salient to the south of Kharkov and to bring Timoshenko's offensive east of Kharkov to a standstill.[2]

A further objective was the occupation of the area to the west of the upper Donets, south-east of Kharkov, in order to secure an assembly area for the later advance eastwards across the river and to destroy in a concentric attack from north and south the Russian advanced elements west of the Donets in the Barvenkovo area.

(c) *Operation 'Wilhelm'*. Attack by Sixth Army in the direction of Volchansk, 10–14 June.

[1] The Field-Marshal is here referring to the second battle of Kharkov in May which, thanks to the skill of the German leadership, ended in a victory and was the last of the great battles of encirclement fought on the eastern front. According to General Schmidt, Chief of Staff, Sixth Army, this battle greatly influenced Paulus when he came to make his decision in Stalingrad in November, because he had realized that, contrary to Field-Marshal Bock's and his own opinions, Army Headquarters had appreciated the situation more correctly than had the Commanders on the spot.

[2] 'Fridericus I' was, in fact, not launched on 17 April but on 17 May, as a counter-stroke to the Soviet offensive launched on 9 May against the German concentrations for the summer offensive.

(d) *Operation 'Fridericus II'*. Attack by Sixth Army and First Panzer Army on Kupiansk.[1]

In practice, these two attacks formed one continuous action. Their objects were to secure suitable starting lines: on the northern wing of Sixth Army for the attack on the enemy's left wing in the hilly country east of Bielgorod: on the southern wing of Sixth Army for the advance of III Panzer Corps and First Panzer Army south-eastwards via Kupiansk.

After carrying out these subsidiary operations, Army Group South was to destroy all enemy forces west of the line Rostov – Voronezh and to reach a position with its northern wing on the Don on both sides of Voronezh and its southern wing and centre in an arc roughly on the line mouth of the Donets – Nizhne Astakhov – Veshenskaya, with a bridge-head across the Don, south of Rostov.

The first objective of the attack on Voronezh was to capture the stretch of the Don from roughly Boguchar to north of Voronezh, as a buttress for a further advance into the Don bend. In addition, a bridge-head was to be established over the river Voronezh, with the object of making possible a later advance on Borisoglebsk, should the situation demand.[2]

---

[1] The following note may shed light on this description written from memory by the Field-Marshal. The Soviet counter-offensive under Marshal Timoshenko (second battle of Kharkov, May 1942) completely wrecked all the original German plans for May. The battle ended at the end of May. It resulted in the annihilation of two Soviet armies consisting of some twenty-two infantry and seven cavalry divisions and fifteen armoured brigades. The enemy losses amounted to 215,000 prisoners, 1,812 guns, 1,270 tanks and 542 aircraft.

In accordance with Fuehrer Directive No. 41 of 5 April, the conquest of the Caucasus was to be achieved in four phases: (1) Break-through to Voronezh (2) Destruction of enemy forces west of the Don (3) Thrust towards Stalingrad (4) Occupation of the Caucasus. This graduated offensive was cancelled by Directive 45 of 23 July, which ordered: Twin-pronged, diverging and simultaneous advances against Stalingrad and the Caucasus and the abandonment of any specific concentration of force; all to be accomplished without committing reserves to battle!

[2] The recollections of the Field-Marshal regarding Phase I are only approximately correct. He does not mention the controversy between Field-Marshal Bock and Supreme Headquarters on how far the advance in the Voronezh area should be carried.

OPERATION BLAU
in four phases as laid down
in the directive of
5 April, 1942

Orel
Army of
Gen.Weichs
XX 2
XX 4
2 HUNG
ARMY
Kursk I
Voronezh
II
Kharkov
GROUP
Kremenchug
Dnieper
SOUTH
Dnepropetrovsk
Zaporozhye
XX 1
XX 6
Donets
Artemovsk
XX 17 Stalino
Wietersheim
Taganrog
Rostov
III
Don
Hills
STALINGRAD
Volga
CRIMEA
Sea of
Azov
Kerch
XX
Tsimly-anskiy
W.Manych
Yergeni
Kotelnikovo
KALMUCK
STEPPES
Astrakhan
Elista
E.Manych
CASPIAN
Kuban
Voroshilovsk
Maykop
Novorossiysk
Tuapse
C A
Elbrus
U
Sukhumi
Mozdok
Terek
Grozny
Ordzhonikidze
SEA
BLACK
IV
C
Kasbek
S
Batum
SEA
Tiflis
Kura Baku
T U R K E Y
N

Miles
0   250
Km
0   200   400

MAP 2

The forces detailed for these attacks were: Fourth Panzer Army, Second Army, Second Hungarian Army and Sixth Army.[1]

The attack opened on 28 June. After reaching the Don in the vicinity of Voronezh, Fourth Panzer Army swung southwards behind Sixth Army's front in order to launch an attack, in conjunction with First Panzer Army, on the lower Don east of the Don–Donets confluence, with the object of cutting off the Russian forces retreating eastwards from Rostov.

In the middle of July, Army Group South was divided into Army Groups 'A' and 'B'.

Army Group 'A' (Seventeenth Army, First Panzer Army) was ordered to advance into the Caucasus and seize the oil fields at Maykop and Groznyy.

Army Group 'B' was given the task of protecting the flank of the Caucasian operations and of advancing to the Volga on both sides of Stalingrad, thus cutting the Russian lines of communication along the Volga waterway and neutralizing a great centre of armament production.

Accordingly, on 23 July Sixth Army advanced from the area north-west of Kalach over the Don in the direction of the northern and central portions of Stalingrad, and Fourth Panzer Army, advancing from the south-west, was directed via Kotel'nikovo against the southern part of the city.[2]

On reaching Stalingrad, Army Group 'B' was to assume responsibility for the defence of the whole stretch from south of Stalingrad to the north of Voronezh.[3] For this task it had under its command Fourth Panzer Army, Sixth Army, Third Rumanian Army, Eighth Italian Army, Second Hungarian Army and Second (German) Army.[4]

---

[1] It would be more correct to say: '. . . part of the Second Hungarian Army and part (XXXX Panzer Corps) of Sixth Army'.

[2] For the sake of brevity the Field-Marshal is here somewhat anticipating events. Fourth Panzer Army was first employed in support of the Caucasian operations, and it was not until 30 July that, on Hitler's orders, it wheeled north-east and was placed under Army Group 'B's' command.

[3] Eventually, Army Group 'B' was made responsible for the defence of some 500 miles of front, stretching from the Kalmuck steppes north-west of Astrakhan to Kursk in central Russia.

[4] The Field-Marshal is again anticipating events. The Third Rumanian Army did not take its place on the left of the Sixth Army until October.

A brief survey of the summer campaign, 1942

Considerable light was shed on Supreme Headquarters' choice of the southern sector for the main effort by a conference held by Hitler at Army Group South Headquarters in Poltava on 1 June. With his entourage, he arrived by air from his Headquarters in East Prussia and flew back the same day. With him were Field-Marshal Keitel, Chief of Staff, Armed Forces, General Heusinger, Head of the Operations Branch, Army Headquarters, General (Eduard) Wagner, Quartermaster-General and Hitler's personal aides-de-camp. The conference was attended by Field-Marshal v. Bock, GOC-in-C Army Group South and his Chief of Staff, General v. Sodenstern, and the following senior officers from what later became Army Groups 'A' and 'B': General v. Greiffenberg, Chief of Staff, General v. Kleist (First Panzer Army), General Ruoff (Seventeenth Army), General v. Mackensen (III Panzer Corps) (all A-G 'A'), and General v. Weichs (Second Army), General Hoth (Fourth Panzer Army) and myself (Sixth Army). Representing the Air Force was General v. Richthofen (Air Fleet 4). The Commanders-in-Chief of the allied armies had not yet arrived.

The subject of the conference was the 1942 summer offensive. Field-Marshal v. Bock outlined his intentions for the execution of the various phases. Stalingrad itself had not yet been mentioned as an objective. Hitler gave his approval to v. Bock's plans and said (among other things): 'If we don't get Maykop and Groznyy, I shall have to pack up ('liquidieren') the war.'[1]

At this conference, Hitler displayed all that ebullient energy that was typical of the man and had not at that time been impaired, and swept aside any and every misgiving that was expressed.

For the summer campaign a whole series of new divisions had been raised and existing divisions brought up to strength in Germany and occupied France. Thus, either in the spring or during the operations, 305, 307, 376, 384 and 389 Infantry Divisions joined the Sixth Army, Fourth Panzer Army was reinforced by 23 and 24 Panzer Divisions and Panzer Division 'Grossdeutschland'[2]. Furthermore, all the

[1] Some doubt exists whether Hitler said 'this war', meaning the war against Russia, or 'the war', meaning the war as a whole.

[2] An error on the Field-Marshal's part. 'Grossdeutschland' at that time was a motorized and not a Panzer division.

divisions at the front itself were brought up to full strength and their arms and equipment deficiencies made good.

Even so, in view of the unduly diverging objectives set, the armies participating in the offensive were still far too weak, numerically, for the tasks allotted to them. To help fill the gap Supreme Headquarters therefore decided to bring the allied armies into the general framework of the operations.

At this juncture of the campaign, the participation of allied troops became an issue of primary importance and one which was destined to have grave repercussions in the future. In principle, the role envisaged for these troops was that of occupying and safeguarding the territories conquered by the German armies. Only the Rumanians, who supplied the major contingent of allied troops, participated, in any considerable numbers, in the actual offensive operations.

Neither in training nor in equipment were the allied troops fit to take part in a major, modern war, and particularly in one fought in the severe climatic conditions of a Russian winter. Furthermore, opinion in allied countries was opposed to the sending of their troops to the Volga and the Don. Nor could it have been easy to explain to, say, an Italian soldier why he should be called upon to fight in the depths of the Russian steppes – and under climatic conditions which were all but intolerable to him.

The same applied, generally speaking, to all the other allies. The Second Hungarian Army was composed of units plucked haphazardly from the whole of the Hungarian Army and of men recruited for the most part from the territories which Hungary had but recently acquired.

The weaknesses inevitable in a force of this composition will be immediately apparent to every soldier. In the circumstances, the fighting spirit and leadership displayed by the Rumanian units in the Army under my command deserve special commendation.[1] With the assistance of heavy weapons of the normal German type issued to them, and thanks to determined leadership by their officers, these troops fought gallantly and showed great steadfastness in the face of all the hardships to which they were subjected.

[1] The Field-Marshal is here referring to the 20 Rumanian Infantry Division and the 1 Rumanian Cavalry Division, which were besieged with him in Stalingrad.

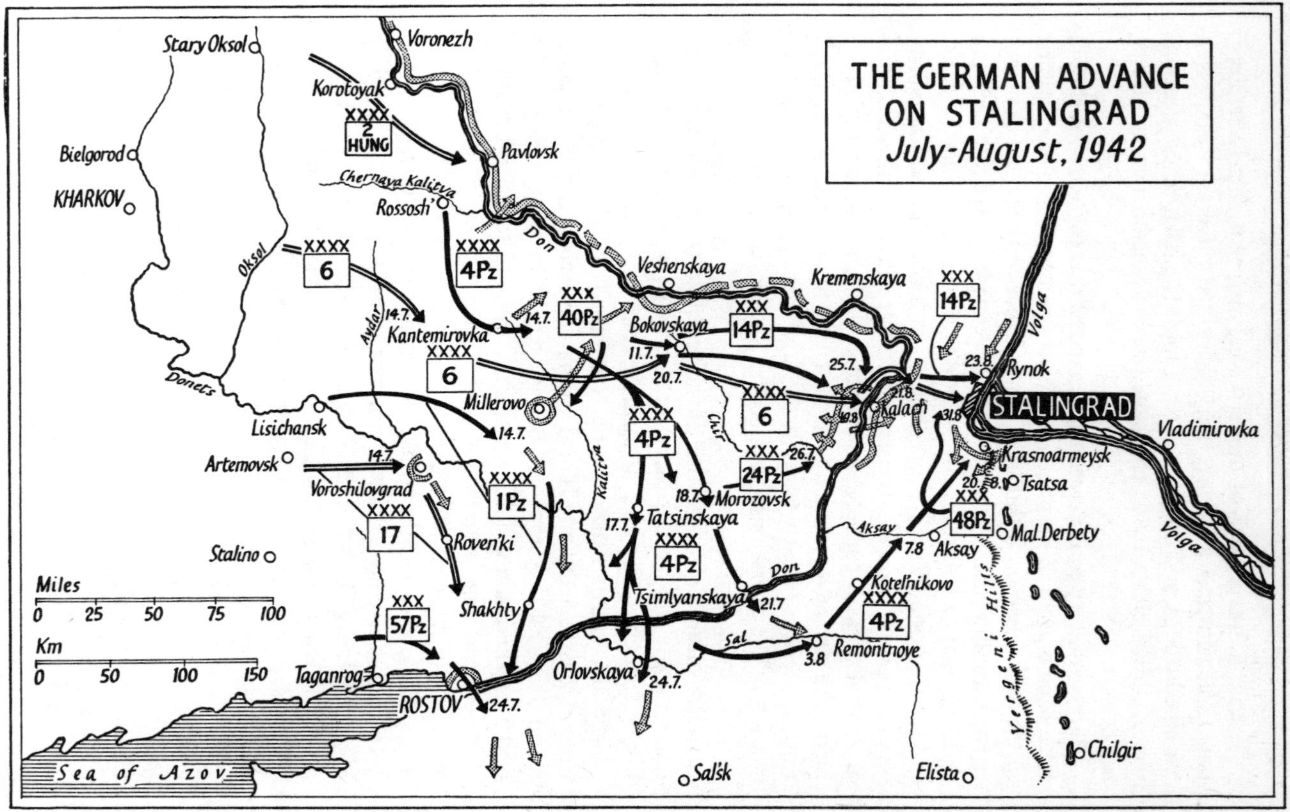
THE GERMAN ADVANCE
ON STALINGRAD
July-August, 1942
Stary Oksol
Voronezh
Korotoyak
2
HUNG
Bielgorod
Pavlovsk
KHARKOV
Chernaya Kalitva
Rossosh'
Oksol
Don
6
4Pz
Veshenskaya
Kremenskaya
14Pz
40Pz
Bokovskaya
14.7.
Kantemirovka
Aydar
11.7.
20.7.
25.7.
23.8.
Rynok
Volga
Donets
Millerovo
STALINGRAD
21.8.
31.8
Kalach
19.8
Vladimirovka
Lisichansk
Chir
26.7.
Krasnoarmeysk
Artemovsk
Voroshilovgrad
1Pz
24Pz
20.8.
Tsatsa
18.7.
Morozovsk
Kalitva
17.7.
Tatsinskaya
48Pz
Mal.Derbety
17
Aksay
7.8
Roven'ki
Stalino
Miles
0
25
50
75
100
Km
0
50
100
150
Shakhty
57Pz
Tsimlyanskaya
21.7
Kotel'nikovo
Hills
Vergeni
Sal
Remontnoye
3.8
Taganrog
Orlovskaya
24.7.
ROSTOV
Sea of Azov
Sal'sk
Elista
Chilgir

MAP 3

It was, however, lack of modern weapons, particularly artillery, tanks and anti-tank weapons, that constituted the main weakness of the allied troops, and the promises to supply them with these weapons were fulfilled either to a very inadequate extent or, in some cases, not at all.

Purely military considerations demanded that these troops should have been employed in quiet or unthreatened sectors of the front or in the back areas; or, if this were not possible and they had to be put in the front line, then they should have been integrated into German formations. For political reasons, however, this could not be done. On the question of their subordination to higher military authority and the issue of orders to them, the prestige of the smaller countries and the very easily ruffled susceptibilities of their commanders in the field were also factors which had constantly to be borne in mind. All this exposes very clearly not only the faulty nature of the whole conception of the operations, but also the weaknesses of Hitler's policy in the forming of alliances.

In the autumn of 1942, with the object of knitting the Rumanians more closely into the pattern of Germany's eastern campaign, Hitler conceived the idea of forming the 'Army Group, Don', to consist of Fourth Panzer Army (composed mostly of Rumanian troops), Sixth Army and Third Rumanian Army, under the command of Marshal Antonescu. Its task was to be the defence of the line from the chain of lakes south of Stalingrad to a point south of Veshenskaya. The organization of this Army Group had not, however, been completed when the major Soviet offensive was launched on 19 November and the whole Don front began to waver.

Instead, an Army Group, Don, was formed, which consisted of Eleventh Army Staff, Fourth Panzer Army, Sixth Army and an improvised Army Group in the area between the Don and the Chir, and was placed under the command of Field-Marshal v. Manstein.[1]

Nevertheless, the fact remains that, notwithstanding their weakness in artillery, armour and anti-tank weapons, allied troops were called upon to defend important sectors of the front, for the whole front – from Stalingrad to Voronezh – was, operationally speaking, important. The explanation is probably to be found in the faulty

[1] Vide v. Manstein: *Lost Victories*, pp. 294 et seq. (Methuen.)

appreciation of the situation made by Supreme Headquarters. For instance, the fact that the Russians had withdrawn according to plan in the great bend of the Don – very few prisoners or booty were taken – was not appreciated, but was, indeed, interpreted as being evidence of the rapidly waning fighting value of the enemy.

And it was on this erroneous assumption that Supreme Headquarters committed the error of ordering the unduly diverging offensives against the Caucasus and Stalingrad and thus adding immensely to the length of the front.

In conclusion, in assessing the results of the 1942 summer offensive, there remains but little to be said, beyond the fact that it failed to achieve the success hoped for by Supreme Headquarters. The Soviet forces had retired in accordance with the strategic conceptions of the Russian High Command and had evaded the encirclement which the German Supreme Headquarters had planned.

In spite of reports to the contrary from formations in the field, Supreme Headquarters had persisted in maintaining that the enemy now had only very weak forces at his disposal and professed to see in the Russian withdrawal from the Don bend a confirmation of this assertion. The assessment of Soviet strength in the late autumn of 1942 led to the conclusion that the Russians were now so weak in reserves that, while still able to put in local counter-attacks, they would be quite incapable of staging any major, strategic counter-offensive.

To assist the reader in appreciating the subsequent course of the battle of Stalingrad and the directives issued during its progress by Supreme Headquarters, I must briefly allude to Supreme Headquarters assessment of the Soviet High Command's intentions for the autumn and winter of 1942–3.

This I can best do by referring to the results of a conference held on 12 September at Supreme Headquarters in Vinnitsa, to which General v. Weichs, the GOC-in-C Army Group 'B', and I, as GOC-in-C Sixth Army, were summoned. The subject of the conference was the battle of Stalingrad and the situation on the Don front from Voronezh to Stalingrad. Both General Weichs and I drew attention to the very long and inadequately held Don front and the dangers inherent in the situation.

Hitler based his appreciation of the situation on the assumption that the Russians were at the end of their resources. The resistance at Stalingrad, he asserted, was a purely local affair. The Russians were no longer capable of launching a major offensive, and as far as the holding of the Don front was concerned, our defences, he said, were being strengthened every day by the arrival of more and more allied troops. In these circumstances he felt quite sure that no serious danger existed on the northern (Don) flank. The vital thing now was to concentrate every available man and capture as quickly as possible the whole of Stalingrad itself and the banks of the Volga. And with this in view, he proposed to reinforce Sixth Army with three more divisions.

That, then, was the situation when we received the first indication that a Russian offensive was imminent and Sixth Army entered upon its last and fateful battle.

Extracts from the correspondence of General Paulus, Commander-in-Chief, Sixth Army

From General Oswald Lutz

Munich   5 January 1942
(The writer describes his tour of inspection of the lines of communication in Rumania . . . dissatisfied with what he saw . . . the three Services acting independently and with no co-operation . . . on returning to Vienna he had discussed the whole matter with Field-Marshal List (GOC-in-C Armed Forces, South East Balkans) . . . the latter expressed himself in no uncertain terms. . . .)

'. . . In short, we must create centres of authority; in each district there must be *one* man responsible for everything and with *everything* without exception under *his* control. If we don't the outlook, in my opinion, is pretty grim. Another thing – the man in charge will have to be completely ruthless. . . .'

(He then goes on to talk about the way in which the Panzer arm is being used, appeals to Paulus, as 'an old Panzer man', and maintains that the Panzer arm should be represented on the staff of Supreme Headquarters, and by 'the very best man we can find', who should be in charge of everything – training, schools, equipment and everything else.)

'. . . I'm quite sure that in your heart you have the same convictions as I myself have, so I need waste no more words on the subject. But I can't help comparing our position with that of the artillery, who have a very good General as their representative at Supreme Head-quarters. . . . But we, with a completely new arm and with completely new ideas, have no one and exercise no influence at all; and all our enemies and detractors scream because we have our own insignia and by means of such superficialities strive to destroy the unity, the feeling of "belonging" and the *esprit* of our fine and proud arm. Such lack of understanding would make us turn in our graves (if we were in them!) . . . With all the vicissitudes and the ebb and flow of events, you've certainly had a pretty hard time during these last few months – and don't look like having it any easier in the future! . . .'

Lutz.

From General Vietinghoff
(Commanding XXXXVI (Mot.) Corps)

11 January 1942

Dear Paulus,

You know that for weeks all we Generals of Fourth Panzer Army, including our deposed C-in-C, have been urging a planned withdrawal. The Fuehrer's orders of 10 January only strengthen my conviction that we are right! The 'steadiness of nerve' displayed by the Russian High Command takes the form of accepting with equanimity a completely ruthless and reckless sacrifice of human life. That, of course, is something quite foreign to us Europeans, although we are always willing to pay the price for things that matter. And in the present situation that means holding on with everything we've got everywhere, *where the Russian is attacking*, and in particular in those places where his attack constitutes a threat to our flanks. It was this narrow-minded stubbornness on the Russian's part that made possible the great battles of encirclement we have fought. And once he was in the cauldron, our main preoccupation was the fear that he might pull out in time and escape, before the ring finally closed. Are we now to copy this mistake and allow ourselves to be surrounded in our turn?

Fully to appreciate our anxieties, you should see the indescribably bad conditions on the autobahn lines of communication of 3 and 4 Panzer Armies (i.e. the road Smolensk–Moscow). We live literally from hand to mouth. Even a temporary interruption of our supply line, be it on account of snow or as the result of enemy action, could well lead to the destruction of both P Armies and the certain destruction of their motorized divisions. Can't they see this? Well, these days I've become a bit of a philosopher!

Yours ever,
Vietinghoff.

From Field-Marshal v. Witzleben
(GOC-in-C, Army Group, West)

12 January 1942

My dear Paulus,

(The writer complains about the mistaken personnel policy being pursued by Army Headquarters, the dismissal of qualified Generals on the grounds of 'unsuitability', and hopes that Paulus will be able to make some use of his views on the subject. He also complains that he has not been given any information regarding the reorganization of Army Headquarters and the intentions underlying it.)

'. . . In addition we are being subjected to constant spying and prying by SS personnel to an extent which is quite intolerable. The Corps of Officers here seems to be completely devoid of any sense of the fitness of things, the younger officers feel that the demise of the old Supreme Command of the Army is a good thing . . . (illegible) . . . You don't need me to tell you where all this is leading to. Please make what use you like of this letter. . . . My cordial good wishes to Halder. And to yourself, my dear Paulus, the best of luck. You are often in my thoughts. Please don't look upon this as a querulous grouse, but as an honest expression of the anxiety I feel.

As always,

Yours, v. Witzleben.'[1]

---

[1] This and the preceeding letter from General Vietinghoff are good examples of the way in which senior Generals, highly critical of the Third Reich, unburden themselves to Paulus, with full confidence in his understanding and discretion. Unfortunately, there is no trace of Paulus' replies.

From Dr Flade

16 January 1942

'. . . But fate has once more stepped in and decided otherwise. Within half an hour of my arrival in Dresden I received the first long-distance call from Army Group Headquarters with the bad news about the Field-Marshal. I at once flew back in an aircraft provided by the Fuehrer. There is, alas, little or nothing that medical science can do. Now I have been given the task of taking the Field-Marshal by air to Leipzig. . . .'

From Colonel Faeckenstedt
(Chief of Staff, III P. Korps)

Corps Headquarters   20 January 1942

'. . . We are all very worried here about the spring and the new offensive. When and whence are we to get the forces (and the material) we shall need? Apart from the fact that attack is the very basis of our unbroken superiority, we shall have to conquer new areas, if we are to survive at all. . . .

'If you have half an hour to spare, Sir, I would be very grateful for a few lines on the plans and prospects for the future. . . .'

Yours, etc.

From Dr Flade

Dresden   12 February 1942

'. . . As you probably know, Sir, I left Poltava in a DO17 aircraft with the Field-Marshal on 17 January for Cracow, where we were to join a later plane bringing Professors Hochrein and Ketter to Leipzig. My pilot thought it would be easier to land at Lemberg and changed course accordingly. At 11.50, while landing, disaster overtook us. How it could have happened I cannot to this day understand. Visibility was quite good, though it seemed to me that our landing speed was much too high. Unfortunately, too, we approached from the wrong direction and did not even land on the runway. In short, having seen the aircraft afterwards, it seems a miracle to me that the whole lot of us were not killed. For myself, I managed to scramble out of the wreckage. Then, with the help of signal pistols we attracted attention to ourselves and were taken by ambulance and stretcher to the airport hospital. . . . After my left leg had been put in splints, I managed, with the help of the airport commandant and Sgt-Major Hein, to attend to the injured Field-Marshal. In the afternoon we were able to continue the flight. . . . The Field-Marshal arrived in Leipzig about 19.30 hours. . . . The whole thing seems like some drama on the films. Even his Field-Marshal's baton was broken in half. . . .'

From Colonel Metz
(GSOI (Ops), Tenth Army)

(At this time with German Military Mission in Rumania)

16 February 1942

(He sends his congratulations on 'your splendid leap, Sir, to the head of Sixth Army'.)

'. . . May Sixth Army under its new leader continue to achieve the same brilliant successes as in the past. . . . Our job here in Rumania is a heartbreaking one. The people are willing enough, but we seem to make little or no progress. There is a vast mountain of wrong ideas, prejudices and confusion of thought to be cleared away. . . . But I musn't complain. "Get on with the job in hand" must be our slogan, and somehow or other we'll get the Rumanians progressing along the right lines.

'The sudden death of Field-Marshal v. Reichenau must have distressed you, Sir, as much as it did me. Shortly before he died he wrote and told me of his appointment as GOC-in-C, Army Group South, and urged me to "stick it". . . . Please remember me to all the Staff and particularly to Heim.'

Yours, etc.

From General Lutz

Munich 22 February 1942

My dear Paulus.

So now you're commanding the Army of which you were Chief of Staff for so long! I am truly delighted to see that you have at last emerged from the wilderness – and not slowly and laboriously, but with one splendid leap. No one deserves it more than you.

(The writer then returns to the theme of his anxiety about the Panzer arm; thinks that he himself might 'fit the bill as Inspector General at home' and is writing to Halder on the subject. Has had a talk with Guderian, who seems more happy about things – 'which, in view of his temperament, is all to the good'.)

Yours, etc.

From Colonel v. Huenersdorff
(Chief of Staff, Third Panzer Army)

20 March 1942

My dear General,

From what my brother says in a letter I gather that my letter of congratulation on your promotion and appointment to Army Commander did not reach you. This distresses me very much, for you must have thought me an ungrateful scamp; but I do assure you, Sir, that no one was more delighted than I. I'm not sure that command of a Panzer army would not have been more appropriate, though, of course, nowadays all the armies are composed of all arms. From what we have heard, Sixth Army has beaten off all the attacks made on it, but Papa Hoth (i.e. GOC Seventeenth Army, Army Group South) is having a harder time of it.

Since February we have been employed as 'gap-pluggers' and have been industriously bunging up the holes in the Gruyère cheese.

All the best people seem to be gathering in the Ukraine, including yourself, Sir, Papa Hoth, my brother and my wife, who is running a soldiers' home in Snamenka. If one can believe what the British radio tells us, there'll soon be quite a lot more friends, relatives and acquaintances there!

Yours, etc.

From General Rudolf Schmundt

Fuehrer Headquarters   20 May 1942

'. . . On the evening of the 16th, as soon as I got back via Poltava and Stalino after visiting Seventeenth Army, I was given the opportunity of telling the Fuehrer all that I had seen. He was intensely interested, and you may rest assured, Sir, that he fully appreciates the successes achieved by the Sixth Army against greatly superior numbers. He also fully realizes all the hardships with which the troops had to contend south of Kharkov. If things go on as they are and the advance of Seventeenth Army succeeds in easing the pressure of the southern front, then the battle of Kharkov will end in a brilliant victory.'

Your, etc. Heil Hitler!

(General Schmundt was at that time Hitler's 'Chief Adjutant' [roughly Military Secretary] and had just returned from a visit to Army Group South at the height of the Kharkov battle.)

From Paulus

To Halder   24 May 1942

(Paulus announces the victorious conclusion of the defensive battle on 22 May; about 100,000 prisoners and 150 guns taken and 450 tanks destroyed.)

'. . . And now the south front has taken the offensive. The steadiness of leaders and men alike was, for the most part, quite exemplary. Some of the formations which have not yet become acclimatized to conditions on the eastern front – e.g. 23 Panzer Division – are still suffering from teething troubles. . . .'

From Halder

To Paulus   25 May 1942

'First and foremost, congratulations on your great victory. With heartfelt eagerness I have followed the course of the action, the planning and preparation of which is a thankless task in comparison with the job of commanding in the field and smashing the enemy! But my twinge of envy has been extinguished by my joy at the success of one who so richly deserves it. More power to you and your troops.'

Yours most sincerely,

From Alfred v. Wietersheim

Neumarkt, Silesia   30 May 1942
(Congratulations on the Kharkov victory)

. . . It is probably unique in the history of both the old Prussian Army and the proud, young German Army that the Chief of Staff of an Army has had the luck in one and the same war to rise and command that same Army in battle. And the fact that you succeeded not only in defeating a major enemy offensive in an 'ordinary' defensive battle, but also in destroying three enemy armies in a brilliant counter-attack must also surely be a feat unique in the history of war; and I can't help feeling that this may well be the first step along the path to final victory. These are the thoughts running through the mind of a miserable and unwilling armchair warrior, and I hope you won't mind, if he puts them into words. . . . (The writer of the above had formerly served on Sixth Army Staff but had been forced to retire for reasons of health.)

From Colonel Metz

5 June 1942

. . . Kharkov has shown that the famous Sixth Army still retains under its new commander all its old flair for winning great victories. Let me at the same time congratulate you on your Knights' Cross – and it won't be long, Sir, before the Marshal's baton follows.

Yours, etc.

From Major Count Stauffenberg

Army Headquarters   12 July 1942
My dear General,

(The writer apologizes for having left without saying good-bye to the General and explains that this was due to a sudden change in departure arrangements. He thanks the General for having received him as his 'personal guest'.)

. . . The days I spent in and around Kharkov, with all the thrill of a bit of adventure, gave me very great pleasure and have put new life into me. And, of course, it makes one realize how much one is missing by being so far removed from the troops and regimental duty. For what could give one more satisfaction than being with the men and being responsible for their and one's own salvation? In comparison such satisfaction as one gets here is a miserable substitute. And all the more so, if one happens to be 'one of the initiated' – as I must now claim to be, after two years here – who, perforce, has to know the limitations imposed upon every action, before ever it begins! But I do realize that we must go on fighting and I do my best to make this clear to all my colleagues. But it is not always easy in the process to preserve one's own enthusiasm. You, Sir, will appreciate better than most how refreshing it is to get away from this atmosphere to surroundings where men give of their best without a thought, and give their lives, too, without a murmur of complaint, while the leaders and those who should set an example quarrel and quibble about their own prestige, or haven't the courage to speak their minds on a question which affects the lives of thousands of their fellow men.

I admit that seeing things in that light does not make life here any easier; but if one doesn't, then the sooner one quits the better!

You, Sir, are now engaged on yet another operation[1] and we shall eagerly follow each step. May your lucky star guide you, now and in the future.

> My deep respects, Sir,
> and my best wishes,
> v. Stauffenberg.

From General Blumentritt
(Paulus' successor as OQuI)

Army Headquarters   21 July 1942

. . . The last two months have brought victory after victory. You, Sir, are familiar with the daily conferences here at 10 a.m. and 10 p.m. Again and again the CGS (i.e. General Halder) has drawn attention to the clear, calm and unerring manner in which the Army has been commanded, and in his voice there has always been a note of quiet satisfaction – evidence of the pride he takes in his former pupil. Recently, too, during all the goading to which we are

[1] Operation 'Wilhelm': the attack on Voronezh.

being subjected to hurry on the advance on a certain great city,[1] the Sixth Army came in for a great deal of praise at the situation conference on 20 July.

I, too, am quite convinced that it is in the open country round this place that the main thrust must not only be made, but be made as a matter of urgent priority. It is a race between the two sides, and I can only hope that fuel supplies will not fail us. I'm crossing all my fingers! . . .

Yours, etc.

From Paulus

To Lutz	5 August 1942
. . . Meanwhile, we've advanced quite a bit and have left Kharkov 500 kilometres behind us. The great thing now is to hit the Russian so hard a crack, that he won't recover for a very long time. . . .

From Colonel Adam
(Sixth Army Staff, on sick leave)

23 August 1942
. . . Here we are all awaiting the news of the fall of Stalingrad, which everybody confidently believes will be the turning point of the war. You, Sir, have become a popular figure. . . .

Yours, etc.

From General Halder

Army Headquarters	24 September 1942
Dear Paulus,

A line to tell you that today I have resigned my appointment. Let me thank you, my dear Paulus, for your loyalty and friendship and wish you further great success as the leader you have proved yourself to be.

As always,
Halder.

[1] This refers to Rostov, in implementation of Hitler's own great plan for yet another battle of encirclement at Rostov. It never materialized.

From Paulus

To General Halder   28 September 1942

My Dear General,

I was, indeed, deeply moved to receive the news contained in
your letter of the 24th.

I am most grateful, Sir, for the unwavering confidence you have
always placed in me and for the kindly friendship you have so
generously bestowed upon me and which I hope I shall also enjoy
in the future. The period I was permitted to spend working with,
and learning from, you has not been turned to my personal advantage alone, but has also been of immense value to me in the
performance of the tasks which I have been called upon to perform.

My deepest respect and my most sincere good wishes accompany
you, Sir.

As always,
Paulus.

From Paulus

To General Schmundt   7 October 1942

(Paulus congratulates Schmundt on his promotion and appointment as Chief of the Personnel Branch, Army Headquarters and
expresses his conviction that this move will be 'all to the good in
every way'.)

. . . The Stalingrad battle continues along its stubborn course.
Things are going very slowly, but every day we make just a little
progress. The whole thing is a question of time and manpower.
But we'll beat the Russians yet!

Best wishes and Heil Hitler!
Yours,
Paulus.

From Colonel Voelter
(Formerly on Sixth Army Staff)

22 October 1942

(He tells Paulus that he has been appointed Chief of Staff V Corps
on the borders of the Caucasus and says he thinks the autumn

offensive has now come to a close – not on account of the weather, but 'on account of wastage'.)

. . . We shall first have to build up our substance again, and then we shall be able to go gaily forward in the spring. . . . Here, thank God, we hear nothing about high policy!

Yours, etc.

From General Kirchheim[1]

26 October 1942

. . . Here, it is difficult to form any accurate picture of how things are with you, but the Russian seems to be fighting with astounding tenacity. I feel that your situation, like that in Africa, is dominated by the question of supplies and reinforcements.

In Africa the British have assumed the offensive.[2] I hope the outcome of the battle will prove me wrong.

Yours, etc.

[1] General Kirchheim, Head of Special Branch, Tropics, AHQ. He was responsible for supplies and reinforcements to the Afrika Korps and a great personal friend of Paulus.

[2] The battle of Alamein.

Appendix:
Documents relating to the advance on Stalingrad

....

Introduction

Among the papers of the late Field-Marshal is a pencilled copy, in his own handwriting, of a note written by Field-Marshal v. Bock on the conduct of operations by the Commander of the Sixth Army during the battle of Kharkov. How Paulus came to hear of its contents is not known. The note says: 'To comment upon the leadership displayed by an Army Commander does not come within the scope of my duties, but is the prerogative of Supreme Headquarters. Were I asked to do so, however, I could only say that in my opinion it was beyond all praise.'

The following report, dated 5 April 1942, by Field-Marshal v. Bock on Paulus is entered in the latter's Record of Services, in the archives of the Personnel Branch: 'Has only been in command of the Army for three months. Absolutely trustworthy, a courageous soldier of mature judgment. Must prove his worth as an Army Commander before being considered for further advancement.'

To judge from its date, this does not in any way contradict the other note, the copy of which Paulus has preserved. Also in Paulus' Record of Services is a report, undated, by Field-Marshal v. Reichenau: 'Sincere and trustworthy char(acter). Clear headed and sound.' GOC.

And under the very shadow of the fateful crisis, on 20 December 1942, General v. Weichs reported as follows: 'Displayed outst-(anding) ab(ility) during 1942 ops. Very much above aver. in both initiative and breadth of vision as well as in strat(egic) and tac(tical) ability. His personal devotion to duty has been an example to the whole of his Army.'

These reports and comments show that Paulus was undoubtedly justified in looking back on the battle with a certain measure of pride. In the account of the 1942 campaign which he wrote while a prisoner in Russia, he does not, however, go into any details regarding his great victory in the second battle of Kharkov. It may be that in this memorandum, which is dated 30 June 1948, he wished to confine himself solely to describing the developments which led up to the final catastrophe. Or perhaps he may have considered it inopportune, as a prisoner of war, to draw attention to a brilliant German victory over an enemy of great susceptibility but of uncertain self-reliance, in circumstances in which only a Pharisee would have the hardihood to cast the first stone.

The extent to which the susceptibility persists to this day on the Soviet side is well exemplified by Marshal Yeromenko's treatise, *The Historic Victory of Stalingrad*. Although the spring battle of Kharkov is undoubtedly part of the history of the battle of Stalingrad, the greatest of Soviet victories, the Marshal does not even mention it.

On the other hand he is frank enough about the difficulties which arose to confront the Soviet Command. At the beginning of August, STAVKA, the Russian High Command (Stalin – Marshal Shaposhnikov), directed that the 'Front Group (i.e. Army Group) Stalingrad' should be divided into two Front Groups, 'Stalingrad' and 'South-East'. The Headquarters of both Groups were to be established in Stalingrad itself.

Yeromenko writes: 'As a result of this dividing up of the Front Group, valuable time was lost in making the necessary administrative arrangements, and the situation from the point of view of the defence, far from being improved, was made considerably more difficult. Five days after the division had been completed, it was realized that a mistake had been made and an order was issued, amalgamating the command of the two Fronts. But though there was then only one Commander, he still had to work with two Staffs – a fact which did not, of course, make his task any easier.'[1]

[1] Unfortunately, Marshal Yeromenko does not say who this Commander was. Was it he himself? Or General Rokossovski? According to Yeromenko, at the end of September, the Front Groups 'Stalingrad' and 'South-East' were renamed 'Don' and 'Stalingrad' respectively. Commander, Don, was Rokossovski, Commander, Stalingrad, was Yeromenko. A report sent by the German Military Mission in Rumania on 2 November 1942 stated that Marshal Timoshenko was presumed to have been appointed GOC-in-C Forces, South-West. But according to official Soviet sources this appointment had been abolished in

After this not uninteresting digression, let us return to the question of the influence exercised by the battle of Kharkov and the opening events of the 1942 summer offensive on the subsequent development of General Paulus' mental outlook, remembering that he was an Army Commander who had just come straight from the General Staff. According to General Arthur Schmidt, his Chief of Staff, the events of May and June and the Reichel – Stumme affair had a profound effect.

To understand what Field-Marshal Paulus was trying to convey in his terse memorandum, 'The basic facts of Sixth Army's operations at Stalingrad' (dated 30 June 1945 – vide Chapters 5 and 6), we must re-examine all the questions regarding both the battle itself and the premature legends to which it gave birth; in this way, but in this way only, can we establish what actually occurred during the course of the battle and what lessons can be learnt from it.

There follow therefore, in elucidation of the Stalingrad campaign as a whole, extracts from the personal diary of Field-Marshal v. Bock, Commander-in-Chief, Army Group South, dealing with the second battle of Kharkov and the Reichel – Stumme affair, which resulted in the imposition of further strict limitations on the liberty of action of responsible Generals in the field; these are supplemented by a report submitted to Paulus by General Stumme himself and found among the former's papers. In their turn, these are followed by extracts from the diary of General Freiherr v. Richthofen, the GOC Air Fleet 4, which was co-operating with Army Groups 'A' and 'B' in the Stalingrad – Caucasus theatres and which, later, was given the task of flying in Sixth Army's requirements after that

---

August. In actual fact, the attack itself, on 19 November, was delivered by: on the left, Front Group South-East (Vatutin), with First Guards Army, Fifth Tank Army and Twenty-First Army; in the centre, Front Group Don (Rokossovski) with Sixty-Fifth, Twenty-Fourth and Sixty-Sixth Armies; on the right, Front Group Stalingrad (Yeromenko) with Sixty-Second, Sixty-Fourth, Fifty-Seventh and Fifty-First Armies. (Vide *Vtoraya Mirovaya Voina* [Second World War], Moscow, 1958, pp. 376 et seq.) As 'delegates in chief' from STAVKA, Generals Voronov and Vasilievski. (Biographic Directory of USSR, New York, 1958.) According to the same source, Rokossovski stated that later (after October 1942) he had been in simultaneous command of both Stalingrad Front Groups.

Army had been surrounded; and finally, by reports taken from the files of the German Military Mission in Rumania on events in the sector of the Third Rumanian Army and the controversy between the German and Rumanian Commands during the first phase of the encirclement of the German-Rumanian forces in Stalingrad, after 19 November.

All these hitherto unpublished reports shed light on the situation as it was at the beginning of Phase II of the battle of Stalingrad.

One final comment on the above sources: Field-Marshal v. Bock's diary is the report of a highly talented disciple of the traditional school of the old German General Staff. Even in those instances where Bock's opinion differs from that of Army Headquarters, he is revealed as a man of independent mind and a great military leader.

As regards the statements made and the opinions expressed, often in a blunt and forthright manner, by General v. Richthofen, it must be remembered that v. Richthofen was a man of considerable intelligence, but also an extremely self-willed man, who was very inclined to harsh and even uncouth criticism. He was what has often been described as 'a difficult character'. Nevertheless he frequently saw things far more clearly and with a far wider outlook than did the more senior officers of his Service, Reichsmarschall Goering and General Jeschonnek, the Chief of the Air Staff.

As regards the Rumanian side, it must be remembered that of all Hitler's allies the Rumanian Army made far and away the greatest military effort and was fully justified in complaining at the inadequacy of the sinews of war with which it had been supplied by the Germans – though in this connection, Bucharest most probably did not fully realize the extent to which the resources of Germany's war potential were overstrained.

Walter Goerlitz

The Second Battle of Kharkov (spring 1942): *extracts from the diary of Field-Marshal v. Bock*

8 *May.* On its eastern front, Eleventh Army has taken the offensive. Enemy appears to have been surprised by both time and place of the attack. In the Sevastopol area enemy is quiet. Short talk with v.

Manstein resulted in complete agreement on the next step in the ops.[1] This morning Kleist's C. of Staff, Faeckenstedt, arrived and gave details about 'Fridericus'.[2] I think the Army Group is too weak in its main thrust and too strong in the subsidiary thrust on Barvenkovo.

Sixth Army requests permission to reinforce VII Corps with 113 Division and to put one regiment of 305 Division, which has just arrived in the Kharkov area, into the Volchansk salient battle, because Russian attacks are expected in both places. The Army justifies its request with the somewhat remarkable statement that ' "Fridericus" will not be jeopardized in any way by these measures'. My fears that the Russians may forestall us with their own attack have not been lessened by this report. Even so, now that orders have been issued for the carrying out of 'Fridericus' in this form – in spite of my protests – I must do my best to see that it is at least given the chance to succeed. I therefore turned down Sixth Army's request.

9 *May*. This morning I informed the Fuehrer of the satisfactory developments in the Crimea. I reported that on the other fronts considerable movement had been observed for several days in the area south-east and east of Slaviansk. . . . Enemy also active in the north-west corner of the Isium salient and in the Volchansk area. . . . Whether this is indicative of an intention to attack is not yet clear. . . .

An article in the *Neue Zürcher Zeitung* of 30 April describes Russian views regarding the anticipated German offensive. The article is highly illuminating, both as regards Russian intentions and the soundness of the Russian appreciation of the situation. We must not underestimate these Russians.

Bad news about the harvest prospects.

10 *May*. In Slaviansk sector and the Volchansk salient local attacks up to battalion strength. Paulus has submitted his plans for 'Fridericus'. Except for one or two minor details, I agree.

11 *May*. In the Crimea, things are going well. . . .

Army Headquarters have agreed, in all essentials, with our

---

[1] i.e. Operation 'Trappenjagd', the reconquest of the Kerch peninsula. (Vide v. Manstein: *Lost Victories*, pp. 231 et seq. (Methuen.))

[2] Op. 'Fridericus I and II', the elimination of the salients gained by the enemy during the winter campaign. Kleist's Army Group consisted of First Panzer Army and Seventeenth Army.

Reinforcements on the way to the front

Soldiers from a regimental band

THE WINTER WAR NEAR THE DON

Tanks approaching the Don bridges

Horse-drawn transport

BEGINNING OF THE ADVANCE ON STALINGRAD

proposals for the major offensive. In the view they express, the idea again crops up that List's Army Group, which is to lead the right wing in the south-easterly thrust in Phase III, might, in certain circumstances, take some part in *Phase II*, and that for this purpose First Panzer Army should perhaps be placed under Kleist's command. This would mean that in the northern sector I should be in command and in the southern sector List – an unnecessary complication.[1]

12 *May*. On Sixth Army front the enemy has launched heavy attacks, supported by strong armoured forces, on the north-western tip of the Isium salient and on Volchansk. As early as this morning it became apparent that he had succeeded in making several breaches in the line in both places. I asked Army Headquarters for permission to use 23 Panzer Division to restore the situation. . . . Army Headquarters have agreed, with the proviso that 23 Pan. Div. is to be committed only to the minimum degree necessary and that Army Group will be held responsible for ensuring that it is available and ready to participate in 'Fridericus' 'on the date already fixed'!

In the afternoon it became clear that the break on VIII Corps front had assumed serious proportions. . . . In the evening enemy armoured forces were within twenty kilometres of Kharkov. . . .

I telephoned to Halder and told him that the carrying out of 'Fridericus' 'on the date already fixed' was now quite out of the question. Halder retorted that the Fuehrer's order was not categorical on the subject, but was intended to convey that, as far as possible, we should adhere to the main object in view – our main offensive – and should not use troops to repair local blemishes. To this I replied: It's not a question of patching up local blemishes, it's neck or nothing!

What I am trying to do is to ensure that the reserves are committed *concentrated* and in *a co-ordinated counter-attack*, and are not wasted in penny packets. My orders to Sixth Army were framed accordingly. Paulus came here late this evening and I personally impressed on him not to be in too great a hurry and not, in any circumstances, to attack without air support. . . .

[1] This refers to Directive No. 41 of 5 April (vide footnote p. 152). Bock's military judgment revolts at the idea of a premature splitting up of command in the Southern Sector of the Eastern theatre of war.

13 *May.* This morning I submitted a report to the Fuehrer on Sixth Army's situation, which is serious enough. . . . The break-through northwards at Volchansk is on a broader front than I had realized yesterday. The premature attack by 23 and 3 Panzer Divisions had been in progress since 0930 hours and had started before I knew anything about it. . . .

The question now arises: can the break-through on the right wing of VIII Corps still be halted by Kleist's envisaged attack north-westwards from the Slaviansk – Alexandrovka area? Or must I confine myself – through lack of forces, both on the ground and in the air – to suggesting that the meagre forces available should be concentrated behind Kleist's left wing and prepare to deliver a *local* counter-attack against the flank and rear of the enemy attacking VIII Corps?

Sixth Army is at the moment completely tied down by the Russian attack. But to seal off the Donets front behind the Russian break-through – i.e. to make a thrust from Slaviansk as far as Balaklea and at the same time screen the thrust from the east – Kleist's force alone seems to me to be far too weak. . . .

Apart from all this, while Kleist cannot be ready for the bigger counter-attack before the 18th, the lesser attack is hardly likely to lead to a complete mopping-up of the Isium salient, and this may well affect the main operations we are contemplating. If Supreme Headquarters do not place at my disposal the divisions now in transit to my sector of the front, I must leave the decision – the bigger or the lesser solution – to them. My primary task, as the Commander on the spot, is to ensure that those formations which would be called upon to undertake the lesser operations are in position and ready, if required. . . .

14 *May.* In the Crimea we have reached Kerch.

This morning the situation of Sixth Army front was somewhat clearer. On VIII Corps' right wing, the enemy had broken through and his advanced cavalry elements are feeling their way forward towards Krasnograd. 454 L of C Division has given way and is holding only a few isolated positions. Our own Panzer attack in the Volchansk salient has achieved nothing decisive and is to be continued this evening. That it will succeed in breaking through is hardly likely. The possibility that a thrust forward from Sixth

Army's southern wing might be able to link up with Kleist's Army Group attacking northwards is therefore receeding.

I telephoned Halder and told him that in these circumstances Kleist's attack, with the forces at his disposal, was hardly likely to meet with the desired success. Kleist, with whom I have just been talking, is of the opinion that his attack would be feasible only provided that the enemy does not forestall it with an attack of his own. He thought he would be able to reach the general line, mouth of the Bereka – Alexandrovka, but 'nothing more'. But if Kleist gets stuck half way, then his attack will have been a failure, which is bound to affect all further plans for the eastern campaign. That is a possibility for which I cannot, *alone*, assume responsibility. Supreme Headquarters must make up their own mind whether they will place at our disposal the forces, on the ground and in the air, that are required for the greater counter-attack, or whether for the moment they feel that they must rest content with the lesser, partial solution. So, from the point of view of the Army Group, with a heavy heart I decided to propose that every man that Kleist could raise – some three of four divisions, one of them a Panzer division – should be concentrated on the left flank of XI Corps and from there deliver an attack against the southern flank of the Russian break-through.

I finished my discussion with Sodenstern (i.e. his Chief of Staff) with the remark: 'Now, I suppose, the Fuehrer will order the "greater" solution, the credit for a bold decision will go to Supreme Headquarters and we shall have modestly to acquiesce.'

At midday, the Fuehrer telephoned and ordered the 'greater' solution. He had given orders that all the air formations in the Crimea and any others that could be spared from elsewhere, were to be made available, and he directed that, with their assistance, the enemy was to be pinned down at the points where he had broken through and held there, until Kleist was able to deliver his attack. This latter, he further ordered, was to be accelerated as much as possible. This was a tremendous weight off my mind, and I happily set about the task. . . .[1]

[1] This decision is said by Schmidt to have made a lasting impression on Paulus. He himself had at first favoured the decision which Field-Marshal Bock had taken with 'a heavy heart'. Later he realized that Army Headquarters had

... By this evening, our Panzer attack in the Volchansk area had made very little progress. In all, Sixth Army has lost sixteen battalions! On the other hand, Kleist now says he'll be ready to attack on the 17th.

15 *May*. At the request of Army Headquarters, I have submitted an appreciation of the situation, the gist of which is: Here it is now neck or nothing.

16 *May*. This afternoon I paid a visit to Krasnograd, to put heart into the weak forces engaged there. As usual in circumstances such as these, the air is full of rumours of catastrophe. When I returned in the evening, I heard that as a result of a number of penetrations on VIII Corps' front and the withdrawal by the Hungarians on his left flank, the Corps Commander had felt obliged to bring his Corps back some ten kilometres. It was not possible for me to countermand this move since, according to Paulus' report, it was both inevitable and was in any case already in progress. This is deplorable, since it means not only that a wide hole has been torn open on VIII Corps' left, opposite 44 Division, but also that the breach to the north of Krasnograd has been further widened. I gave a strict order that no further withdrawal in divisional strength upwards would take place without my prior, personal permission.[1]

17 *May*. Kleist's Army Group has launched its attack and is making good progress on the whole front. Russian cavalry attacks on Krasnograd, heavy enemy armour attack on VIII Corps and in the Volchansk salient have all been repulsed, most of them with the utmost difficulty.

I have submitted a further appreciation of the situation to the Fuehrer to the effect that the action cannot be brought to a successful conclusion with the forces available and that I therefore request a reply from Army Headquarters regarding the proposals I submitted.

---

appreciated the situation better than those on the spot. There is no doubt that the credit for persuading Hitler to make this decision belongs to General Halder.

[1] This order, too, and the uncompromising leadership displayed by Army Group Headquarters in a critical situation were accepted by Paulus as a lesson to be borne in mind. Sixth Army's task, as he now saw it, was to hold on, regardless of how critical the situation might be, until the effects of the relieving counter-attacks could make themselves felt. Cf. the situation in Stalingrad in November 1942.

18 *May*. Kleist's attack continues to make good progress and has reached the high ground immediately south of Isium on the lower reaches of the Bereka. . . .

Flew to Panzer Army. Kleist and I are in complete agreement. In the evening I telephoned to Halder. I told him that I had no option but to go on pestering Army Headquarters with the same arguments, because I feared that they were underestimating both the severity and the significance of this battle. The enemy, I told him, was attacking VIII Corps with eight or nine armoured brigades, Volchansk with seven or eight armoured brigades and strong infantry forces. VIII Corps was at its last gasp. When Halder said something about wheeling Kleist's attack to the west, I replied: 'Until the Bereka crossings are in our hands, any wheel is, in my opinion impossible.' I added that the object of the attack, as I saw it, was firstly to bring swift relief to VIII Corps and then to destroy the enemy forces in the Isium salient.

During the night Halder telephoned to Sodenstern and asked: 'Don't you think that your Chief is, perhaps, exaggerating things a little?' Sodenstern replied – with most refreshing clarity! – that he did not.

19 *May*. The right wing of Kleist's attack has forced the crossings over the Bereka and captured the high ground to the west of Petrovskaya, where enemy resistance is now stiffening.

In the evening I informed the Fuehrer of the situation and told him of the success at Kerch. I also told him that with today's events, I hoped that the *defensive* crisis in this Kharkov battle has now been overcome. In contradiction of the viewpoint so far held by Army Headquarters, the Fuehrer now suggested that it might perhaps be a good move to thrust further up the Donets with Kleist's right wing. That is exactly what I intend to do!

20 *May*. During the night came an order from the Fuehrer that the date for Operation 'Blau' (the major summer offensive) must be adhered to and that the attack on Sevastopol must begin, if possible, on 5 June.[1]

---

[1] The start of Operation 'Blau' was originally fixed for the end of May. Marshal Timoshenko's Kharkov offensive, if it can be said to have accomplished anything at all, did, in fact, cause the postponement of the whole German timetable by some four weeks.

... Kliest reported on his further intentions: to halt his westward attack and to thrust northwards with all available mobile forces. Sixth Army proposed to concentrate as strong a forces as possible in the Balaklea – Andreievka area and from there to launch an attack southwards. ... These were moves which we had discussed many times, and I agreed. In the evening I issued orders accordingly, aimed at the complete cutting off of the Isium salient. So everything is going to be all right after all!

22 *May*. Army Headquarters informed that the attack on Sevastopol cannot take place before 10 June and that for this and other reasons a postponement of the launching of our major offensive is inevitable.

23 *May*. In the Kharkov battle, the enemy is making desperate efforts, from within and without, to break the ring. ...

25 *May*. The cauldron is being still further compressed. ... The possibility of bringing the enemy advance via Savintsi to a halt by making a thrust from Balaklea, north of the Donets, has been under discussion for some days. The very enterprising new Chief of Staff, Sixth Army, is strongly opposed to any such move. If we are to reach a line which we have any prospect of holding, we cannot content ourselves merely with the capture of one deep-lying locality, Savintsi, but will have to push on to the sector north of Isium. That would be costly in both time and men, and, particulary, in tanks; but the latter are now in urgent need of rest and overhaul, if they are to be ready to take part in the major offensive. ... I do not therefore feel justified in agreeing to the operation at this juncture. ...

26 *May*. I paid a visit to Breith's Group, 44 Division, 23 and 16 Panzer Divisions and on to 60 (Mot) Division and 1 (Mountain) Division. The picture is the same everywhere. The enemy is being hedged in more and more closely, and though he is still making sporadic attempts to break out, he is obviously on the verge of complete collapse. From some high ground south-east of Losovenka I could see the shells from our batteries all round bursting in the smoking cauldron. The reply from the Russian guns was very feeble. Swarms of prisoners are streaming back, and close by our Panzer Division and some units of 1 Mountain Division are advancing to the attack – an overwhelmingly impressive sight. ...

27 *May*. The battle is drawing to a close. ...

In the evening came the order that the Fuehrer had now decided after all to attack the enemy between Isium and Savintsi and – in the Volchansk salient! He is anxious to exploit our victory to destroy as many enemy forces as quickly as possible, before the start of the main offensive operations.[1]

29 *May*. Nothing of importance at the front. The booty taken in the battle has now risen to 239,306 prisoners, 2,026 guns and 1,249 tanks. Approximately 540 aircraft were shot down. Our own losses amount to about 20,000 men.

The Reichel Affair and the action taken by Supreme Headquarters : extracts from the diary of Field-Marshal v. Bock

13 *June*. Swift advances by 22 Panzer Division from Northern Group and 305 Division from Southern Group have closed the ring round the enemy south-east of Volchansk. Some made good their escape; even so, by evening we were reported to have taken 20,000 prisoners, more than 100 guns and about 150 tanks. . . . At midday I talked to Schmidt, who suggested that we should now assault and capture the commanding high ground at Olkhovatka, where the enemy is weak. Now that the main object, the encirclement of the enemy, has been achieved, I fully agreed and directed that III Panzer Corps should remain under the command of Sixth Army for the purpose. It was, I said, in my opinion of more importance that the left wing of VIII Corps should throw the enemy back over the Nezhegol and thus secure as broad and favourable a springboard as possible for the launching of the main offensive. Schmidt agreed.

20 *June*. The weather at last seems to be improving.[2]

To ensure against all possible contingencies in the Olkhovatka

---

[1] A typical example of the hasty manner in which, in this summer offensive, Hitler kept on setting new tasks without the slightest regard for the troops.

[2] As is apparent from previous entries in the Field-Marshal's diary, heavy and continuous rainstorms had repeatedly played havoc with all the German timetables. As a result both Supreme and Army Headquarters had revived the idea of carrying out Operation 'Fridericus II' (First Panzer Army attack on Kupiansk) before initiating Phase I of the main offensive, Operation 'Blau'.

area, I ordered the bringing forward of 3 and 23 Panzer Divisions, which were in the Kharkov area, preparatory to the start of the main offensive. In their new area they would be equally well placed both for their approach march in Operation 'Blau II' and to deal with any local counter-attack the enemy might launch in the Olkhovatka area. Major Joachim Reichel, a Staff Officer of 23 Panzer Division, with the operation orders for the first phase of Operation 'Blau' on his person, flew forward by helicopter and either crashed or was shot down four kilometres beyond our front line. An assault party was immediately sent forward and found a hole in the fuel tank, but no sign of fire or blood. It would therefore seem probable that the complete operation order has fallen into the enemy's hands. This is yet another reason for making an immediate start with Operation 'Blau I', particularly as it is nearly the end of June and there is no time to lose.

21 June. This morning I told Halder that I had given orders to launch 'Fridericus' tomorrow and that, in view of the enemy concentrations in the Olkhovatka area, it was important to launch 'Blau I' *swiftly*. I asked him to point this out to the Fuehrer, who is still in Bavaria. Halder doubted whether he would be able to contact him today. But I urged him to try to emphasize the extreme urgency of my request. . . .

22 June. . . . First Panzer Army has launched the 'Fridericus' attack. In the vicinity of Isium and to the north-west of it, the Donets was quickly crossed and Savintsi captured. The attack on Kupiansk, which has met with stiff opposition, is progressing more slowly and is only half-way to its objective. . . . According to air reconnaissance reports, portions of the enemy forces concentrated in the Olkhovatka area appear to be retreating northwards. This may well be one of the repercussions caused by the finding of the papers on the dead Staff Officer.[1]

Have received instruction to be ready to launch Operation 'Blau I' on 26 June, if so ordered.

23 June. This business of the loss of the secret documents on the

---

[1] The operation order for 'Blau I' contained details of the orders for the attack on Voronezh in the north. The bodies of the officer and his pilot were recovered by the patrol, but there was no evidence to indicate that the papers might have been destroyed.

19th is taking a serious turn. Halder has therefore been trying to persuade me to fly home and see the Fuehrer tomorrow. I telephoned to Schmundt in Berlin and told him that until the Fuehrer had studied the detailed statements taken by the court of inquiry, there did not seem much that I could do. But, I added, if, after reading the evidence, the Fuehrer is still of the opinion that disciplinary action should be taken against anyone, then I would request an interview before he proceeded any further, since I was convinced that no serious blame could be attached to anyone, except, of course, the dead Staff Officer.

During the night Schmundt telephoned to say that the Fuehrer would not reach East Prussia until tomorrow afternoon and would therefore not be able to see me tomorrow in any case. He would phone again tomorrow.

25 *June*. Flew to Fuehrer Headquarters. The proceedings of the court of inquiry sent yesterday to Halder have not yet been submitted to the Fuehrer, because, I was told, the moment did not seem opportune! I first saw Field-Marshal Keitel. He was obviously very ill at ease and took an extremely serious view of the case. The Fuehrer, he said, insisted on making an example of someone; he was of the opinion that the Generals were not obeying his orders and he had directed him, Keitel, to tell me that I must not try to dissuade him from punishing those who deserved to be punished. Keitel then read out to me a summary of the charges which he had himself drafted. This summary, which had been drawn up without any knowledge of the statements made by those concerned, contained so many unjust fallacies, that I strongly advised Keitel not to use it.

The Fuehrer received me in an exceptionally sombre mood. Schmundt was also present. I outlined the facts of the case as they had been submitted to me in the reports and statements of those concerned. Only rarely did the Fuehrer interrupt me with a question. I was allowed every opportunity to state my case, the gist of which was that, while the Staff Officer had been guilty of an almost incredible piece of criminal folly, I could find no evidence that pointed to deliberate disobedience or criminal negligence on the part of anyone else; I did, however, feel that the General Officer Commanding XXXX Panzer Corps deserved a reprimand for having, in his *written* orders to his divisional commanders, gone into too great detail regarding the task of the Corps as a whole. That, in my opinion, I said, had been a bad blunder, which might well have grave consequences. And as such, as a *blunder*, it was deserving of censure.

In conclusion, I well knew, I said, how worried the Fuehrer had been by the thought that obedience was lacking in the Army and particularly among the more senior officers. Of any anxiety on this score, I assured him, I could relieve him, for as an old and experienced soldier I knew that his fears were groundless. He could rest assured that I myself and, I was sure, all the other senior officers would intervene without mercy wherever and whenever we encountered any case of disobedience. The Fuehrer listened quietly and attentively to all I had to say. As was only to be expected, he did not come to a decision on the spot, but after a long discussion on the general situation he took his leave in a friendly manner and obviously in a far better frame of mind than he had been when the interview started.

26 June. Returned to Poltava.

27 June. At 1800 hours I received a telegram from Keitel, stating that the Fuehrer had decided to dismiss the GOC XXXX Corps, his Chief of Staff and the Commander of 23 Panzer Division. The exact time of their relief was left to my discretion. The Generals selected to replace them have already arrived here. Quite apart from the merits of the case, the removal of these first-class and experienced Panzer officers could not have come at a more unfortunate moment – just as XXXX Panzer Corps was about to become the spear-head of Sixth Army's main attack.

In conversation with them, both Halder and Schmundt agreed with my impression that the Fuehrer had been in a much calmer frame of mind after my interview with him. But it appears that, later, when he was going through the reports on the case, he came across a recommendation that disciplinary action should be taken against a clerk in 23 Panzer Division. This immediately aroused the suspicion in his mind that an attempt was being made to put the blame on a subordinate! I had already assured him in my interview on the 25th that there was no question of any action being taken against this clerk. I had at the time seen no reason, I had said, to prefer any charge against him, but had not intervened, because I had thought that perhaps some further light might in this way have been shed on the matter. But in actual fact proceedings against this NCO had been dropped on the 23rd, as there was not a shred of evidence against him! All this excitement at the highest level has therefore been quite unnecessary!

I telephoned to the Fuehrer and told him all this and added that I felt very guilty for having failed to make it clear to him at our interview and having thus caused all this trouble. This the Fuehrer denied, but admitted that the suggestion of initiating proceedings against a subordinate had angered him. I pointed out that the fact that the Corps Commander himself had ordered proceedings against this NCO to be dropped was, surely, proof enough that there was no suggestion of any attempt to put the blame on a subordinate. When I finally asked him whether the orders he had given were still to stand, the Fuehrer answered: 'Yes.'

28 June. When I heard that Paulus was contemplating asking that disciplinary action in this case should be taken against him, as the General Officer Commanding-in-Chief, Sixth Army and the Officer ultimately responsible, I told him: 'Out of the question! Keep your eyes on your own plate and get on with the job!'

30 June. Sixth Army has assumed the offensive. Its main attack between Volchansk and Nezhegol has come up against stiff opposition with large numbers of dug-in tanks. . . .

3 July. At 0700 hours, the Fuehrer arrived. Although he must have left his Headquarters at about four o'clock in the morning, he was alert and in a friendly mood. He confirmed what Halder had told me yesterday and left it to my discretion to abandon Voronezh as an objective, if I found that its capture would involve too severe fighting. . . .

. . . Finally, Halder raised the question of splitting the command for Operation 'Blau' Phase II. I adhered to my old objections, pointing out that all the planning, preparation and concentration of the requisite forces etc., were still my responsibility and that any division now into two Army Groups would only complicate the function of command. No decision was reached. . . .

The Fuehrer was merrily sarcastic about the way in which the British always sacked any General when things went a bit awry for him and how this led in their Army to a great reluctance to show any

initiative and enterprise! . . . Sixth Army has defeated the enemy.
5 *July*. Orders have been received that List is to take over command
of Eleventh Army and First and Seventeenth Panzer Armies
with effect from the 7th. The battle has thus been split into two
parts. . . .
13 *July*. This morning I telegraphed to Halder: 'Enemy opposite
Fourth Panzer Army and northern wing Army Group "A" withdrawing some formations eastwards and south-eastwards, and bulk
of his forces southwards. Do not believe destruction of enemy in
any great numbers can be achieved in an operation strong in the
centre and weak on the flanks. . . . In my opinion main thrust
Fourth Panzer Army, whose rear and eastern flank would require
protection, should be directed via Morozovsk towards mouth of
Donets and on eastwards.'

In the afternoon Keitel informed me by telegram that, on the
Fuehrer's orders, Fourth Panzer Army was now to be placed under
command of Army Group 'A', as had been envisaged by Supreme
Headquarters. He further informed me – to my complete surprise –
that General v. Weichs had been ordered to assume command of
Army Group 'A' and that I myself had been placed at the Fuehrer's
disposal!
15 *July*. v. Weichs assumed command at 0600 hours. At 0700 hours I
left by air for Berlin.

Extract from a letter from General Georg Stumme to Paulus

Gera

14 August 1942

Dear Paulus,
   . . . And now I feel in duty bound to give you some account of
my own miserable affairs. After a short halt in Poltava and a very
friendly farewell dinner with Field-Marshal v. Bock, who told me
of the strenuous efforts he had made to persuade Hitler not to
exaggerate the importance of this business and punish people who,
in the Field-Marshal's opinion, were innocent, we three flew on
home. On arrival we were kept for several days, cut off from everybody, in Field-Marshal Keitel's special train, where we were in-
terrogated by a member of the Judge Advocate General's Depart-

ment and were then left in peace to await developments. We rather hoped that proceedings had been quashed, but the Fuehrer ordered an inquiry before a special Court, with Reichsmarschall Goering as president and Generals Model, v. Thoma and the Deputy Judge Advocate General as members. The President adopted a reasonable and friendly attitude. He thought that . . . (illegible in the original letter) . . . but that the written statements were faulty. My own representations were of no avail. The prosecution demanded the maximum penalty of five years fortress imprisonment on a charge of culpable negligence and, in addition, loss of rank under a law specially framed by the Fuehrer for this case. The judges rejected the demand for loss of rank on the grounds that my honour was not in any way involved, but imposed the maximum penalty. My Chief of Staff Franz got three years, while Boineburg (i.e. his GSO I Ops) was found not guilty. At the same time, the Court forwarded a strong recommendation for mercy to the Fuehrer. . . .

In Berlin, I saw Field-Marshal v. Bock again, who is still wondering why he is there at all. Finally, let me thank you most sincerely for the boundless support, both officially and as a friend, that you have always given me. I shall remain always in your debt.

With best wishes,

Heil Hitler!

Yours sincerely and gratefully,

Stumme.

The advance on Stalingrad as seen from the air: extracts from the War Diary of Air Fleet 4 and the personal diary of General Freiherr v. Richthofen, GOC Air Fleet 4

2 *August* 1942. Sixth Army's advance on Stalingrad is making no progress, partly as the result of stiff opposition, but mainly because of lack of supplies. In some places the Russians are actually attacking. South of the Don, Fourth Panzer Army has wheeled northeastwards, where it encountered no enemy at all. The Russians are

flinging troops into the Stalingrad area from every point of the compass. VIII Air Corps has been detailed to support Sixth Army, to bomb railway traffic and shipping on the Volga and to transport supplies for Sixth Army. . . .

7 *August*. Orders received from the Fuehrer to attack and destroy Russian bridge-head at Kalach. VIII Air Corps and Sixth Army have stepped up their efforts. Paulus very confident. . . .

10 *August*. To cope with the situation here, I have issued the following orders on my own responsibility: The main effort of the Air Force will be directed against Stalingrad itself. Air reconnaissance units will at once make available air lift to a capacity of 3,000 tons to carry supplies to the army. One Anti-Aircraft Division and all Air Fleet 4's road transport companies will be sent to Stalingrad.

15 *August*. Conference at Air District Rostov. Ordered General Vierling to Stalingrad to cope with supply difficulties. Demanded a special effort by technicians and transport personnel. Gist of my remarks: How do things stand as regards my orders for the movement of transport to the Stalingrad area, in order to ensure that our fighter formations (and I mean the whole lot of them) can operate from that area? As the railway eastwards via Stalino is no longer usable, we shall have to transport our stuff a further 350 kilometres ourselves – a difficult problem. And a completely new one, since it has always been accepted that fighter formations must be supplied by rail. I therefore dealt gently with them. They seemed mildly astonished by my views and the things I said could be done. I felt quite sorry for the wretched people – no one ever seems to have spoken to them like this before. . . .

20 *August*. Another conference with Paulus on the situation and his intentions. No further attack before 23 August. Our main job is to knock out tanks! Paulus is worried about his left flank.

21 *August*. Visited LI Corps, which is holding a new bridge-head up north on the right flank, from which the armoured forces are to break out. I went out with reconnaissance flights and visited observation posts and Corps Battle Headquarters. All goes well. Enemy much weaker than I expected. Army always seems to have far too high an opinion of the enemy, partly because the troops are over-tired and, as the saying goes, have 'had it'! . . .

23 *August*. A sudden alert sent out by VIII Air Corps put the whole

of Air Fleet 4 into the air, with the result that we simply paralysed the Russians and helped Wietersheim's Panzer Corps to advance 60 kilometres almost without firing a shot. At 1600 hours they reached the Volga.[1]

25 *August*. Flew to 76 Infantry Division, where I met General Paulus and v. Seydlitz – 'situation critical, because no reinforcement is possible. The infantry are pinned down on the right and left and at the moment cannot get forward to support Panzer spear-head, and won't be able to do so for another three days!' General Paulus in consequence very anxious. From 1300 hours onwards further heavy air raids on Stalingrad. Many large fires observed.

27 *August*. General Paulus still in an anxious frame of mind. Nothing much happening at the front. Paulus and Hoth[2] did not intend to attack until 29 August. I sent my GSO I Ops., Colonel Schulz to submit a personal report to Jeschonnek and the Reichsmarschall on '*the jitters and poor leadership of the Army!*'

31 *August*. Advance on Stalingrad continues.

2 *September*. Sixth Army and Fourth Panzer Army have at last made contact ten kilometres west of Stalingrad.

10 *September*. The same old 'throttling process' in the Stalingrad area. . . .

13 *September*. At 0730 hours went myself with General Fiebig (Commander VIII Air Corps) to the fighter airfield fifteen kilometres from Stalingrad. Personally accompanied several sorties. Poor results.

16 *September*. Went again to fighter airfield. The mopping-up in the city is progressing only very slowly, in spite of the fact that the enemy is weak and in no shape for hard fighting. The truth is that our own troops are both few in numbers and listless in spirit, and the High Command already has its eyes turned towards Astrakhan. The same applies to LI Corps. I had to stir up VIII Air Corps, too. I told them they were slack and lacking in enterprise and were not pressing home their attacks on the enemy lines of communication. Sorties lacked dash and determination. I therefore gave some pretty

---

[1] On the evening of 23 August XIV Panzer Corps reached the Volga on a narrow front at Rynok. For a whole week, until infantry support reached them, the Corps' hold was somewhat precarious.

[2] General Hoth, GOC-in-C Fourth Panzer Army.

sharp orders, but at the same time I expressed complete optimism. 'As the Army is a lame duck,' I said, 'the Air Force alone cannot do very much. But with a little more combined and spirited action we could finish off Stalingrad in a couple of days.'[1]

In the north, the enemy is concentrating for another attack. I shall bomb these concentrations heavily tomorrow.

19 *September*. Orders from the R–M (i.e. Goering): 'On conclusion of Stalingrad operations, report immediately to me.' That won't be for quite a long time still!

22 *September*. In the town, some minor progress. Sixth Army attack is suffering from constipation, primarily because such a large portion of its forces is pinned down by constant enemy pressure from the north and because reinforcements – infantry divisions – are coming up so slowly. It's just a filthy slogging match from ruin to ruin and cellar to cellar!

26 *September*. Today's attack is going well. Height 107.5 in the north has been taken, and the day's objectives have all been reached – and in some cases exceeded. Over Stalingrad not a Russian aircraft to be seen. Perhaps they, too, are suffering from lack of fuel!

3 *October*. Went to Stalingrad with Jeschonnek. Visited battle command post of VIII Air Corps. Flew over the front by helicopter. A great deal of dust and smoke. Had long discussion with Paulus and Seydlitz. Both agreed that, but for the lack of infantry, we could certainly succeed. Jeschonnek very impressed by what he saw of the battlefield. I again made it quite clear to him what I thought: 'What we lack,' I said, 'is some clear thinking and a well-defined primary objective. It's quite useless to "muck about" here, there and everywhere, as we are doing – and doubly futile, with the inadequate forces at our disposal. One thing at a time, and then all will go well – that's obvious. But we must first finish off what we've started, of course, especially at Stalingrad and Tuapse. . . .'

5 *October*. Surprisingly, Paulus has decided to call off all further attacks until reinforcements arrive and the whole army can be regrouped. . . . That, I suppose, will take five or six days.

---

[1] This and his entry on 21 August are typical examples of v. Richthofen's slap-dash, snap judgments.

6 *October*. Our chief headache here is worry about supplies and reinforcements!

14 *October*. The attack on Stalingrad, with the maximum possible support from VIII Air Corps, is making good progress. The Russians seem to have been taken rather by surprise. The dreaded tractor factory has been captured and we've reached to Volga on a front of three kilometres.

19 *October*. Stalingrad situation very confused. It seems that divisions have been too optimistic in their reports. No one knows exactly what the position is, and all the divisions are sending contradictory reports. Attack on Spartakovka has been halted north of Stalingrad. Fiebig is furious, because the infantry don't exploit the chances his air raids make for them. . . .[1]

1 *November*. Early this morning I went to the fighter airfield and from there on to a conference with Paulus and Seydlitz. I told them that proper use of the air arm was not being made, 'Because the artillery won't fire and the infantry make no attempt at all to exploit the air raids to their advantage'. They trotted out all the same old arguments (which are only partly true) – numerical inferiority, lack of training in this type of warfare, shortage of ammunition and so on. I said that I would place transport at their disposal for ammunition supplies and would use my influence to see that properly trained reinforcements would be forthcoming. The same evening I telephoned to Jeschonnek and demanded the despatch at once of four Pioneer assault battalions. . . . The real explanation is to be found in the weariness of both troops and command and in that rigid Army conservatism, which still accepts without demur 1,000 men in the front line out of a ration strength of 12,000, and which leads to the Generals being content merely to issue orders, without bothering to go into any detail or to make sure that the preparations required for this type of fighting are properly made. That is what I told Paulus, who, of course, didn't like it, but couldn't refute the truth of it. . . .

9 *November*. Real winter weather. On the Don front it is cold and clear.

---

[1] Quite simply, because, in this grinding battle of attrition, the infantry, with no reliefs and no reserves, could do no more – a fact which the Air Force Generals seemed very reluctant to grasp.

11 *November*. VIII Air Corps carried out sorties against Stalingrad and the Russian concentrations on Third Rumanian Army's front.

12 *November*. On the Don, the Russians are resolutely carrying on with their preparations for an offensive against the Rumanians. VIII Air Corps, the whole of Air Fleet 4 and the Rumanian Air Force are keeping up continuous attacks on them. Their reserves have now been concentrated. When, I wonder will the attack come! At the moment there appears to be a shortage of ammunition. Guns, however, are beginning to make their appearance in the artillery emplacements. I can only hope that the Russian won't tear too many big holes in the line!

14 *November*. Weather still atrocious, with mists that cause wing icing and freezingly cold rain storms.

On Stalingrad front all quiet. Our bombers have carried out successful raids on the railways east of Stalingrad, dislocating the flow of reinforcements and supplies. Fighters and fighter bombers have been concentrating on smashing up the Russian approach march to the Don.

16 *November*. Weather still bad! I had a long telephone conversation with Zeitzler (i.e. Halder's successor as Chief of the General Staff): 'Let us either get on at once with the battle or abandon the attack altogether. If we can't clear up the situation now, when the Volga is blocked with ice floes and the Russians are in real difficulty, we shall never be able to. The days, too, are getting shorter and the weather worse.' Zeitzler agrees with this and says he will report to this effect to the Fuehrer.

During the night Fuehrer's orders in the above sense came through by 'phone. But I don't for a moment suppose anything will be done about it. While talking to Zeitzler, I emphasized that both the command and the troops themselves were so listless that, without the infusion of new blood, we should get nowhere. I suggested that the senior officers, who, after all, had all given proof of their intrinsic merit, should be granted a little leave and should be temporarily represented by others. But those at the top haven't the guts to do anything like that.

The poverty of enterprise displayed by the present commanders is demonstrated by the fact that here we are, with three Panzer divisions, standing around, waiting for a Russian attack, instead, as

of old, of advancing with a strong striking force and smashing them![1]
19 *November.* From their bridge-head at Kremenskaya on the Don
the Russians have launched their long expected offensive against the
left wing of Sixth Army and have succeeded in breaking through on
a broad front in the direction of the Chir. Reports are confused and
contradictory. But Russian tanks are already operating behind the
front of Eleventh Army and Third Rumanian Army. One and a half
Rumanian Army Corps are said to have disintegrated. Our reserves
are about to counter-attack. Attacks on Stalingrad are being halted
immediately, and all available troops are being hurried up to stop the
gap in our line. Once again, the Russians have made masterly use of
the bad weather. Rain, snow and icy mists have put a stop to all
flying. VIII Air Corps managed with great difficulty to get one or
two aircraft into the air. To seal off the Don crossings by bombing
is not possible. It's not even possible to get a general picture of the
situation by air reconnaissance. I can only hope that the Russians
won't get as far as the railway, the vital artery for all our supplies. . . .

The advance on Stalingrad as seen through the eyes of our allies: the operations of the Third Rumanian Army on the Don, 19 – 23 November 1942 (Report by General Heim, Head of the German Military Mission to Rumania)

1. The Background

The Commander-in-Chief of the Third Rumanian Army, General
Dumitrescu, insisted from the outset that the task allotted to his
Army, the defence of the sector from Kletskaya to the mouth of the
Tishaya, could only be carried out successfully if the Don itself
were in our hands, to form a tank obstacle and to counter-balance,
at least to some extent, the Rumanian lack of anti-tank weapons.

---

[1] Another quite unjustifiable comment. The three Panzer divisions did not,
as v. Richthofen infers, constitute 'a strong striking force' but were nothing
more than the essential nucleus of the defensive fire-plan against Russian
counter-attack.

When he reported for duty to Army Group Headquarters at the end of September, he therefore suggested that German and Rumanian forces, which happened at that moment to be available, should be used to throw the enemy back across the Don. Army Group Headquarters recognized the soundness of his suggestion, but rejected it in view of the requirements of the situation as a whole.

On 10 October 1942, General Dumitrescu assumed command of the Army on the Don.

On 16 October, he requested permission to undertake a local operation, designed to improve his position in the vicinity of Blinov. This, too, was rejected by Army Group on the grounds that the Rumanian troops were required for the relief of further units of the Italian Army.[1]

In his teleprinter memoranda of 18 and 21 October, the Rumanian Army Commander replied that the relief by Rumanians of further Italian units would require the prior concurrence of the Rumanian Head of the State. Army Headquarters nevertheless decided that the Rumanians would have to take over from one more Italian division. This decision was conveyed to the Third Rumanian Army with the explanation that acceptance of the risks involved in holding the line thinly and with meagre reserves was justified by the current situation on the enemy's side. Accordingly, a further Italian division was relieved by the Rumanians towards the end of October. The front held by each division (of seven-battalion strength) was approximately twenty kilometres. It was immediately after the relief of this Italian division (the Celere Division) that Rumanian Army Headquarters first gained the impression that the enemy was preparing for a major attack. (Increase in the number of Don crossings in rear of the Russian front, statements by deserters, continuous local enemy attacks, the sole object of which must have been to find the soft spots and to pave the way for the major attack. . . .)

A report to this effect was first sent to Army Group Headquarters on 29 October. When air and ground reconnaissance and the statements made by prisoners (evacuation of civilian population) confirmed the correctness of this impression, I went myself to Army Group Headquarters in Starobielsk on November 9 and submitted a

[1] The Sixth Italian Army, under General Garibaldi, had originally been made responsible for the whole of the Don sector.

report with the following details: three new infantry formations with some tanks had been identified in the Kletskaya area, and one new armoured, one new motorized, and two new infantry formations were thought to be concentrated in the same area; and in the Blinov sector the presence of two new infantry formations with a few tanks had been definitely established. A major enemy attack, it was considered, could be expected at any moment. Army Group Headquarters thereupon immediately initiated the following measures:

That same day, 9 November, the close support group under Colonel Simons (one anti-tank company, one motorized rifle battalion, one section heavy assault artillery) was ordered to move into position behind Third Rumanian Army. On 10 November XXXXVIII Panzer Corps (22 Panzer Division, 1 Rumanian Panzer Division, one anti-tank battalion (less one company, with Simons) and one motorized Artillery battalion) began to concentrate in Third Rumanian Army's sector. The German units were placed under command of XXXXVIII Corps as Army Group reserve.

Units of Air Fleet 4 effectively attacked areas in which the enemy was known to have concentrated, and preparations were completed for the intervention of the whole Air Fleet when the enemy attack was launched. Ammunition available at the start of the operations amounted to full authorized scale, plus a 50 per cent reserve. Stocks had not been built up prior to the Army's advance and could not be supplemented later because of lack of transport facilities. On 19 November we were by no means sure that our supplies would prove adequate in the event of heavy expenditure. In actual fact, however, further supplies arrived by rail on 19 November, so that with the exception of the Lascar Group[1] the shortages that occurred later during the battle must be attributed to faulty arrangements by the Rumanians.

It was, however, on the days immediately preceding the enemy attack that this lack of ammunition was most keenly felt, for, with the very limited stocks available, the artillery was compelled to refrain from engaging and breaking up the enemy forces massing for the assault. The position was further aggravated by the fact that in

---

[1] 5, 6, 15 and remnants of 12 and 14 Divisions, surrounded in the Raspopinskaya cauldron, were formed into a Group under General Mihail Lascar, GOC 6 Division.

the Rumanian Artillery individual gunfire is not practised, and the Rumanian method of engaging any target is to bring to bear on it the fire of at least one complete battery. This involves a very heavy expenditure of ammunition.

The situation as regards anti-tank guns caused grave anxiety. The Army had three motorized anti-tank companies with twelve 4.7 cm guns each. Corps were without any anti-tank units under command. Each division and regiment had one anti-tank company with twelve to sixteen 3.7 and 4.7 cm guns, and in October 1942 each division had been given six 7.5 cm German anti-tank guns. The Rumanian artillery possessed no armour-piercing shells, and mines and incendiaries were in very limited supply.

The construction of defensive positions left much to be desired. They had been badly constructed before the Rumanian Army took over, and, in view of the advanced season of the year, the first task was to build shelters for men and animals. In this connection it must be remembered that the Rumanians are inclined to concentrate first on the construction of large dug-outs for the command posts and only after that to turn their attention to the front lines. Although the Rumanians set to work with a will, the front line defences were well constructed in only a very few places.

During the time between the take over and the enemy attack, rations for the Rumanian troops were inadequate. Reason: no local produce was available, and reserve stocks had not been accumulated before the Army advanced. . . .

In the local defensive actions fought between the taking over of the sector in September–October and the enemy main attack on 19 November, the Rumanians, on the whole, fought gallantly, and most of the attacks were beaten off. On the other hand, there were almost invariably some individual units which gave way prematurely. It was therefore felt that, when the enemy main assault came, some breaches in the line would be inevitable.

We failed completely to persuade the Rumanians to concentrate their reserves in immediate readiness for an instant counter-attack behind those sections of the line where a possible break was anticipated, or to organize L of C units into emergency formations. It was only when Army Group Headquarters intervened with orders to this effect that the 15 Infantry Division was brought forward as far as Gromki and the 7 Cavalry Division to Seniutka. In spite of all our efforts, no emergency formations were organized.

The Rumanian Army Command, the GOC XXXXVIII Panzer Corps and the German Liaison Staff were all in agreement in considering that the allied forces available would suffice for all eventualities, provided that the Panzer Corps was brought up to full strength and that the Rumanian Army maintained its high defensive fighting qualities which its previous efforts entitled us to expect of it. The enemy, however, allowed us no time to bring the Panzer Corps up to strength. According to the Daily State for 18 November, XXXXVII Panzer Corps had the following:

14 Panzer Division	..	51 tanks
20 Panzer Division	..	40 tanks (of which 5 were 38-T's)
1 Rumanian Panzer Division	..	108 (of which 87 were 38-T's)[1]

A total of 107 modern tanks and 92 Mk. 38-T's.

2. The Course of the Operations

At approximately 0500 hours, on November 19, the enemy opened a heavy artillery bombardment along the whole front. Between 0530 and 0600 hours, his infantry advanced to the attack, with the main thrust north-west of Kletskaya and on Blinov. Against the latter the enemy attacked with armour from the very outset, but north-west of Kletskaya enemy tanks did not intervene until about 0700 hours. In the initial stages, the attacks were repulsed along the whole front. With very few exceptions no withdrawals occurred anywhere until after strong enemy armoured forces had broken through and over-run our own artillery and anti-tank positions.

The 1 Cavalry Division held on to its position throughout the 19th and during the afternoon was placed under the command of Sixth Army.

On 13 Division front, the 87 Infantry Regiment was forced to withdraw at 0700 hours, but very quickly what remained of it halted and fought on. The 1 Infantry Regiment maintained its position and was eventually surrounded with the Lascar Group. Twenty-five

[1] Mark 38-T, the Czech Skoda tank, was much too light in the Russian campaign.

enemy tanks were destroyed on 13 Division's front on 19th. The counter-attack by 15 Division was eventually driven off by enemy tanks, which remained in possession of the commanding high ground previously re-gained by the counter-attack. 15 Division held on to the second position allotted to it, to the west of Gromki, against all subsequent attacks. At 1400 hours, twenty-five enemy tanks reached Gromki, and a little later a few isolated tanks got as far as Kalmykov. IV Rumanian Corps, to which 14 Panzer Division had been attached during the course of the day, was not able to initiate any effective counter-measures. On the evening of the 19th the remnants of 13 Division were attached to 6 and 15 Divisions, and command of all troops to the east of a line Kletskaya – Yevstratovskiy was assumed by Sixth Army. The enemy had succeeded in breaking through to a depth of seven or eight kilometres on an eighteen-kilometre front. In addition, in the Gromki sector, the Rumanian front had been breached on a front the extent of which was not yet known.

Blinov (II Rumanian Army Corps sector) was abandoned early on the 19th by the 36 Infantry Regiment of 9 Division. This enabled the enemy to press rapidly forward and over-run the positions of 9 Division's artillery, south of Blinov. 14 Division thereupon bent its left wing back on Klinovoy. At 0900 hours strong enemy armour broke through on 14 Division's front. The regiment on the right of this division held on to its original position. 5 Infantry Regiment finding itself separated from the other units of 14 Division, joined up with this regiment. By the time anti-tank units of 22 Division appeared in the vicinity of Peschany at 1330 hours, 14 Division was already in process of disintegration. 7 Cavalry Division did not arrive in time to put in a counter-attack and had to be content with sealing off Blinovsky. This Division fought gallantly until early on the 20th.

In the centre, 5 and 6 Divisions, lightly attacked, maintained their positions.

In the 9 and 14 Divisions' sector, the enemy opened a breach fourteen kilometres wide and ten kilometres deep on the 19th.

On the same day, admirably led by its Commander, 11 Division repulsed strong attacks on its right wing, 7 Division was not attacked.

XXXXVIII Panzer Corps had received orders at 1010 hours from Army Group Headquarters to attack Kletskaya; at 1130 hours, however, this order was cancelled and the Corps was directed to restore the situation at Blinov as quickly as possible.[1] For this purpose II Rumanian Army Corps, consisting of 7, 9 and 14 Infantry Divisions, was placed under XXXXVIII Corps' command. The Panzer Corps was ordered to concentrate 22 Panzer Division in the Peschany area and 1 Rumanian Panzer Division in the vicinity of Shirovskiy, in preparation for an attack on Blinov early on the morning of the 20th. Both Divisions became engaged with the enemy while moving to their assembly areas on the 19th.

Early on 20 November, 22 Panzer Division encountered strong enemy armoured forces in the vicinity of Peschany and was heavily engaged throughout the day. In the evening, to escape from the encirclement with which it was being threatened, 22 Panzer Division withdrew southwards. Contact with 1 Rumanian Panzer Division was lost. Early on the morning of the 20th, 7 Cavalry Division withdrew, under pressure, to the high ground north of Pronin, but was not at once pursued by the enemy who, apparently, were tied down by 22 Panzer Division. In the evening, while advancing on St. Seniutkin with the object of regaining contact with the enemy, 7 Cavalry Division was surprised by enemy tanks, which it was unable to drive off. The Division retired on Chistiyakovka. Some elements of 14 Infantry and 7 Cavalry Divisions were gathered together by their divisional commanders in the Chernyshevskaya – Bokovskaya area of the Chir sector and organized for the defence of Chernyshevskaya (Battle Headquarters, Third Rumanian Army).

9 and 15 Divisions were still holding on to their positions on the 20th. Strong enemy armoured forces advanced via Blinov south-westwards towards Perelasovskiy and beyond, where they attacked and dispersed IV and V Corps. 15, 6 and 5 Divisions and the remnants of 12 and 14 Divisions held on throughout the 20th and

---

[1] XXXXVIII Corps, poorly equipped as it was and faced in any case with an arduous task, found its difficulties greatly increased by a stream of orders and counter-orders, issued by Hitler direct to Army Group Headquarters. At the end of November, the Commander, General Heim, was made a scapegoat and was dismissed by Hitler, who wanted to have him shot. He was saved only with great difficulty by Field-Marshal Keitel.

were then incorporated into the Lascar Group and placed under the command of General Heim, XXXXVIII Corps. On 21 November, Heim was ordered by Army Group to attack northwards with 22 Panzer Division with the object of relieving the Lascar Group and re-establishing contact with I Rumanian Panzer Division. 9 Division was attached to I Rumanian Army Corps, and I and II Rumanian Army Corps (the latter with weak forces scraped together on the Chir) were placed under the command of German XVII Corps (General Hollidt), which was advancing to join the battle, and the whole was given the designation Hollidt Group.

Headquarters, Third Rumanian Army, on orders from Army Group Headquarters, moved back to Morozovsk on the afternoon of 20 November.

Third Army now issued orders that all units in retreat were to be halted at the Chir and were there to take up new defensive positions.

On 20 November the Lascar Group heroically repulsed all attacks made upon it. Demands that it should surrender were rejected.

22 Panzer Division, heavily engaged all the way with enemy armour, thrust its way forward as far as the area to the west of Perelasovskiy, where it was surrounded by the enemy. Contact with I Rumanian Panzer Division and with the Lascar Group was not established. On 21 November the enemy armour advanced in strength from Perelasovskiy on Kalach in rear of Sixth Army.

On 21 November, 9 Infantry Division, though not severely pressed by the enemy, retired to Gorbatovo, abandoning most of its artillery. As a result, at 1300 hours 11 Division was ordered to withdraw its right wing to Dubovskoy. When darkness fell, the withdrawal was carried out without interference.

Early on 22nd, attacking with armour from the west and from the rear, the enemy overran 5 Infantry Division's front.

At 1930 hours on 22nd, General Lascar, who had just been awarded the Knights' Cross with Oak Leaves by the Fuehrer, on his own responsibility ordered the forces under his command to try to break through the ring to Chernyshevskaya. Four thousand men, without any heavy weapons, succeeded in breaking out and while so doing made contact at Bolshaya Donshchinska with 22 Panzer Division, which was itself surrounded. On 24th, these remnants of the Lascar Group and 22 Panzer Division broke their way through to Chernyshevskaya, being heavily engaged *en route* at Donshchinska and in the vicinity of Chernyshevskaya itself. In this engagement, according to General Heim's report, the Rumanian forces in general and 15 Infantry Division under General Sion in particular fought extremely well. General Sion was killed in this action. The remainder of the Lascar Group was either killed or taken prisoner. Some held out until 24 November. . . .[1]

To sum up. The bulk of the Rumanian troops fought well and displayed high devotion to duty. Acts of gallantry by individuals and by units were numerous. The unexpectedly strong mass of enemy armour and the inability to hold them in check, however, had paved the way for the enemy's success, prevented the German Panzer force from making any effective intervention and precluded any possibility of restoring the situation. . . .

A contributory factor to the enemy's great success was the mist which throughout the 19th and 20th prevented the Rumanian artillery and the Rumanian and German air forces from playing any effective part in the battle. . . .

[1] The fate of the Lascar Group in the Raspopinskaya cauldron led to sharp controversy between the Rumanian and German High Commands. General Steflea, the Rumanian Chief of the General Staff, who was in Rostov, demanded that early permission be given to Lascar to fight his way out. Hitler directed that the Group was to stand fast at all costs. To send supplies by air to General Lascar proved impossible. On the night of the 22nd, Marshal Antonescu himself intervened and telegraphed to Hitler, who replied that he had already given his consent to an attempt to break out!

5. The Stalingrad Cauldron (Phase I):
break out or await relief?
19 November – 12 December 1942

(*Vide* Sketch Maps 4 and 5)

• •

Introduction

'During the day, alarming reports have been coming in from the Chief of the General Staff regarding the Russian Don offensive in Third Rumanian Army's sector, which the Fuehrer has been expecting for a long time and which was launched this morning. . . . ' Thus runs Supreme Headquarters War Diary entry for 19 November 1942.

While Hitler, the 'Fuehrer' and Supreme Commander of the Armed Forces, had been staying in South Germany since 7 November, first in Munich where, at a ceremony in commemoration of the 1923 Putsch, he had spoken in the most boastful terms regarding the situation at Stalingrad, then at the Berghof in Obersalzberg, it so happened that on 19 November General Stiflea, the Chief of the Rumanian General Staff, was in Rostov, where he was joined a few days later by General Pantazi, the Rumanian Minister of Defence. It had been their original intention to visit the Rumanian troops in the southern sector of the eastern front and at the same time to finalize the arrangements for the creation of the proposed Rumano-German 'Army Group Don'.

The Commander-in-Chief designate of the Army Group was the Rumanian Head of State, Marshal Antonescu. Since, for reasons of prestige, he had not yet appeared on the scene, the Chief of the German Military Mission to Rumania, General Hauffe, who, with a 'mobile echelon', was already in Rostov and was functioning as Chief of Staff, Army Group Don, suggested that General Dumitrescu (Third Rumanian Army) and General Paulus should be appointed as the accredited representatives of Marshal Antonescu and the German Armed Forces respectively.

On this same, fateful day, General v. Richthofen, the Commander-in-Chief, Air Fleet 4, had flown to IV Air Corps in Maykop (north Caucasus), because there, in contrast to the Don-Volga front, weather conditions were excellent for flying.

At this time, a number of very different problems were causing Hitler acute anxiety. Rommel's Panzer Army in Africa, defeated at El 'Alamein, was retreating into Libya. On 8 November strong Anglo-American forces landed in Morocco and Algeria, and German and Italian troops had been rushed to Tunisia by air. On 11 November, Operation 'Anton', the occupation of the whole of France by German and Italian troops, began. And it was in the midst of all these events that the news of the Soviet Don offensive reached him.

On 19 November, the Twenty-First Soviet Army and the Fifth Soviet Tank Army, each with two armoured and two cavalry corps and infantry estimated at twenty-one infantry divisions, broke through the front of the Third Rumanian Army on the Don. The next day, 20 November, the Fifty-First and Fifty-Seventh Soviet Armies, with strong armoured support, broke through the front of Fourth Panzer Army and Fourth Rumanian Army to the south of Stalingrad. XXXXVIII Panzer Corps, the sole formation in reserve behind the Don front, was immediately ordered to counter-attack, but failed to do so.

Thus the enemy had succeeded in making deep breaches in the line on both flanks of the Sixth Army. Similar situations had arisen before, during the previous winter. In the middle of January 1942, II Army Corps, with approximately 100,000 men under General Count Brockdorf-Ahlenfeldt, was surrounded in the Demyansk area, had held out for three months, completely cut off and supplied by air, and had then transformed itself into a bridge-head, which it held until further German ground forces arrived – all in accordance with Hitler's orders! It is therefore not surprising that Sixth Army at its Battle Command Post in Golubinskaya on the Don, while realizing that the position was somewhat serious, did not at first appreciate the full gravity of the situation.

For the one very simple reason that in the midst of all the confusion their vision of the situation as a whole was not obscured, General v. Weichs, the Commander-in-Chief, Army Group B, and General v. Sodenstern, his Chief of Staff, at once grasped the full

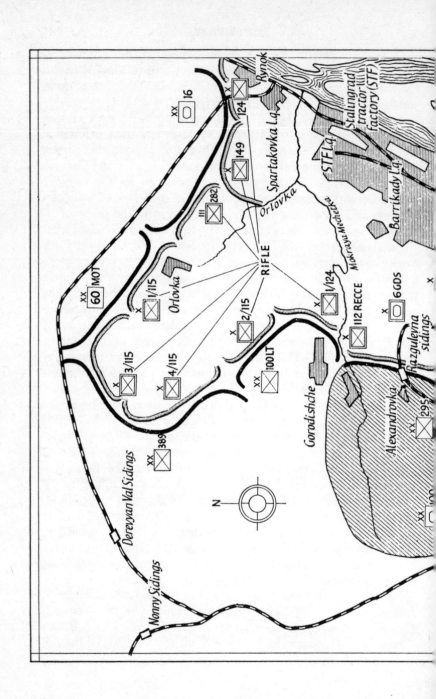

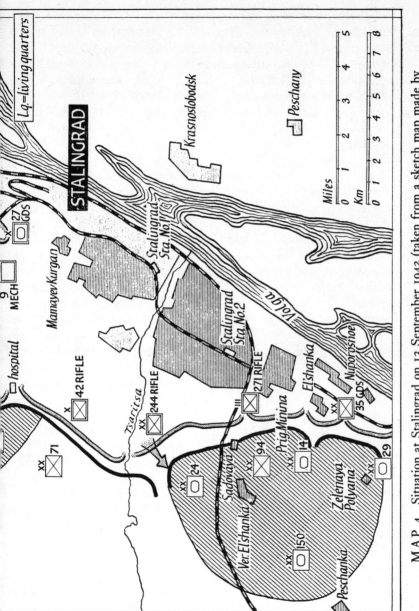

MAP 4 Situation at Stalingrad on 13 September 1942 (taken from a sketch map made by Marshal Zhukov in Moscow, 1958).

implications of what had happened. On 19 November itself, they ordered Sixth Army to halt all attacks in the Stalingrad area and to concentrate all mobile units behind its left flank, west of the Don, in readiness to counter-attack under the command of General Hube (Commander, XIV Panzer Corps). Additional measures were also taken by Army Group Headquarters itself, and at first there seemed to be justifiable grounds for hoping that these steps would lead either to the situation being restored or at least to the sealing-off of the breaches in the line.

In considering this initial situation, there are two points which cannot be too strongly emphasized: firstly, that the whole of the eastern campaign had been full of crises of a similar nature – crises which General Paulus had experienced either as OQuI at Army Headquarters or first-hand and on the spot during the winter and spring battles in the Kharkov area; and secondly, the fact that the tactical skill of German leadership and the superiority of the German troops had invariably succeeded in overcoming every crisis had given rise to a feeling of self-confidence that was by no means unjustified. True to his own methods of leadership, Hitler, in addition to intervening and giving Army Group orders regarding the tactical employment of XXXXVIII Panzer Corps, at once took certain steps of a politico-personal nature. He surrendered the commissar-like command he had been exercising over Army Group A in the Caucasus in favour of General v. Kleist and appointed Eleventh Army Commander, Field-Marshal v. Manstein, to command the Army Group Don, which, with effect from 22 November, was to consist of Sixth Army, Fourth Panzer Army and Third and Fourth Rumanian Armies in the Don-Volga sector.[1]

It was not until 21 November that Paulus and his Chief of Staff, Schmidt, who were still in Golubinskaya on the Don, fully realized the deadly peril confronting them. Soviet tanks had appeared only a few kilometres from their battle headquarters. The bridges over the

---

[1] Cf. v. Manstein: *Lost Victories*, pp. 294 et seq. Manstein, who had been directed at the end of October to report to Hitler in Vinnitsa, was there told that his Eleventh Army would probably be transferred to the Vitebsk area (central sector), where the 'Fuehrer' was expecting a major attack. Manstein himself was to take over command of Army Group A, when Hitler left Vinnitsa for the winter! On 20 November orders were issued that Manstein was to assume

Don at Kalach, which were vital links in Sixth Army's lines of communication, had been captured by the Soviet Group North. As a result, it was obvious that those portions of the Sixth Army, the Fourth Panzer Army and the Fourth Rumanian Army in the area between the Don and the Volga were now in danger of being surrounded. Whatever Sixth Army Commander now decided – whether he decided to avoid encirclement by withdrawing his Army to a position on the Don-Chir, or whether he decided to stand and fight in his present position, he would, in either case, have to organize a hedgehog system of all-round defence, if he were to avoid the risk of having his Army rolled up from the rear.

Accordingly, he transferred his Headquarters eastwards to Gumrak railway station, just west of Stalingrad itself. Having done so, Paulus then flew, with his Chief of Staff, to Nizhne Chirskaya on the Don, to direct the organization of fronts facing south and west. He still felt that only by advancing westwards could the enemy break-through be neutralized.

The gist of the first order issued by Army Headquarters on the evening of 21 November was as follows: Stalingrad and the Volga front will be held and strong forces will be concentrated west of the Don for a counter-attack. When Schmidt telephoned to General v. Sodenstern at Army Group Headquarters that same afternoon and said that the situation on Third Rumanian Army's front was catastrophic, Sodenstern had replied airily: 'You must work out your own salvation.'

If the immediate object was to gain time by organizing an all-round, hedgehog defence, then supplies would, inevitably, have to be transported by air. But all the responsible air commanders, from General v. Richthofen himself downwards, declared that an air lift over any considerable period of time would be out of the question.

On 22 November General Hoth, whose Fourth Panzer Army, like the Fourth Rumanian Army, had been scattered piecemeal,

---

command of the new Army Group Don, which was about to be formed. At the time he was paying a visit to the central sector of the front. Bad weather had made flying impossible, and he was compelled to travel by train. Held up again and again by partisan activities *en route*, he did not reach Army Group B Headquarters in Starobielsk until 24 November, by that time the role to be played by Sixth Army had already been settled.

arrived at Nizhne Chirskaya, *en route* to Headquarters, Army Group B. His formations had been split and driven apart in two different directions by the Russian attack. IV Corps, under General Jaenecke, had been placed under Sixth Army command and had been withdrawn north-westwards; the Fourth Rumanian Army retreated south-westwards into the Kalmuck steppes. On the same day, 22 November, Soviet armoured forces, estimated at about 100 tanks and advancing from north and south, joined hands in the area Marinovka-Kalach. (According to Soviet sources, this junction was not affected until 23 November.)

At 1400 hours on 22 November General Paulus with his Chief of Staff and a skeleton staff flew from Nizhne Chirskaya to his new battle headquarters at Gumrak railway station. West of the Don, XI Army Corps and XIV Panzer Corps found that they were not able even to hold on to their positions, let alone to launch any effective counter-attack, and, contrary to instructions from Army Headquarters, both Corps had to withdraw to the east bank of the river.

On the afternoon of 22 November, fresh orders arrived from Army Headquarters: Stand fast and await further orders. On receipt of this, Paulus turned to his Chief of Staff and said: 'Well – now we'll have time to think over what we ought to do. This we'll do separately. Meet me, please, in an hour's time and we'll compare the conclusions we have reached.'

The Army Commander and his Chief of Staff found that their conclusions were identical: There was only one possible course of action. To avoid being surrounded, they must break out south-westwards just as soon as the formations still engaged west of the Don had been withdrawn and the requisite re-grouping had been completed.

On the other hand, on the evening of 22 November Hitler repeated his order to stand fast in the current position, but without giving any specific instructions as to how this was to be done. That same evening he travelled in his special train from Obersalzberg to Leipzig and from there flew to his Headquarters in East Prussia on the 23rd.

On 23 November, General Zeitzler, the Chief of the General Staff, ordered Major v. Zitzewitz to fly that same day with an echelon of Headquarters Communications Regiment to Stalingrad, where

'Sixth Army is presumed to be surrounded'. 'Your task,' said Zeitzler, 'will be to report direct to me in as great detail as possible and as quickly as you can. You need not concern yourself with questions affecting the conduct of operations. General Paulus is doing very well, and we have no anxiety on that score.'

The Chief of the General Staff, the Commander-in-Chief, Army Group B and the Commander-in-Chief, Sixth Army, were unanimous in their conviction that there was only one possible solution – to withdraw Sixth Army to a position on the arc formed by the Don and Chir. It was calculated that, if orders to break out were issued on 24 November, Sixth Army could be ready to start to do so by the 27th.

On 23 November General Zeitzler tried to persuade Hitler to accept this solution. During the night of 23–24 he telephoned to Army Group Headquarters and said he believed he had succeeded and that Hitler would sign the order on the 24th.

On the evening of 23 November, the GOC LI Corps, General Seydlitz-Kurzbach, the most vehement of the Generals who supported a break out – with or without permission from Army Group or Army Headquarters – took independent action. Without obtaining the sanction of Sixth Army Headquarters and amid dramatic scenes of the burning of supplies and equipment, he withdrew his corps some eight or ten kilometres from its position in the Yersovka area on the northern front of the cauldron. In the course of the withdrawal, 94 Infantry Division was pinned down by the pursuing enemy and was destroyed. It was not until the next day that his Chief of Staff informed Sixth Army of what had been done, adding as justification that the Corps Commander had hoped in this way to make it easier for the Army Commander to decide to retreat!

In view of the heavy fighting on the western and southern fronts and of the fact that both v. Weichs and Paulus had repeatedly requested the permission of Army Headquarters to act as they saw fit, both Army Group B and Sixth Army Headquarters were confident that orders to withdraw would be received on 24th. Instead, there came an order from Hitler that the cauldron was to be held until relief arrived. The order gave precise, detailed instructions as to how this was to be done and stated that Sixth Army would be kept supplied by air! The Commander-in-Chief of the Air Force,

Reichsmarschall Goering, had guaranteed, through his Chief of Staff, Jeschonnek, that this would be done.

That these decisions had been reached for reasons of internal policy and Party political prestige is obvious. Hitler, the People's Tribune and the Leader of the Masses, had paralysed the liberty of Hitler, the War Lord, by boldly declaring that we had got Stalingrad, the vital point on the Volga, and could rest content; Goering hoped that by guaranteeing adequately to supply Sixth Army by air he would be able to restore his sorely tarnished reputation as C-in-C of the Air Force. But all this was something which the responsible leaders at the front could not possibly have realized. The whole of their minds and energies were concentrated on the struggle against a merciless and mighty enemy, freshly equipped with the most formidable weapons. The Sixth Army stood in deadly peril, and the sole question exercising the minds of Paulus and his Chief of Staff was, how could they maintain the fighting power of their Army, preserve its existence as a corporate entity and save the lives of the hundreds of thousands of men entrusted to them? It was as simple as that.

At 2100 hours on the evening of 24 November Hitler, still in ignorance of the bold but ill-advised independent action taken by General Seydlitz-Kurzbach, issued a further order: 'The GOC LI Corps will assume unified command of the northern and eastern fronts of the cauldron' (i.e. of just those fronts which would have to be the first to be given up, if Sixth Army decided to re-group its forces with a view to a general retreat!). The order added that the GOC LI Corps would be personally responsible to the Fuehrer for the holding of these fronts, though this did not in any way affect the overall responsibility of the GOC-in-C, Sixth Army.

Before calling upon Field-Marshal Paulus to carry on with the story, and before giving extracts from the archives of the German Military Mission to Rumania and the War Diary of Air Fleet 4, it is, I think, essential that I should give the reader a general outline of the purely chronological sequence of events. Field-Marshal Paulus divided his memorandum into two main parts: the 'fundamental facts' and an appendix on specific factors. The former was countersigned by General Strecker, GOC-in-C XI Corps, who held the northern front of the cauldron and did not surrender until

2 February 1943, and by General Seydlitz-Kurzbach. The appendix bears no signature or counter-signature and is the only surviving paper that has been typewritten.

It is easy to be wise after the event. There can be little doubt that, in theory, the immediate withdrawal of the Sixth Army from its critical position in the Volga-Don area in November 1942 would have been the correct course; but, in war, the theoretically correct, as I have already suggested, is not always correct or even feasible in practice. And there is no doubt whatever that to those conducting Sixth Army's operations there appeared to be no over-riding all-compelling reason for them to decide, in direct disobedience of Army Group and Supreme Headquarters' orders, to withdraw on their own responsibility. They had been promised that relief was on its way; they had been assured that adequate supplies would reach them by air. As regards the latter, there is no concealing the fact that the senior Air Force Officers were, it is true, sceptical; but as regards the former, they could not but assume that this was no empty promise.

For obvious reasons, there can be no documentary evidence to prove or disprove that General Beck, the Chief of the General Staff who was dismissed in 1938, felt in his enforced exile at the time of Stalingrad that Paulus could have emulated Yorck's feat and that he had it in his power to break out on his own responsibility and thus give the signal for 'action by the Field-Marshals', which would have compelled Hitler to surrender at least the supreme military command.

But as far as 'action by the Field-Marshals' is concerned, it must be remembered that the only two Field-Marshals who, in the autumn of 1938 or the winter of 1939–40, had given any serious thought to the possibility of direct action against Hitler, Erwin v. Witzleben and Wilhelm Ritter v. Leeb, had both retired – the former for reasons of health and the latter at his own request as the result of divergencies of opinion between himself and the 'Fuehrer'. In spite of the caustic and critical comments on the National Socialist régime in which his wife constantly indulged, it never for a moment entered Paulus' head that an Army Commander, by acting arbitrarily on his own responsibility, could raise the standard of political revolt against the régime at home or on less active sectors of the front. During those November days, he once said to his Chief of Staff that he would willingly give his head for the Sixth Army, but that he felt it was useless to do so. Was he really wrong in this?

Though appeals to revolt against the Third Reich play an important part in the history of the Second World War, it is nevertheless quite impossible to pass judgement on military decisions – or perhaps I should say on decisions based upon soldierly ethics, solely from the viewpoint of revolt and resistance.

In addition, there is another aspect which deserves mention, though the extent to which the cases quoted may have influenced General Paulus cannot, of course, be assessed. During the winter crisis of 1941–2 in the battle for Moscow, the Commanders-in-Chief of the Second and Fourth Panzer Armies, Generals Guderian and Hoepner, were peremptorily dismissed by Hitler for having carried out tactical withdrawals on their own responsibility. Their Army Group Commander, Field-Marshal v. Kluge, must either have refused to accept responsibility for their actions or have failed entirely in his endeavours to defend them.

At the end of December 1942, General Count v. Sponek, Commanding XXXXII Army Corps, in the face of landings by superior Russian forces, ordered the evacuation of the Kerch peninsula in the Crimea, contrary to the intentions of both the GOC-in-C Army Group South (Field-Marshal v. Reichenau) and the GOC-in-C Eleventh Army (Field-Marshal v. Manstein). He was immediately relieved of his command by v. Manstein.

Paulus himself knew all about the Major Reichel case and the extraordinary manner in which Generals Stumme and v. Boineburg had been treated.

And there is yet another, classical example (which occurred, admittedly, after Paulus had ceased to be an Army Commander in the field) of the way in which Hitler was wont to punish what he was pleased to call 'disobedience in the higher ranks'. During the January 1945 Soviet offensive on Army Group Centre, when there seemed to be every chance that East Prussia and the Army Group would be cut off from the Reich, the Commander-in-Chief, Fourth Army, General Hossbach, decided to act on his own responsibility. Contrary to the intentions of Supreme Headquarters, but with the concurrence of the Army Group Commander, General Reinhardt, he launched an attack from the Loetzen position westwards in the direction of Elbing. In the middle of this operation, both Reinhardt and Hossbach were relieved of their commands. But neither of them felt that it was in any way possible to revolt against this order from the 'Fuehrer', even though Hossbach, in particular, was a most enterprising and self-willed character.

Inevitably, then, the question arises: What, exactly, would have happened if Paulus had decided in November or December to take matters into his own hands?

Walter Goerlitz

The basic facts of the Sixth Army's operations at Stalingrad (Phase I) by Field-Marshal Friedrich Paulus

Foreword

This memorandum has been written from memory and may therefore be incomplete in certain aspects and inaccurate on points of minor detail. I have endeavoured to draw a sharp distinction between the manner in which I regarded the orders issued to me at the time of issue and the manner in which I now see them in retrospect. Even so, the outline of my views at the time may well seem today to give the impression that my appreciation of the situation was more pertinent and comprehensive than my then knowledge of events and their background would have permitted.

My primary purpose in writing these notes is to clear my own mind. Later, revised and amplified, they will, I hope, be included in a more comprehensive study, which in its turn may perhaps make some contribution to a proper understanding of the war and its outcome.[1]

It is, I feel, incumbent upon me to set down the basic facts regarding the struggle for Stalingrad against the background of the situation as a whole as I saw it at the time.

[1] The more comprehensive study referred to was never written.

SOVIET COUNTER-OFFENSIVE
up to the encirclement of the
SIXTH ARMY*(19-23 November 1942)*

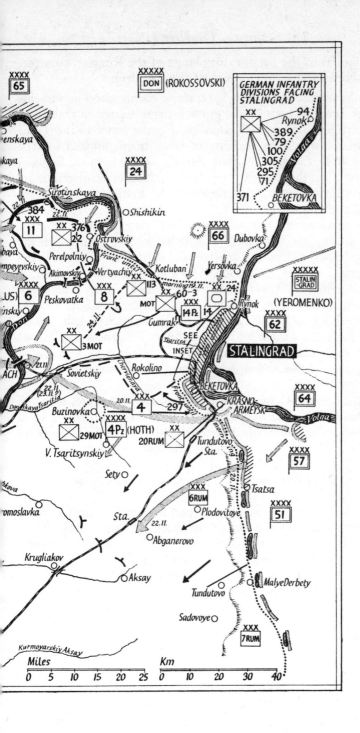

XXXX
65

XXXXX
DON (ROKOSSOVSKI)

GERMAN INFANTRY
DIVISIONS FACING
STALINGRAD
XX
94
Rynok
389
79
100
305
295
71
371
BEKETOVKA

enskaya

kaya

Sirotinskaya
22.II.
Shishikin
XXXX
24

XXXX
66
Dubovka

XXX
384
22.II.
11

XX 376
22
Ostrovskiy

Perelpolniy
Kotluban
Yersovka
XXXXX
STALIN-
GRAD

bava

mpeyevskiy
Akimovskiy
Vertyachiy
Front unter
XX
113
morning19.II.
XXXX
XX 24:
(YEROMENKO)

US
XXXX
6

Peskovatka
XXX
8
MOT
XXX 60-3
XXX
14 Pz 14
Rynok
XXXX
62

nskiy

Don

24.II.
Gumrak
XX
3 MOT
Tsaritsa
SEE
INSET
STALINGRAD

ACH
21.II.
Sovietskiy
Rokolino
Chervlenaya
BEKETOVKA
XXXX
64

22.II.
(23.II.?)
DonskayaTsaritia
20.II.
XXX
4
297
KRASNO-
ARMEYSK
Volga

Buzinovka
XX
29 MOT
XXXX
4 Pz (HOTH)
20RUM
XX
Tundutovo
Sta.

V. Tsaritsynskiy

Sety
XXXX
57

kova
Sta.
XXX
6RUM
Tsatsa
XXXX
51

omoslavka
Plodovitoye
20.II.

22.II.
Abganerovo

Krugliakov
Aksay
MalyeDerbety
Tundutovo

Sadovoye
XXX
7RUM

Kurmoyarskiy Aksay

Miles
0 5 10 15 20 25

Km
0 10 20 30 40

I. Period from the preparatory stage of the Russian counter-offensive to the encirclement of the cauldron

From the middle of October 1942, major enemy troop movements were observed by both air and ground reconnaissance in the area to the north of Kletskaya — Serafimovich, in the sector of the Third Rumanian Army. The majority of these troops appeared to be moving from the area of Sixth Army's northern front, between Stalingrad and the Don. At the same time, east of Stalingrad more troops were observed, moving south and south-west on Fourth Rumanian Army's front.

These movements were interpreted as being preparations for a major attack, the first object of which was presumed to be the cutting-off of the German forces engaged in the Don bend and in the Stalingrad area east of the Don. This appreciation of the situation was submitted to the Commander-in-Chief, Army Group 'B' (Field-Marshal v. Weichs), and all further information obtained was at once passed on to him. His attention was also repeatedly drawn to the weakness of the neighbouring armies (Rumanian and Italian) as regards armament in general and lack of anti-tank weapons in particular, and the consequent dangers in the event of a major enemy attack.

At the end of October, as a precautionary measure, a mixed force composed primarily of anti-tank units had already been moved into position behind Sixth Army's left flank (i.e. behind XI Army Corps), ready to intervene on the right flank of the Rumanian Army.[1] On 12 November, 14 Panzer Division, less its infantry regiments, which were engaged elsewhere, was moved to the same area and placed under the command of XI Corps.

In spite of the reported Russian preparations for a major attack and contrary to the representations made by Sixth Army, Army Group Headquarters directed that the attacks on Stalingrad should be continued. As a result, the intended relief of all the units of XIV Panzer Corps, for which all preparations had long since been completed, had to be delayed.[2]

On 19 and 20 November the enemy launched his attacks on the

[1] This refers to the Simons Group. According to the German Liaison Staff with Third Rumanian Army, this move did not take place until 9 November.

[2] In the event, this relief never took place.

neighbouring armies to the west and south of Sixth Army respectively, XIV Panzer Corps, with 16 and 24 Panzer Divisions, which were withdrawn from the front line, was thereupon ordered to move behind the Army's left flank and from there to attack westwards against the flank of the enemy's northern offensive and bring it to a halt.

On 21 November, the Russian northern attack reached the high ground north-west of Kalach. The enemy southern attack was found to have developed into a two-pronged thrust, one moving westwards and the other south-westwards in the direction of Kotel'nikovo. IV Army Corps of Fourth Panzer Army was being pressed back on to the southern flank of Sixth Army. The mass of Fourth Panzer Army (Rumanians) was withdrawing south-westwards.

At 1300 hours, Sixth Army's Battle Headquarters was transferred from Golubinskaya on the Don to Nizhne Chirskaya, where all the necessary administrative installations had long since been prepared in anticipation of such a move. In the afternoon, the following proposals were submitted to Army Group Headquarters:

Sixth Army to withdraw to the Don and the Chir – i.e. to the arc which had previously constituted Sixth Army's front; the move to be timed to harmonize with the situation on neighbouring fronts; the forces of the Army's southern wing, which would then become available, to thrust against the flank of the enemy advancing on Kotel'nikovo and, in co-operation with Fourth Panzer Army and elements of Army Group Caucasus, to bring the enemy advance to a halt. Had this solution been accepted, the following troops would have been available for operations against the front and flanks of the Russian northern attack:
(a) XIV Panzer Corps, together with other Sixth Army formations as they became disengaged.
(b) the reserves already in the hands of Army group, plus those which had been promised by Army Headquarters.

At the same time, particular attention was invited to Sixth Army's inadequate stock of supplies.

Army Group accepted Sixth Army's proposals. But later in the evening further orders were received, the gist of which was: By order of Army Headquarters, Sixth Army will hold the Stalingrad-

Volga front whatever happens. Should breaches on the flanks call
for the organization of an all-round, hedgehog defensive position,
this will be created further eastwards.[1] The Army's Battle Headquarters will be transferred to the area east of Kalach. IV Army
Corps and Fourth Panzer Army (three German and one Rumanian
divisions) will be placed under Sixth Army command. Large-scale
counter-measures are being initiated. Further orders will follow
in due course.

At about 0700 hours on 22 November, the GOC-in-C, Fourth
Panzer Army, passed through Nizhne Chirskaya on his way back to
report to Army Group Headquarters. He was not able to give any
detailed information regarding the confused situation on his own
front.

At 1400 hours, the Army Commander, Sixth Army and his Chief
of Staff flew into the cauldron to the Army's new Battle Headquarters established to the west of Gumrak railway station. During
that afternoon, the Army Commander gained the following impression of the situation:

IV Army Corps (General Jaenecke) was holding on to the pivot at
the southern end of Stalingrad, while its south-western flank was
slowly giving ground in the direction of Zybenko.

LI Army Corps (General v. Seydlitz), holding the northern front
from the Volga to Kotluban, had not been attacked.

VIII Army Corps (General Heitz) on the left of LI Corps, except
for an attack on 76 Division, on its left flank on the Don, had also
not been engaged.

XI Army Corps (General Strecker) was heavily engaged west of the
Don to the south of Kletskaya, and its western flank was being bent
back southwards.

XIV Panzer Corps (General Hube) was in action on the Don plateau
to the west of Vertyachi – Golubinskaya. Its movements were
hampered by shortage of fuel and by the terrain.

During the afternoon, on Sixth Army's south-western flank, which

---

[1] According to General Schmidt, who has had the opportunity of refreshing
his memory by studying Sixth Army's War Diary, this order did not say that an
all-round defensive position was to be adopted, but ordered Sixth Army to
attack westwards and at the same time maintain its positions in the Stalingrad
area.

was only protected by flank guards, Russian tanks, coming from the north-west and the south-east, joined forces in the area Marinovka-Kalach. Estimated strength – about 100 tanks.

This picture further confirmed the conclusions which I had previously reached and which I had already submitted to Army Group on 21 November.

On the afternoon of 22 November I had a personal meeting and discussion with the Commander of LI Corps, General v. Seydlitz. He urged that the whole Army should forthwith fight its way out. I told him of the proposals I had already submitted on 21 November and of the further steps I proposed to take.[1]

During the night of 22–23 November[2] I sent a further detailed report to Army Group and to Army Headquarters, the salient features of which were:

(a) In the area (the Steppes) in which the western and southern fronts of the envisaged cauldron are to be formed, there are no prepared defensive positions. Moreover, there is no wood with which to construct such positions – and it is now mid-winter.

(b) Whether the creation of an all-round defensive hedgehog is tactically possible appears to be doubtful. Today, on the western front, which has not yet been closed, 100 Russian tanks have appeared to the east of Kalach.

(c) The available forces are not strong enough to hold for any lengthy period a cauldron position of sufficient size to include an adequately secured airfield (Pitomnik).

(d) Even while our rear lines of communication were still open and secure, supplies have latterly been quite inadequate for our needs. According to information available here, adequate supply by air, as a long-term policy, will be quite impossible. The supply situation will nevertheless rob the Army in the near future of its capability to offer further resistance.

[1] Vide Paulus' wireless report to Army Headquarters on page 233.

[2] Not quite correct. In reality this message was signed by Paulus at 2130 hours on the 23rd and was despatched at 2345 hours. The message refers to the supply situation only in general terms . . . 'the timely arrival of adequate supplies is not possible'. The question of supply by air had not at that time been decided, so Paulus could have done no more than express doubts on the subject. As he says in his foreword memory may have played him false.

(e) All my Commanding Generals agree with my appreciation of the situation and my proposal that the Army should fight its way out south-westwards to the Chir-Don position. I therefore repeat most urgently the proposals submitted on 21 November and ask to be given authority forthwith to act as I see fit.

On 23 November[1] Army Group sent on a fresh order from Army Headquarters for the formation of a hedgehog, the precise delineation of which was given in detail. This 'fortress' was to be held 'with every available means'. Army Headquarters, it was stated, then intended, with a strongly reinforced Fourth Panzer Army, to re-establish contact with Sixth Army and transform the current crisis into a victory. The relief operations would be initiated, it was hoped, at the beginning of December. Arrangement for the flying-in of adequate supplies to Sixth Army were in process of completion by Air Fleet 4.

By 23 November the Army was completely surrounded, while inside the cauldron itself the movement of troops to their ultimate positions and the requisite re-grouping of formations continued.

II. Defence of the cauldron up to the failure of Fourth Panzer Army's relief operations

On 24 November, the Commander of LI Corps submitted a report

---

[1] Again not quite correct. According to available information, the sequence and timing of these exchanges appears to have been as follows: *21 Nov.* (*evening*). Army Headquarters order: Stalingrad-Volga front will be held at all costs. Sixth Army will concentrate strong forces for a counter-attack west of the Don. Major counter-measures are being initiated. Further orders follow in due course. *22 Nov. 1800 hours.* GOC-in-C, Sixth Army, reports to Army Group that his Army is surrounded and the supply situation is critical. Army intends to hold on to Stalingrad-Don area, provided that southern front is successfully closed and adequate supplies are flown in. Asks for freedom of action in the event of failure to create the defensive 'hedgehog'. *Later.* Repeat order from Army Headquarters via Army Group: Hold on and await further orders. Then yet another order from the Fuehrer: 'Sixth Army will adopt hedgehog defence and await relief from outside.'
23 Nov. 1845 hours. C-in-C Army Group 'B' wireless message to Chief of General Staff, supporting Paulus' proposal to withdraw and break out, and emphasizes that supply by air is impossible.
Later. Paulus' wireless report to Army Headquarters.
24 Nov. Reply thereto, after Hitler had made his final decision.

on the state of his Corps and the supply situation, which culminated in:

(a) a statement that the supply situation and the fighting qualities of his Corps could not be relied upon for any considerable further period.

(b) a demand that the GOC-in-C, Sixth Army, should ignore the Fuehrer's order and, mindful only of his responsibilities to the German people, should abandon Stalingrad and the Volga front and break out to the south-west.

This report was sent by air courier to v. Manstein's Army Group, which had in the meanwhile assumed command in place of that of General v. Weichs.[1] With it went a covering note from myself, (a) stating that the Corps Commander's summing-up of the situation agreed with the repeated reports I had myself submitted, and (b) repeating my requests of 21 and 22 November to be given authority to act as I thought fit.

The other Generals of Sixth Army[2] agreed with the attitude I had adopted and rejected the idea of acting contrary to the Fuehrer's orders. In these circumstances, I felt there could be no question of my withdrawing on my own responsibility as suggested by General v. Seydlitz, for the following reasons:

(1) The holding of the Volga front was the basis upon which Army Headquarters' operational plan had been built (the 'Volga corner-stone' as it was called).

(2) Army Group and Army Headquarters were linked by a wireless system of communication which was functioning perfectly. My own Headquarters, too, was directly connected by wireless telephone and teleprinter with Army Group, and there was, in addition, the air

---

[1] Not correct. Field-Marshal v. Manstein, the newly appointed Commander-in-Chief, Army Group, Don, did not arrive at Group Headquarters in Starobielsk until 24 November, to take stock of the situation. He was convinced that Paulus should have retreated at once on 19 November, but that as he had not done so, Sixth Army had no alternative but to hold out until relief arrived. On 26 November v. Manstein set up his Headquarters in Novocherkask. From 28 November onwards, Sixth Army came under command of Army Group Don. (See v. Manstein: *Lost Victories*, pp. 303 et seq., and Paulus' letter of November 26 to v. Manstein.)

[2] i.e. Generals Jaenecke, Heitz, Strecker and Hube, commanding IV, VIII, XI Army Corps and XIV Panzer Corps respectively.

link. The higher formations, therefore, always had a complete, up-to-date and detailed picture of Sixth Army's situation. Further- more, they were all – the Chief of the General Staff, the GSOI Ops. and the GSOI Intelligence, Army Group Headquarters – kept constantly informed of the situation by their own Liaison Officers attached to Sixth Army in the cauldron itself. Army Head- quarters, too, sent a Liaison Officer to my Headquarters.

(3) We had been told that we could expect an early raising of the siege by strong Panzer, motorized and infantry forces.

(4) At a short distance from the cauldron, the Chir front still stood firm, with a bridge-head across the Don.

The essential pre-requisites for the relief operations and the restoring of the situation, therefore, were undoubtedly there.[1] In these circumstances, and particularly as it was quite impossible for me to form any authoritative appreciation of the situation as a whole, to have acted independently and against orders would have destroyed the foundations upon which the High Command was basing its plan of operations. To act, on principle, thus independent- ly and contrary to the strategic concept of operations would have led to a state of anarchy among responsible commanders in the field.

Early on 25 November there arrived from Army Headquarters a further order, the gist of which was: 'The eastern and northern front up to the strong-point south of Kotluban will be placed under the command of General v. Seydlitz, Commanding XI Corps, who will be responsible directly to the Fuehrer for the holding of this front. This order does not, however, affect in any way the general responsi- bility of the Army Commander for the conduct of the operations of his Army.'

I handed this order personally to General v. Seydlitz at his Headquarters, which were close to my own, and asked him what he proposed to do about it? He replied that in the circumstances he had no option but to obey. This he did with soldierly devotion to duty

---

[1] As the situation then was, the Field-Marshal had every justification for this assumption. If, instead of resorting to stop-gap improvisations, Hitler had concentrated major forces in the Volga-Don area and had withdrawn the Caucasian Army Group in good time, he would have had ample forces with which, in spite of the North African crisis, to relieve Sixth Army.

to the very end, though that did not prevent him from urging me all the time to act on my own responsibility, regardless of orders from above!

When this order reached Sixth Army, neither Army Group nor Army Headquarters had yet any knowledge of the memorandum submitted to me by the Corps Commander of LI Corps.

Field-Marshal v. Manstein's reaction to this latest order is reflected in the message he sent me, which ran:

'This order from Army Headquarters on the question of command within the envisaged cauldron displays a mistrust of the Army Commander which is totally unjustified. Nor do I think it would be possible to obey it in practice. I have protested to Army Headquarters and asked that the order be cancelled.'

To this protest, Army Headquarters vouchsafed no reply. Later, however, Field-Marshal v. Manstein issued an order, stating that as far as he himself was concerned, full responsibility still rested with the Army Commander. This, however, did not wholly remove the anomaly created by Army Headquarter's order.

In the days that followed, we were fully occupied in taking steps to ensure that the cauldron could be successfully held and in making preparations for a break-out as soon as the relieving force drew near.

To Army Group and Army Headquarters I reported that in my opinion, even after the siege had been raised, Sixth Army should in no circumstances be called upon to remain on the Volga front for the winter, but that, as soon as the Panzer Army drew near, we should break out to meet it and should then take up a position further back. To this, Army Group replied: 'We agree with Army Commander's intention to make all necessary preparations for a break-out. Army Headquarters decision, however, must be awaited. Pending receipt of latter, current orders will remain in force.'

During this time, frequent and urgent messages were sent by Sixth Army, requesting an increase in the inadequate volume of supplies being sent in by air, to enable the fighting capability of the Army to be maintained.

Appendix to the basic facts, Sixth Army's operations at Stalingrad (Phase I)

I. Exchange of views with higher authority before the beginning of the Russian offensive on 19 November 1942

Before ever the events in the great bend of the Don began, a series of lively discussions took place between Army Group Headquarters and Sixth Army on the subject of the northern flank, which was becoming longer and longer and was but weakly held, on the one hand, and the decreasing strength of the offensive spearhead, which was constantly being called upon to provide yet more troops as flank guards, on the other.

The arrival of allied forces on the Don had brought about a relief that was apparent rather than real.[1] In reality, the allied forces were quite inadequate, not only in numbers, but also and even more so in their fighting quality and their material equipment. An episode that occurred while the Italian defensive front was in process of creation gave significant indication of things to come. About the end of August, a minor, exploratory thrust by weak Russian forces in the Serafimovich area resulted in a twenty mile, precipitate retreat by a whole Italian division.

About this time, the OQuI of the General Staff, General Blumentritt, was paying a visit to Sixth Army, and I called upon him to bear witness to the correctness of my reports and warnings on the subject, by going personally and seeing for himself what things were like in the Italian sector and passing on his impressions to Army Group and Army Headquarters. I took this step, which did not really come within my competence as an Army Commander, in the interests of both my own Sixth Army and of the operations as a whole.

On 12 October, while at Fuehrer Headquarters, I drew attention to (a) the weakness of the Stalingrad front and (b) the dangerous situation on the flank and the desirability of stiffening the allied

---

[1] On 5 August, the Italian Eighth Army, which consisted only of XXXV Corps (two infantry divisions), one cavalry group and one group of 'Black Shirts', took over the protection of the whole of Sixth Army's northern flank.

formations by interpolating some German troops and stationing German reserves behind their front.[1]

At the end of September I sent the Army Headquarters Liaison Officer with Sixth Army, Major Menzel, to Army Headquarters to submit once again my views on (a) increasing the fighting power of my Army, (b) the protection of my flanks and (c) the need to improve the reliability of the channel of supply and to increase the volume of supplies being sent to me.

In the same way, I briefed various senior officers visiting Sixth Army – General Ochsner, General Fellgiebel, the Head of the Armed Forces Communications Branch, and General Schmundt, Hitler's Military Secretary, and asked them to pass on what I had told and shown them.

The last-named I took with me on a visit to 767 Infantry Regiment, which was engaging Russian forces that had crossed the Don and advanced southwards to a point quite close to VIII Army Corps' battle headquarters.

I also took the somewhat unconventional step of approaching General Dumitrescu, the GOC-in-C, Third Rumanian Army, in an effort to do something to strengthen my northern flank. I urged him to press, through his own High Command, for German anti-tank guns and artillery, to reinforce the Rumanian Army.

With the object of completing the capture of Stalingrad and thus eliminating a potential danger spot, I asked that Sixth Army should be reinforced by three infantry divisions. The assistance granted in response to this request was of no practical value. It is true that 14 and 24 Panzer and 94 Infantry Divisions were transferred from Fourth Panzer Army to Sixth Army; but in return Sixth Army was called upon to take over two divisional sectors from Fourth Panzer Army, with the net result that our strength was in

[1] Supreme Headquarters War Diary entry for 22 October reads: 'The Fuehrer has decreed that Air Force ground divisions are to be located in rear of all three allied armies, to put some stiffening into them.' Cf. also GOC-in-C Air Fleet 4's diary, 15 October: 'Discussed with Jeschonnek question of raising twenty Air Force ground divisions. I don't like the idea. But the RM (i.e. Goering) won't surrender these men as recruits to the Army, where they properly belong. I only hope we don't make a real mess of things!' Incidentally, the divisions, which Hitler decreed should be so employed, existed, at that time, only on paper!

reality increased by only one division. Furthermore, all three divisions transferred to my command were battle weary in the extreme and, indeed, 94 Infantry Division was shortly afterwards broken up and its troops were transferred to other divisions.

In the second half of October, I requested permission to halt the attacks on Stalingrad, in order to be able to bring up two Panzer and one motorized divisions to relieve XIV Panzer Corps. For both tactical and strategic reasons I wished to withdraw the latter, give it a well-earned rest and then retain it in reserve behind the front line. All necessary administrative and supply arrangements in its new location had, I said, already been completed.

In spite of the fact that from the middle of October onwards it had been generally accepted that the Russians were preparing for an offensive and reports to that effect had continued to be sent on, not only was my request refused, but I was also ordered to launch a fresh attack on Stalingrad. For this purpose five pioneer battalions were flown in to reinforce Sixth Army.[1] These, however, were of little fighting value. They were composed for the most part of young, untrained soldiers and were in any case under strength.

As will be seen from what I have said above, the response of the High Command to all my pleas, reports and representations regarding reinforcements, flank protection and supplies had remained woefully inadequate. This, however, did not deter Hitler from issuing the following appeal in the middle of November: 'Of the men of the Sixth Army, who have so often in the past given eloquent proof of their gallantry, and of their seasoned leaders, I expect one final, supreme effort that will carry them to the banks of the Volga from one end of Stalingrad to the other and thus secure the basis on which to build our defence of this most important pivot on the river Volga.'

Sixth Army's response to this appeal was to make available two of the above-mentioned pioneer battalions for local raids within the confines of the city. It is typical of the man that Hitler's telegram made no mention of the main danger point – the flanks.

In the midst of all these abortive discussions it had become ob-

---

[1] General v. Richthofen claims that these 'assault' pioneer battalions were sent to reinforce Sixth Army as the result of his initiative in the matter. Vide his diary entry of 1 November.

vious that the Russians were intensifying their preparations for a major offensive on the northern flank – in the area to the west of Kletskaya on the Third Rumanian Army's front and further to the west against the Italian Army.

Reports reaching Sixth Army from XIV Panzer Corps, VIII and XI Army Corps were consistently unanimous on the subject, and their contents were confirmed by air reconnaissance carried out on Sixth Army orders. In addition, I satisfied myself of their accuracy by personal observation from the high ground in 384 Infantry Divisions' sector.

Corresponding reports sent to Army Group and Army Headquarters by their own Liaison Officers were given but scant credence. 'Air reconnaissance by Air Fleet 4,' Army Headquarters replied, 'has established that there is no unusual concentration of enemy forces in the areas mentioned by Sixth Army. The general situation in this respect would appear to be normal. The troop movements reported by Sixth Army are probably nothing more than routine supply traffic.'

Towards the middle of November – a few days before the launching of the main offensive – all Sixth Army's previous reports were suddenly confirmed by Air Fleet 4.

Faced with this situation, the new Chief of the General Staff, General Zeitzler, issued an order more or less in the following terms: 'The Russians no longer have any reserves worth mentioning and are not capable of launching a large-scale offensive. In forming any appreciation of enemy intentions, this basic fact must be taken fully into consideration.'[1]

---

[1] According to Greiner: *War Diary, Supreme Headquarters*, pp. 412 et seq., the CGS himself was by no means clear in his own mind regarding the situation and enemy intentions. (The War Diary entry for 9 October states that 'the CGS does not deny that there is more than a possibility of an enemy winter offensive!') On 20 October Hitler expressed anxiety over a possible attack over the Don on Rostov. At the situation conference on 27 October Zeitzler said that the violent Russian agitation calling for a major offensive could be regarded as little more than propaganda. On 7 November he reported that, according to agents' reports from Moscow, the 'Supreme Council' had decided on 4 November to launch a major offensive either on the Don or in the central sector. Manstein in *Lost Victories*, p. 294, states that even as late as 21 November AHQ did not seem to have grasped the full gravity of the Stalingrad situation.

The difference between this assessment of enemy strength and intentions and the actual facts is a clear indication – as subsequent events proved – that the Supreme Command, by adhering to its insistence on the capture of Stalingrad as the main object when the vital need was to concentrate every available man for the protection of our flanks and the repulse of the enemy winter offensive, was now more than ever indulging in pipe-dreams and wishful thinking that were nothing less than a betrayal of the troops in the field.[1]

The defensive measures which it was within the scope of my authority to take consisted in the main of putting a stop (contrary to orders from above) to all major attacks, confining offensive action to local raids, reinforcing my left flank, withdrawing troops (14 Panzer Division) from the line into reserve behind the Army's left flank, making preparations for the withdrawal into reserve of further forces (XIV Panzer Corps) and calling upon the Air Force to engage such enemy concentrations as had been located. In this way, Sixth Army did all that lay in its power to do.

In taking the decisions outlined above, I was actuated by considerations which extended far beyond the confines of Sixth Army operations into the broader context of the operations of Army Group and, indeed, of the conduct of the war by Supreme Headquarters in the whole theatre of operations. These broader issues figured thus prominently in my deliberations, because I knew that the fate of the Sixth Army would depend upon the decisions and measures taken by Army Group and by Supreme Headquarters, and that these latter would have to be based upon the strategic situation as a whole. To have confined my thoughts solely to the interests of Sixth Army and independently to have ordered it to break out, on the other hand, would have jeopardized the fate of the neighbouring armies and of the whole of the southern front.

II. Co-operation with higher authority at the beginning of, and during, the Stalingrad winter campaign

I have already dealt in some detail with the co-operation between Sixth Army and higher authority. There remain nevertheless certain aspects which deserve mention:

---

[1] This is a conclusion which the Field-Marshal reached in 1945 – after the catastrophe! In 1942 his confidence was unshaken.

(1) My urgent recommendation of 21 November that Sixth Army should withdraw to the Don was approved by Headquarters, Army Group 'B'; but in what form and with what emphasis the latter forwarded it to Supreme Headquarters I do not, of course, know – any more than I know the reasons upon which Army Group and Army Headquarters based their confidence that the breaches in our lines could be sealed and Sixth Army relieved.[1] But, as a generalization, I would say that all the senior commanders, including myself, were hampered by the paralysing effects of an order which Hitler issued towards the end of October and which was worded more or less as follows: 'No Army Group Commander, and certainly no Army Commander, has the right to give up a locality or even a single co-ordinated trench system without my prior sanction.'[2] This was an order which quite deliberately deprived the senior commanders of any authority to make even minor tactical adjustments, let alone decisions of a strategic nature.

I cannot remember exactly whether it was in this order or in one he had previously issued that Hitler said that he could not grant to a senior officer the right to refuse to carry out an order or to take up any given appointment, any more than he could do so to a private soldier; and the latter, certainly, could not refuse, for that would be desertion.[3]

---

[1] The full text of Army Group's telegram of 23 November to the Chief of the General Staff is given in Doerr, *Stalingrad*, pp. 71 et seq. In it General v. Weichs gives full and unqualified support to Paulus' recommendation and says, among other things: 'Supply by air of the twenty divisions comprising Sixth Army is not possible.' Paulus, who wrote this memorandum in 1945 in Russian captivity, could of course have had no knowledge of this. Incidentally, General v. Weichs makes it plain that he did not feel either that he was competent to take independent decisions or that the situation justified his acting on his own responsibility, against the instructions of both Army and Supreme Headquarters – which is exactly what Paulus himself felt!

[2] There is no trace of the original of this order. It is, however, a fact that during the winter crisis in the battle for Moscow in December 1941, Hitler issued an order that any front line adjustment required his prior sanction.

[3] No official order, in this form, was ever issued. But Hitler certainly expressed views of this nature, as, for example, when Field-Marshal v. Rundstedt requested to be relieved of his command of Army Group South at the end of November 1941. Otto Dietrich, the Nazi Press Chief, summed up Hitler's attitude at that time in these words: 'As far as Hitler is concerned, there is no

(2) Field-Marshal v. Manstein, who had been appointed General Officer Commanding-in-Chief, Army Group Don, with Fourth Panzer, Sixth and Third Rumanian Armies under his command, at the outset also shared my views on the situation, though he, too, was no more successful than Field-Marshal v. Weichs in his endeavours to persuade Hitler to accept them.[1]

(3) On 23 November, in order to obtain troops for the southern front of the hedgehog we were in process of forming, I had to shorten my front on the northern perimeter. This I did on my own responsibility contrary to Hitler's basic order mentioned in sub-paragraph (1) above. On 25 November I received a signal, couched in the most peremptory terms, demanding my reasons for having taken these measures.[2]

(4) That same day,[3] an Army Headquarters telegram, the gist of which is given on page 224, arrived. Inevitably I connected this blunt expression of no confidence in myself with the signal mentioned in sub-paragraph (3) above, on the one hand, and, on the other,

---

such thing as "retirement at one's own request" or "placing one's office at the disposal".' . . . All he recognized was – 'obedience of orders' or 'desertion'. During his tenure of the post of OQuI Paulus must undoubtedly have heard Hitler express views of this nature.

[1] This is only partially correct. Field-Marshal v. Manstein only took over Army Group Don on 27/28 November, after the decision had already been taken that Sixth Army was not to try to fight its way out. He had therefore neither any reason nor opportunity to make any further representations to Supreme Headquarters on the subject. Indeed, by that time he had himself come to the conclusion that the correct course now was for Sixth Army to hold out until relieved, although up to 24 November he had advocated the immediate withdrawal of Sixth Army. Vide v. Manstein, *Lost Victories*, pp. 304 et seq.

[2] This refers to General Seydlitz's withdrawal, on his own responsibility, from the Yersovka area on 23 November, of which the Army Commander was only informed after the event. Paulus makes no mention in this memorandum of Seydlitz's disobedience of orders, but, very decently, as Army Commander he accepted full responsibility for the move. Beyond delivering to him a homily on the errors of his ways, Paulus took no action against v. Seydlitz.

[3] An error. The order making v. Seydlitz responsible personally to the Fuehrer for the northern front was sent off, as already stated, at 2100 hours on 24 November and could not, therefore, have reached Sixth Army before late on that day.

personal side, with the disclosure made to me at the end of October by General Schmundt, Hitler's Military Secretary and Head of the Personnel Branch, when he was paying Sixth Army a visit. Schmundt then told me that I was to be offered a new appointment in the near future and that v. Seydlitz, who enjoyed Hitler's particular confidence, was to be my successor.[1]

The Stalingrad Cauldron (Phase I): documents and letters

Paulus' wireless signal to Army Headquarters, 23 November 1942[1]

To Army Headquarters
Secret

23 November 1942

My Fuehrer,

Since receipt of your wireless signal of 22 November, the situation has developed with extreme rapidity.

In the west and south-west we have not succeeded in completing our hedgehog position. Further enemy breaches are anticipated.

Ammunition and fuel are running short. Many of my batteries and anti-tank units have expended all they had. A timely and adequate replenishment is not possible.

Unless I concentrate every available man and inflict a decisive defeat on the enemy advancing from the south and west, my Army will be faced with imminent destruction.

To do this, I must forthwith withdraw all the divisions from Stalingrad itself and further considerable forces from the northern perimeter. As, in these circumstances, it will not be possible to hold

[1] There is no definite information regarding the 'new appointment' envisaged for Paulus. Schmundt was probably thinking of the suggestion that Paulus, in view of his family connections, should be appointed permanent German Deputy Commander-in-Chief of the German-Rumanian Army Group Don, under Marshal Antonescu. Later there was also, apparently, some talk of Paulus succeeding General Jodl. At the Nuremberg trial, Schmundt said he could not remember having mentioned this to Paulus. (Perhaps he did not wish to!)

[1] Vide p. 221 and Footnote (1).

the eastern and northern fronts with the weak forces still available, I shall then have no option but to fight my way out south-westwards.

We shall, it is true, suffer heavy material losses, but the majority of these fine fighting men and at least a portion of their arms and equipment will be saved.

Although my subordinate commanders, Generals Heitz, Strecker, Hube and Jaenecke, all agree with my views, I personally accept full responsibility for this grave communication.

In view of the situation, I request you to grant me complete freedom of action.

Heil mein Fuehrer!

(signed) Paulus.

2130 hours, 23 November 1942

Despatched 2345 hours 23 November

Copy to:

Headquarters, Army Group 'B'.

. . . . Lieut.

Extracts from a letter from General Paulus to Field-Marshal v. Manstein[1]

Gumrak Railway Station

26 November 1942

(Written by hand of officer)

From: The General Officer Commanding-in-Chief, Sixth Army
To: The General Officer Commanding-in-Chief, Army Group Don

My dear Field-Marshal,

I beg to acknowledge your signal of 24 November and to thank you for the help you propose giving.[2]

To assist you in forming an appreciation of my position, I am taking the liberty to report the following:

(1) When the large-scale Russian attacks on the Army's right- and

---

[1] The full text of this letter is given in Manstein: *Lost Victories*, Appendix I.
[2] At midday on 24 November a signal arrived from v. Manstein, advising Paulus to hold on, in accordance with the Fuehrer's orders, and saying: 'We will do all we can to get you out of the mess.'

left-hand neighbours started on 19 November, both my flanks were exposed within two days and were quickly penetrated by Soviet mobile forces. When our own mobile formations (XIV Panzer Corps) were pulled westwards across the Don, their spearheads ran into superior enemy forces west of the river. This put them in an extremely difficult situation, particularly as their movements were restricted by fuel shortage. Simultaneously, there developed an enemy thrust from the west against the rear of XI Corps, which, in accordance with orders, had fully maintained its position facing north. Since it was no longer possible to withdraw forces from the front to ward off this danger, I was left with no alternative but to fold XI Corps' left wing back to the south and subsequently to allow the Corps to fall back into a bridge-head west of the Don, in order to save the elements on that side of the river from being cut off from the main body.

While these measures were being carried out, an order was received from the Fuehrer calling for an attack on Dobrinskaya by XIV Panzer Corps' left wing. This order was overtaken by events and could not be complied with.

(2) Early on 22 November, IV Army Corps, which had hitherto belonged to Fourth Panzer Army, was placed under my command. Its right wing was retreating northwards, via Buzinovka, which meant that the entire south and south-west flank was laid open. To prevent the Russians from marching unchecked across the Army's rear towards Stalingrad, I had no alternative but to pull forces out of the city itself and from the front of the northern perimeter. There was just a chance that these would arrive in time, whereas troops drawn from the area west of the Don would certainly not have done so.

With the forces thus supplied by us from the Stalingrad front IV Army Corps succeeded in establishing a weak front facing south, with its western wing on Marinovka. This front, however, was penetrated several times on 23 November, and the outcome is still uncertain. On the afternoon of 23 November, strong enemy armour, including at least 100 tanks, was identified in the area west of Marinovka. In the whole of the area between Marinovka and the Don there was nothing but flimsy German protective screens. The way to Stalingrad lay open to the Russian tanks and motorized forces, as did that to the Don bridge at Pestovatka.

For the past thirty-six hours I had received no orders or information from higher authority. In a few hours I was liable to find myself confronted with the following situation:

(a) Either I must remain in position on my western and northern fronts and very soon see the Army front rolled up from behind (in which case I should be formally complying with the orders issued to me), or

(b) I should have to take the only possible decision and turn with all my might on the enemy who was about to stab the Army from behind. In the latter event, clearly, the eastern and northern fronts could no longer be held and the only alternative would be to fight my way out south-westwards.

In the case of (b) I should, it is true, be acting as the situation demands, but should also – for the second time – be guilty of disobeying an order.

In this difficult situation I sent the Fuehrer a signal, asking for freedom to take such a final decision, if it should be necessary. I wanted to have this authority in order to guard against issuing the only possible order in that situation too late.

I have no means of proving that I should only issue such an order in an extreme emergency and I can only ask you to accept my word for this.

I have received no direct reply to this signal. . . .

Today's situation is being communicated to you by map. Even though it has been possible to move more forces up to the south-western front, the situation there is still strained. . . .

The air-lift of the last three days has brought only a fraction of the calculated minimum requirements (600 tons daily). In the very next few days the supply situation can lead to a crisis of the utmost gravity.

I still believe, however, that the Army can hold out for a time. On the other hand – even if anything like a corridor is cut through to me – it is still not possible to tell whether the daily increasing weakness of the Army, combined with lack of accommodation and wood for constructional and heating purposes, will allow the area round Stalingrad to be held for any length of time.

As I am being daily bombarded with numerous, understandable inquiries about the future, I should be grateful if I could be provided with more information than hitherto, in order to increase the confidence of my men.

Allow me to say, Herr Feldmarschall, that I regard your leadership as a guarantee that everything possible is being done to assist Sixth Army. For their own part, my commanders and gallant troops will join me in doing everything to justify your trust.

Yours, etc.

Paulus.

P.S.—In the circumstances I hope you will overlook the inadequacy of the paper and the fact that this letter is written by hand.

The Stalingrad Cauldron (Phase I) as seen from the air : extracts from the War Diary of Air Fleet 4 and the personal diary of General v. Richthofen, GOC-in-C, Air Fleet 4

20 *November*. Very bad weather. On the Don, the Russians, by and large, have made no more progress. Russian tanks are cruising about in the back areas behind the front. A German defensive front, manned by reserves and troops from Stalingrad, is being formed. The Air Force, too, is scraping the barrel and putting every available anti-aircraft and ground unit and everybody else it can find into the Don battle. V. R(ichthofen) says: 'I think that if we had a short period of fine weather and threw in everything we've got, we could smash this Russian effort to bits. . . . But fine weather we must have, if we are to save anything at all!'

21 *November*. Weather bad everywhere. No flying possible anywhere. Any effective intervention to help the defence is just not possible. This morning the Russians had already captured the bridge at Kalach, which is an absolutely vital link in Sixth Army's supply line. Not only was the bridge not destroyed, but it doesn't seem even as if any attempt was made to defend it! Sixth Army's left flank is being pushed further and further eastwards. They now don't think they will even be able to hold Kalach. Sixth Army seems to be havering and can't make up its mind one way or the other. They are

now talking of making a hedgehog between Stalingrad and the Don.
... The airfields in the Kalach area have been overrun by the
Russians, particularly those of the close support squadrons. From
2 Stuka Squadron only a small group got away. The fighters, under
Lieut Hitzschhold, just managed to get off the ground at the very
last moment. ...

On the evening of 21 November, General Fiebig, commanding
VIII Anti-Aircraft Corps, telephoned to Sixth Army Commander
and his Chief of Staff at their Headquarters in Nizhne Chirskaya
and gave them a brief outline of the situation at Kalach. Schmidt
said: I do not see any immediate danger for the bridge. There are
ample protecting forces on the high ground near Kalach. The Army
Commander is thinking of forming a hedgehog. ...

General Fiebig then at once asked him how he thought the Army
could be supplied, now that its lines of communication had been
interrupted? 'By air,' replied Schmidt. To which Fiebig retorted,
with the Army Commander listening-in on a second telephone: 'To
supply a whole Army by air is quite impossible. We haven't the
requisite number of transport aircraft.'[1]

In his personal diary, General v. Richthofen noted on 21 November: 'Sixth Army expects to be supplied by the Air Fleet. We
have done our utmost to prove to them that this is not possible,
since we have not sufficient transport aircraft available. The same

[1] The above entry, from the words 'The Army Commander' to the end, is
underlined in the original. All General Schmidt's arguments about supply
by air were based on the idea that, if Sixth Army was to avoid being, as Paulus
put it, 'stabbed in the back', it had no option but to assume a posture of all-
round defence and that, in that case, supply – by air and for a brief period –
would have to be organized. It is of interest to compare the above with an
appendix in General Fiebig's own diary, dated 26 January 1943. Writing of a
telephone conversation which he had with Paulus and Schmidt early on the
evening of 21 November, he says: Turning to the possibility of creating an all-
round defensive hedgehog, I asked how in that case they thought the Army could
be supplied, as its lines of communication would shortly be severed? General
Schmidt replied that supplies would have to be flown in. I explained to him
that I did not think it would be possible to supply a whole army by air, particularly
as heavy claims on our transport aircraft were being made to meet the situation
in North Africa. I warned him against being too optimistic in this respect.
General Paulus had listened to our conversation on a second telephone and had
himself intervened on one or two occasions.

arguments were repeated to the Commander-in-Chief of the Air
Force and to Army Headquarters and Army Group.[1] I spent the
whole night telephoning to Corps, to Jeschonnek, Meister (C of
Air Staff) and various others. . . .'

22 *November.* This morning a conference was held at Sixth Army
Headquarters with General Hoth, Fourth Panzer Army, at which
General Pickert (Commander, 9 Anti-Aircraft Division) was asked
by Sixth Army Chief of Staff what he thought should be done.
'There's only one thing to do,' replied Pickert, 'you must break out
at once south-westwards.' General Schmidt did not agree. 'We can't,'
he said, 'because we haven't got the necessary fuel. And if we tried
we should end up with a catastrophe like that of Napoleon.' Pickert
then offered Sixth Army his 160 2-cm guns, complete with gun teams
carrying their own ammunition. 'No – the Army is going into a
"hedgehog"! Its orders are to hang on to Stalingrad.' General
Pickert then retorted, as General Fiebig had done, that it would be
impossible to keep the whole army supplied by air, particularly in
winter. But General Schmidt refused to listen. '*You've just got to
do so,*' he retorted. 'And don't forget there are plenty of horses in
the cauldron, and we can eat them, too!'[2]

[1] It is clear today that General Paulus, his Chief of Staff and the GOC-in-C
Army Group 'B' all fully realized that Sixth Army could not be adequately
supplied by air for any considerable period of time. On the other hand, as
General Schmidt has with justice pointed out, limited, albeit inadequate supplies were, in fact, flown in over a short period. The real problem was not that of
supply by air, but that of relief by the ground forces.

[2] Once again, the following aspect must be emphasised: The basis of all the
deliberations of Paulus and his C of S was as follows: Regardless of whether the
Army later attempts to break out or stands fast and awaits relief, we have no
option, at the moment, but to organize an all-round defence position; and
for this phase, it is essential that we should be supplied by air. In this connection, both Paulus and Schmidt felt with justice that they could rely on
General v. Richthofen's energy and initiative – qualities to which the GOC-
in-C Air Fleet 4 had himself frequently laid claim and of which, indeed, he
had given ample proof in the past. It is unfortunate that in his book: *Die Luft-
waffe ringt um Stalingrad* Herhudt v. Rohden reproduces the diary entries in a
garbled, press reportage style which gives the impression that Sixth Army
was obsessed with the idea of a hedgehog defence, whereas in reality the Army
Commander and his Chief of Staff both wanted to fight their way out, though
not, admittedly, against the orders of the Chief of the General Staff and the
Army Group Commander.

23 *November*. Weather on the Donets a little better, but still poor in the areas where the enemy has broken through, so that only a few sorties can be flown and we can still get no clear picture of the situation as a whole. A few supplies were flown in to Sixth Army and Fourth Panzer Army. V. R(ichthofen) describes the position in the following terms: 'By and large, the general picture confirms that, after their success in breaking through both Rumanian Armies, which came as a surprise to them, the Russians are now turning everything they have against the Stalingrad cauldron, with the object of destroying the forces in it and freeing the Volga. The remaining Russian troops wandering about the countryside are in weak groups and engaged in nothing more than probing tactics. VI Rumanian Army Corps, which had been given a large sector to hold, has proved to be a broken reed – a bad show.'

Colonel Stahel's 2 Ground Combat Group, which is being raised midway between the Don and the Donets, has been given the task of freeing and holding the railway running eastwards as far as the Don; it consists of ground personnel of Air District VIII (Rostov), two sections of tanks and odds and ends of German and Rumanian troops, who have become separated from their units. V. R(ichthofen) says: 'If this succeeds, it may well pave the way for the creation of a corridor into the Stalingrad cauldron itself.'

24 *November*. Weather in the Stalingrad-Don area a little more favourable. All formations have been sent off on sorties against Russian transport columns and troop concentrations. A few isolated tanks destroyed. Russians again suffered bloody losses. Russian fighters are interfering very seriously with the supply air lift. We have been forced to station some of our fighters in Stalingrad itself; and there, of course, their own needs have to be met from the supplies flown in for Sixth Army. We have not managed to master the Russian fighters completely, and, of course, the Russians are able to attack our forward airfields any time they like. The situation on the ground, as v. R(ichthofen) sees it, is: 'It seems highly improbable that Sixth Army will be able to hold the fronts of its cauldron and quite out of the question that we shall be able to fly in enough supplies even to maintain the Army's present fighting strength, let alone increase it. Consequently, I feel that if the Army is given orders *now* to fight its way out westwards, it would probably be able

l Field-Marshal v. Bock, Supreme Commander of Army Group, South;
r Col v. Huenersdorff, commanding officer of 11 Panzer Regiment

On the steppe before Stalingrad (Paulus centre)

Bombed bridge over the Don

Inside Stalingrad

A SECOND VERDUN

to do so; but if the order is delayed, with its fighting power proportionately decreased, the Army's chances of success will be very much less rosy. . . .'

25 *November*. All our JUs employed today in flying in supplies. But we now have only thirty of them left. Of yesterday's forty-seven, twenty-two were lost, and today another nine were shot down. We have thus been able to fly in only 75 tons, instead of the 300 tons as directed from above. We simply have not got the transport aircraft to do it.

v. R(ichthofen) says: 'For six weeks the Sixth Army will have to carry on as best it can. How we can possibly be expected to supply it by air is a complete mystery to me. Since, as a result of the contraction of its bridge-head over the Don, the Sixth Army cannot now break out from the northern corner of the cauldron, the only remaining possibility is a thrust south-westwards. The Fuehrer is against this. I again made urgent representations to Jeschonnek and Zeitzler in this sense. We must, I said, maintain the fighting strength of Sixth Army, even at the cost of heavy material losses, and the Army must at once fight its way out! Weichs has been saying the same thing until he's tired of the sound of his own voice. I urged Jeschonnek and Zeitzler to submit this appreciation of mine to the Fuehrer and to co-opt the Reichsmarschall in support. But he's in Paris. . . . Whether anything will come of it, goodness knows!'

I (i.e. the officer responsible for maintaining the War Diary) have taken the following extract from notes made by v. R(ichthofen): 'Report in above sense submitted to Fuehrer. Latter listened to what was said and then decided against the recommendation, because he believes that the Army can hold out, but that if we once leave Stalingrad we'll never get it back again. I disagree. But orders are orders, and we'll do our best to carry them out. The tragedy is that no local commander on the spot, even of those who enjoy the Fuehrer's confidence, can any longer exercise any influence. As things are, we commanders – from the operational point of view – are now nothing more than highly paid NCOs!'

*The Stalingrad Cauldron (Phase I) : as seen
through the eyes of our allies*

The Destruction of the 'Lascar Group'. Documents

Secret   Headquarters,
                                          German Mil. Mission, Rumania.
No. Ia. Nr. 1682/42.   22 November 1942
Subject: Conference between General Steflea and General Hauffe,
            22 November 1942, 0820–0900 hours.
            Minute for file.

General Steflea stated that the Lascar Group had been called upon to surrender, but had refused. Arrangements were in hand to supply the group by air. He suggested that 62 Division should be brought forward as quickly as possible.

General Hauffe replied that the advanced elements of the leading regiment of 2 Division had arrived today. The situation, he said, was undoubtedly serious. But the essential thing now was to maintain one's own confidence and thus preserve the morale of the troops themselves. It was not now German and Rumanian military honour alone that was at stake; there were other, very grave, issues – the fate of the Sixth Army, of the Fourth Panzer Army and of Stalingrad itself was also involved. The main point was not that an isolated military formation should be rescued, but that German and Rumanian troops should stand and fight where they had been ordered so to do. General Hauffe therefore requested General Steflea to use his influence and bring this aspect to the attention of both Third and Fourth Rumanian Armies and Rumanian Supreme Headquarters, and thus to ensure that an exemplary attitude adopted by all concerned would lead to both a moral and practical mastering of the situation. He had, he said, already addressed the German Military Mission in this sense two days ago.

Retreat without orders by individual formations must be prevented, in order to guard against panic. Stragglers must be collected and led back to the front by officers determined to do their duty. General Hauffe further suggested that all available officers should be sent to the help of the Rumanian Armies and said that with this in view he had himself closely combed through the Staff of the German Military Mission.

General Steflea reported that he had already ordered an inquiry to be held in all cases where a breakdown had occurred. Steps to collect and reorganize stragglers were already in hand. It was hoped that all stragglers would be stopped at the latest at the Donets, where frontier guard battalions and Staff Officers from Rumanian Supreme Headquarters were in charge of arrangements. He added that the only stragglers so far had all been from supply units. . . .

In the name of Marshal Antonescu he had issued an order to the Rumanian forces to co-operate in every way with the German military authorities and to hold their positions at all costs. He would, however, bring the points mentioned by General Hauffe once again to the attention of the Rumanian forces.

General Hauffe suggested that something also might be done to sustain the morale of the Lascar Group – perhaps by awarding decorations in the name of the Marshal – and that perhaps the Marshal himself might pay a brief visit to the front as an encouragement to his troops. General Steflea replied that, in view of the Fuehrer's letter to the Marshal, that, unfortunately, would not be possible, but that the War Minister, on the other hand, was arriving that day.

Bartsch, Major,
General Staff.

Distribution:
Copy No. 1 General.
   ,,   ,,   2 Ia.
   ,,   ,,   3 War Diary.

TELEGRAM FROM
THE CONDUCATORUL, MARSHAL ANTONESCU
TO
THE FUEHRER AND SUPREME COMMANDER, THE ARMED
FORCES
22 NOVEMBER 1942

To Colonel Jon Gheorghe.[1] Please pass on the following to German Supreme Headquarters for immediate submission to the Fuehrer, Adolf Hitler:

[1] The Rumanian Military Attaché in Berlin.

(1) According to reports received from the Rumanian General Staff, with whom I have been in contact throughout the day, it is obvious that the Third Rumanian Army is in a very serious situation and has no more reserves available.

(2) We have noted that four major German formations had already reached the Rumanian sector by 18 November. But I have been informed that these will not be able to intervene in the battle before 28–30 November. This means that Third Rumanian Army will have to hold out for another 6–8 days, and that, in my opinion, is quite impossible.

(3) General Lascar, commanding a group of four divisions which has been surrounded, reports that he has no ammunition, although supplies had been promised to him, and that if he is to try to fight his way out with any prospect of success, he must do so forthwith. He has, however, received orders from Army Group 'B' to hold on and now requests direct orders from me.

(4) I have refused to issue any orders supplementary to those already issued by the responsible authority in the field.

(5) In view of the situation described and of the long delay before the troops concentrated for the purpose can intervene, I should prefer to see General Lascar pull out and join forces with 1 Armoured Division and 22 German Panzer Division and such other units as still remain in existence, and form a group to hold the line at present being held by 22 Panzer Division, until the relief promised by the four major formations mentioned above materializes. If this is not done, the Lascar Group – since any effective replenishment of its ammunition and supplies is not possible – may well be destroyed *in situ*, before German help arrives.

(6) I am putting forward this suggestion, not because the situation causes me anxiety, but because of my political responsibility to my country and because I quite rightly do not wish to sacrifice the Third Rumanian Army, which I should never be able to replace. I therefore request the Fuehrer to take these facts into consideration in making his decision.

TELEGRAM FROM THE FUEHRER, ADOLF HITLER
TO
THE CONDUCATORUL, MARSHAL ANTONESCU

23 November 1942. 1000 hours. (Eastern European Time.)

Your Excellency,

When, on the night of 22/23 November, I received the news that 1 Rumanian Armoured Division had with a brilliant attack joined forces with 22 Panzer Division, I at once and before receipt of your Excellency's telegram, gave orders that the Lascar Group was to exploit this avenue which had been cleared for it and fight its way out southwards, in order to join forces with XXXXVIII Panzer Corps. I am convinced that the Lascar Group, the commander of which has shown himself to be a soldier of exemplary merit, will succeed in doing so. The Sixth Army will stand fast, and the divisions advancing from the west will, in conjunction with I Rumanian Corps, strike at the deeply extended flank of the enemy. I am also convinced that, as has happened so often before in this campaign against Soviet Russia, superior leadership and finer troops will once again triumph over initial enemy success. I would be most grateful if this conviction of mine could be conveyed to your commanders as an encouragement. The exemplary conduct of General Lascar has commanded my particular appreciation. In recognition of his outstanding services, I yesterday awarded him, the first allied officer to be so decorated, the Oak Leaves to the Knights' Cross of the Iron Cross.

> With my sincere good wishes and respects,
> Adolf Hitler.

CONFLICT WITH GENERAL STEFLEA
Chief of the Royal Rumanian General Staff

Secret.   Headquarters,
No. Ia Nr1/706/42   German Military Mission Rumania.
(Four copies)   25 November 1942
Copy No. 2

Subject: Note, for file, on a conference with the Rumanian Chief of Staff, 23 November, 2100 hours.

On the evening of 23 November I had my usual conference with General Steflea, the Chief of the Rumanian General Staff. General Pantazi, the Rumanian Defence Minister, who happened to be in Rostov, a number of other Rumanian Staff Officers and Colonel Zoeller and Major Bartsch were also present.

The conference opened on a friendly note. I first of all read out Marshal Antonescu's telegram of 22 November, in which the Marshal leaves the decision regarding the Lascar Group to the Fuehrer, and the latter's telegram in reply. (Copies of both these telegrams are attached to this memorandum.) I concluded by saying that these two great historical figures had given further proof of the mutual esteem in which they held each other, and I congratulated the Rumanian Army on the award of the Oak Leaves to General Lascar.

There followed a brief report on the situation of Third and Fourth Rumanian Armies, in which, I said, a slight easing of Third Army's position had become apparent. Some elements of the Lascar Group had set off to effect a junction with XXXXVIII Panzer Corps. I then made a brief reference to the operational value of the Lascar Group.

At this point, General Steflea, with whom for the past ten months and more I have been working harmoniously, intervened and declared in an exceptionally agitated tone:

'The order to the Lascar Group to fight its way out was issued too late. I asked for sanction of this move on the morning of 21 November, but my request was rejected by the Fuehrer. On the afternoon of 21 November I directed General Lascar to make all necessary preparations for an attempted break-out. On 22nd this would still have been possible, but by the 23rd it was too late. General Lascar has probably been killed without having heard that permission to break-out had been granted. The Rumanian Air Force officer, who yesterday landed at General Lascar's battle headquarters, today saw nothing but burning houses and Rumanian corpses. The order to fight their way out could not have been known to the units of the Lascar Group, and the 120 officers, 140 NCOs and 2,000 men who have broken out will therefore be tried by court-martial. The delay in sanctioning the break-out has been responsible for the loss of four Rumanian divisions.

'All the warnings which I have for weeks been giving to the German military authorities – to Supreme Command, to General v. Weichs and General Hoth and the Head of the German Military Mission – have passed unheeded. My warnings that the Rumanian forces had been allotted too broad a front have all been in vain, and, in fact, the enemy has succeeded in breaching the line only at those points where battalions have been called upon to hold a five- or six-kilometre front. I wanted to hold the 7 Rumanian Division in reserve, and I protested against the Third Army being called upon to hold so broad a sector of the front. I repeated my warnings to Fourth Panzer Army. Of the three divisions of the Fourth Rumanian Army there are now only three battalions left, and the whole of their equipment has been lost. I warned General Hoth on all these points in good time, when he visited the Rumanian forces.' (Here he once more repeated his oft enunciated theory of defence, namely, to hold the front thinly, to withdraw in the face of attack and then to destroy the enemy with a counter-stroke.)

'For four days,' General Steflea continued, '4 Rumanian Armoured Division remained without fuel, having been forced to surrender some of its reserve fuel to the German 22 Panzer Division. As a result, the Rumanian division lost most of its vehicles, including thirty-five tanks. No contact with the Heim Group was established, the Russians having succeeded in misleading the Rumanians with bogus wireless signals. The anti-tank guns with the Lascar Group were ineffective against enemy heavy tanks, even at a range of five metres. German Army Headquarters failed to meet Rumanian requirements, and that is the reason why two Rumanian armies have been destroyed.'

I listened to this agitated speech without interrupting, and then I said quietly: 'I take note of your statement and will pass on your complaints to Army Headquarters.'

If the responsible German military authorities had been unable to meet Rumanian requirements, I said, there had been important reasons for their failure to do so, and these had been explained to him or to his Staff. If General Lascar had fallen, then a gallant Rumanian General had fallen in the execution of a vital task and in the midst of his men, and we German soldiers would always remember him, the first of our allies to be awarded the Oak Leaves, with affection and high soldierly esteem. The Rumanian Armoured Division and the elements of the Lascar Group had fought with great gallantry, I said; whether all the Rumanian divisions had emulated their example, only the history of the war would reveal.

There were two points in his remarks upon which I said I would like to comment:

(1) The Rumanian defensive concept, namely, on principle to hold the front line thinly, to withdraw in the face of attack and then to halt the enemy with a counter-attack was not a concept that was acceptable to German military thought. The conduct of defensive operations in the eastern theatre of war must conform to one, uniform pattern, applicable to all troops engaged in them, and in this respect the directions issued by the Fuehrer must be considered binding on both Marshal Antonescu and the Rumanian General Staff.

General Steflea here intervened to say that the Rumanian concept was more in the nature of a theory, to which Marshal Antonescu in particular subscribed.

'My second point,' I said, 'is this: You say yourself that on 21 November you issued orders to General Lascar to make all preparations for an attempted break-out southwards. This order may well have encouraged the troops under General Lascar's command to turn their whole thoughts to an effort to fight their way out, rather than to hold on at all costs. It can, I suggest, also be regarded as an interference with the plans of those responsible for the conduct of operations, namely, Army Group "B", which, of course, has not yet been placed under the command of "Don Staff".'

This latter point caused General Steflea considerable embarrassment. The cipher instructions, he said, had been addressed to General Lascar personally.

To this I retorted that the contents of the signal must, nevertheless, have been known to a considerable number of Rumanian soldiers. General Steflea emphasized that he had never deliberately interfered in questions affecting the conduct of operations, though he had sometimes found it difficult to refrain from doing so. As regards permission for the Lascar Group to fight its way out, he had appealed to Marshal Antonescu only after all his other representations had been rejected. Permission had ultimately been given on the Marshal's recommendation; but by then it was too late.

I expressed regret that, after what had happened, we should be quarrelling about who was to blame and who was not, instead of making a determined and joint effort to give all the help we could. General Steflea replied that he was not concerned with apportioning blame, but had felt that he had to give expression to the pain which the failure of all his efforts had caused him. I repeated that all the German authorities had done, and were still doing, all they could to render every possible assistance to the Rumanian Army. I reminded him that I had consistently advocated the assumption of command by Marshal Antonescu, for, as he well knew, the primary task for which the German Military Mission had been created had been to stand at his side and render such help as he required. To this General Steflea made no reply.

I closed the discussion with an emphatic request – quoting one specific case – that every possible means should be adopted to bring the movement of Rumanian formations to the rear to a halt. This, General Steflea assured me, would be done.

(signed) Hauffe.

Distribution:
Copy No. 1 Lt-General Rotkirch.[1]
  ,,   ,, 2 General Hauffe.
  ,,   ,, 3 Chief of the General Staff (for War Diary).
  ,,   ,, 4 Destroyed on 26 November 1942.

---

[1] The Commander of the security and lines of communication troops, Don area.

6. The Stalingrad Cauldron (Phase II) : break out or sacrifice ? 12 December 1942 - 2 February 1943

(*Vide* Sketch Maps 6 and 7)

....

Introduction

'I stand and fight – those are my orders!'

That is one of the few sentences which can with some certainty be said to have figured in the last letter which General Paulus wrote to his wife, but which has not been preserved.[1] It was written shortly before he was promoted to Field-Marshal and shortly before the end came; and it was sent by one of the last aircraft to fly out of the cauldron. It shows that to the very end Paulus felt that it was his bounden duty to obey orders.

Unlike the first phase in November, this second phase of the great battle in the wintry Steppes between the Volga and the Don and in the ruins of the Great Russian industrial metropolis leaves unanswered the question of whether obedience to orders or obedience to the dictates of his conscience was the overriding consideration in Paulus' mind. This was no political problem, such as had confronted General v. Yorck at Tauroggen in 1812. This was a purely military problem and a question of soldierly ethics.[2]

[1] Presumed to have been destroyed by Frau Paulus when she was arrested by the Gestapo in November 1944.

[2] Cf. the biographical introduction. Vide also General Pickert's diary, 27/28 November. Therein he states that on 27 November he flew at Paulus' request, to see v. Manstein and v. Richthofen, to try to 'ginger up' the air supplies. When he returned on the evening of 28 November he told Paulus that on the previous evening v. Manstein expressed the opinion that an attempt to break out, under enemy pressure or as the result of enemy pressure, would lead to a complete catastrophe, and that therefore he need say no more on the subject. Only operations co-ordinated with those of the forces advancing to the relief, he had added, held out any prospect of ultimate success.

According to an appreciation of the situation sent by Field-Marshal v. Manstein to the Chief of the General Staff on 9 December,[1] the 'Stalingrad fortress area' was surrounded by Twenty-First, Twenty-Fourth, Fifty-Seventh, Sixty-Second, Sixty-Fourth, Sixty-Fifth and Sixty-Sixth Soviet Armies. These, according to German calculations, totalled some forty-four infantry divisions, seventeen independent infantry brigades, twenty-nine armoured brigades and twelve motorized brigades. To the south-west, opposite the German-Rumanian front on the Chir, the encircling ring was protected by the Fifth Soviet Tank Army, which consisted of seventeen infantry divisions, five cavalry divisions and two motorized cavalry brigades, eight armoured brigades and three motorized brigades. To the south, east of the Don, protection was furnished by the Fifty-First Soviet Army, with four infantry and four cavalry divisions, two armoured brigades, one motorized and one independent infantry brigade. In addition in this area there was an unspecified number of additional motorized formations.

Supply by air from the two great air bases at Tatsinskaya and Morozovsk, 240 and 200 kilometres west of Stalingrad respectively, had, as had been anticipated, proved to be inadequate, in spite of all the efforts of German Air Transport Command and the Supply Officer, General Cargunico, who at the start had some 320 aircraft at his disposal. Initially, Sixth Army had asked for a daily lift of 500 tons, but this was later reduced to 300 tons. In practice, however, only on very rare occasions was a maximum lift of about 300 tons achieved, and the daily average was 97.3 tons for the period 1–12 December, and 137.7 tons for 12–31 December. After that the average sank steadily, while Sixth Army stood more in need of additional supplies than ever.

The plan for the relief of Sixth Army in December envisaged simultaneous advances by relieving forces from two directions. From the Chir, elements of XXXXVIII Panzer Corps were to thrust eastwards, while from the south, from the Kotel'nikovo area, General Hoth's Army Group (Fourth Panzer Army and what remained of Fourth Rumanian Army, together with additional Panzer forces) was to advance on Stalingrad. General Hoth's orders were to move east of the Don and, taking the shortest

[1] This appreciation is given in full in Manstein: *Lost Victories*, Appendix II.

possible route, make contact with Sixth Army. Army Group Don's orders, based on Hitler's directive, ran: 'The Sixth Army will be relieved, but will continue to hold the Volga "pivot", with a view to future operations in 1943.'

General Hoth himself, however, felt that Sixth Army would have to advance some distance to meet him. With the object of enabling the armoured and mobile forces inside the cauldron to do so, he planned, as soon as his relieving forces were near enough, to send a lorry convoy with fuel, escorted by armour and moving under cover of darkness, to burst its way through into the cauldron.

In his appreciation mentioned above, Field-Marshal v. Manstein had already recommended that Sixth Army should not be left in the Stalingrad area for the rest of the winter, but should be 'pulled out' as soon as contact with the relieving forces had been established. There was, then, a possibility of two separate operations merging into one: Operation 'Wintergewitter', the relieving thrust on Stalingrad, and Operation 'Donnerschlag', the break-out by the whole of Sixth Army and its incorporation in the new German southern front that was in painful process of being created.

From the outset it very soon became obvious that the armoured forces on the Chir would be quite unable to take part in the relieving operations – a possible contingency of which v. Manstein had issued a warning on 9 December. They were, in fact, tied down in heavy defensive fighting. The carrying out of Operation 'Wintergewitter' had therefore to be left to Hoth's Army Group alone. As the main spearhead of its attack it had at its disposal the LVII Panzer Corps (General Kirchner), which consisted of the battle-worn 23 Panzer Division with thirty tanks and transferred from Army Group 'A' in the Caucasus, and the 6 Panzer Division, newly arrived from France and at full strength with 160 tanks and forty assault guns – a truly welcome reinforcement. Later, 17 Panzer Division, another division well equipped and at full strength, was placed at Hoth's disposal. At the start, however, he only had two Panzer divisions with which to carry out a relief operation involving an advance of 120 kilometres, in the course of which he would have to break through strong and well prepared enemy forces!

In Stalingrad, a force, composed of the only sixty tanks available,

MAP 6

was concentrated under General Hube in the southern sector of the cauldron, in readiness to break out and effect a junction with Hoth when the opportunity occurred. This force, however, was, of course, greatly handicapped, as far as its mobility was concerned, by lack of fuel. It could advance perhaps 20 or 30 kilometres, but no more. Then again, it had to keep in hand enough fuel, should the attempt to break out end in failure, to enable it to return into the cauldron, where the tanks would be urgently needed in a defensive artillery role. For a 'real' break-out to the south-west Sixth Army calculated that it would require an additional 1,000 tons of fuel, ammunition and rations. It was further considered that to carry out the requisite reliefs, re-grouping and measures to deceive the enemy – in a cauldron that measured about 40 kilometres in diameter – some five days would be required, before the Army would be ready to move.

On 12 December Hoth's attack was launched. A week later, on 19 December, the decisive hours for Sixth Army began. The 6 and 23 Panzer Divisions, reinforced by 17 Panzer Division, the arrival of which had been delayed, thanks to Hitler's intervention,[1] had fought their way forward against exceptionally stiff resistance by the Soviet Fifty-First and Second Guard Armies across the Myshkova to within some 48 kilometres, as the crow flies, from the cauldron.

On the previous day, 18 December, although General Schulz, the Chief of Staff, and Colonel Busse, the GSOI, Operations, Army Group Don, had recently paid a visit into the cauldron to see the situation for themselves, Field-Marshal v. Manstein sent his Intelligence Officer, Major Eismann, on a mission to Sixth Army Headquarters. In his memoirs, v. Manstein attaches great importance to the Eismann mission. The Major's task was to explain Army Group's ideas to Sixth Army Commander, namely, that Operation 'Wintergewitter' should be regarded as the first step.[2] With decisions

---

[1] On Hitler's orders, this division, while in transit to Kotel'nikovo, was unloaded *en route* and initially sent to Army Group Don's left wing, there to be held in reserve, ready to launch a counter-attack against an anticipated major enemy offensive on the Don. v. Manstein considers that the holding back of this division contributed very greatly to the failure of Hoth's attack.

[2] Cf. v. Manstein, *Lost Victories*, pp. 332, et seq. v. Manstein directed

of such vital importance in the balance and with a second step in view which, in practice, would have amounted to a disobedience of the Fuehrer's directive, the question may well be asked why did the Field-Marshal not himelf fly in to Stalingrad? (The reason he gave for not doing so is given on page 75.)

Apart altogether from the Eismann mission, however, the fact remains that during these decisive days Sixth Army Headquarters felt that they had not been kept well informed either as regards Army Group Don's intentions or as regards the progress made by LVII Panzer Corps (upon which, of necessity, temporary wireless silence had been imposed).

At 1435 hours on 19 December v. Manstein sent a signal to Army Headquarters requesting permission to order the whole of Sixth Army to fight its way out – i.e. to initiate Operation 'Donnerschlag'.

On the same day, at 1800 hours, he sent a signal ordering Sixth Army to commence Operation 'Wintergewitter' as soon as possible. LVII Panzer Corps, said v. Manstein's signal, had reached the Myshkova sector. Sixth Army was to be ready to cross the Donskaya Tsaritsa, if need be, in order to ensure making contact with LVII Corps and taking over the fuel convoy destined for it. The further development of the situation might well necessitate an extension of Operation 'Wintergewitter' to include an advance by Sixth Army as far as the Myshkova. 'In that case, it is essential that Operation "Donnerschlag" should follow immediately upon

---

Eismann to urge Sixth Army to be prepared to regard both relief and break-out as potentially one continuous operation. v. Manstein regarded General Schmidt, the Chief of Staff, Sixth Army, as the principal opponent of the break-out idea. The latter, with every justification, contests this, though he admits that he was averse to any attempt to break out contrary to orders from Army Group and Supreme Headquarters – particularly as Sixth Army's mobility had been greatly reduced by the failure of the air lift to fly in the requisite additional supplies. On page 334 of *Lost Victories*, v. Manstein quotes Schmidt as saying 'Sixth Army will still be in position at Easter. All you people have to do is to supply it better.' This, says Schmidt, was, of course, only a figure of speech. During a discussion on the inadequacy of the supplies being flown in, he did, in fact, say something to the effect that if the Sixth Army were kept adequately supplied it could probably hold out till Easter.

Operation "Wintergewitter". This, however, will be implemented only on receipt of an express order: "Donnerschlag." [1]

Had the great hour now struck for the break-out – even though a few days must elapse while the necessary re-groupings in the cauldron were completed and even though lack of fuel and other supplies meant that the greater part of the Army's heavy equipment and all its hospitals would have to be abandoned to fall into enemy hands? Had the moment come for Sixth Army Commander, covered as far as the Fuehrer was concerned by this signal from one of the most highly esteemed of all the Field-Marshals, to act on his own responsibility and to justify his action by pointing out that the larger – and forbidden – operation had been forced upon him by the outcome of the smaller?

Manstein, who wrote his memoirs in 1955 and presumably had only some of his former files at his disposal for reference, confined himself to giving the order for Operation 'Wintergewitter', which he issued at 1800 hours on 19 December. In the meanwhile, however, it transpired that Army Headquarters, where Zeitzler was arguing in vain with Hitler,[2] was not prepared to accede to v. Manstein's request made at 1435 hours. At 1816 hours the Commander-in-Chief, Army Group Don, informed Sixth Army that the orders already given would remain in force. In reply to Paulus' query whether it would be possible to incorporate in Operation 'Wintergewitter' the corps standing by to launch 'Donnerschlag', v. Manstein replied: 'Wait until this evening's conference.'

The telephonic conference between Army Group and the Chief of Staff, Sixth Army, on the evening of 19 December brought but little consolation. Schmidt declared that any advance southwards over the

---

[1] The full texts of this signal and that mentioned in the immediately preceeding paragraph are published as Appendix III and IV in *Lost Victories*. Of interest, too, is the entry for 18 December in the diary of General Pickert (the Air Force General in the cauldron with Paulus): 'Sharp frost. Clear. Considerable enemy activity in the air. News of the advancing Panzer Army sounds good. Enemy withdrawing strong forces southwards from our front. What a pity we can't make a sortie and stop him! But we can't afford to make more than one sortie, though when it comes – as soon as the Panzer Army is near enough – it will be a decisive one.'

[2] Manstein, *Lost Victories*, p. 329, quotes Zeitzler as saying: 'Hitler does nothing but put spokes in our wheel.'

Donskaya Tsaritsa would not be possible, if the 'fortress' was still to be held. All that could be managed would be a short, forward thrust by armour. If the hold on Stalingrad was to be maintained, Sixth Army could not take any offensive action until the relieving LVII Corps had reached the vicinity of Buzinovka.

For the next few days the situation remained unchanged. Paulus, greatly though he was, in principle, in favour of Operation 'Donner-schlag', was not willing to act without clear orders from Army Group, possibly against the orders of Supreme Headquarters; and Army Group was unwilling to give the code signal 'Donnerschlag' without permission from Army Headquarters. And in the meanwhile a fresh catastrophe had occurred on the Don. The Eighth Italian Army had been overrun by strong Soviet forces, enemy tanks, probing deeply southwards, were threatening the two great air bases from which Stalingrad was being supplied and had approached to within 170 kilometres of Rostov. Manstein was forced to with-draw some Panzer forces from Hoth's command. All chance of the relief of Stalingrad had vanished. It was Christmas 1942.[1]

The student of military history will inevitably ask himself: For the sake of his Army, which was still a powerful fighting force which was hoping eagerly to be allowed to fight its way out and which would have fought like lions, should not Paulus have taken action, without asking Manstein or Hitler or anybody else? Particularly as v. Manstein, an officer of the old Prussian style, would almost certainly have supported his action? A Charles XII of Sweden would perhaps have done so; perhaps Field-Marshals v. Reichenau and Model, too, would have acted independently, employing in the process their usual tactics of reporting to Hitler that 'in anticipation of your concurrence, I have . . .'. That is exactly what v. Reichenau did in December 1941, when he withdrew Army Group South to the Mius against Hitler's orders. But Paulus, the painstaking, traditional soldier, who weighed every aspect thrice before reaching a decision, was a man of a different type.

Nor, indeed, is that the sole aspect. No one can say for certain

[1] Cf. General Pickert's diary, 19 December . . . 'If the Italians collapse like the Rumanians, not only will our own situation be hopeless, but the whole of the southern front, including the Caucasus, will collapse, too. Then – God help Germany!'

that an Army, whose heavy weapons and armour had become immobilized, would have succeeded in fighting its way out through an
encircling Soviet ring that had but recently received such strong
reinforcements, particularly of artillery. No one can be sure that, if
Sixth Army had succeeded in breaking out, it could at once have
been incorporated in a new front on the Myshkova or the river
Aksay. Nor can anyone judge how swiftly the Soviet Command
would have reacted – whether, with the vast number of divisions
thus freed from the Stalingrad front, the Russians would not have
made a complete switch and thrust in strength south-westwards to
the Sea of Azov, completely disintegrating the German southern
sector and cutting off Army Group 'A' in the Caucasus. Nor,
equally, can anyone say – and this, too, must be taken into consideration – how Hitler would have reacted. Would he not perhaps
have summarily dismissed Paulus and Schmidt in the middle of the
battle, placing General v. Seydlitz or some other General in command and thus rendering confusión worse confounded still?[1]

For the next four weeks and more, in view of the absolute necessity of reorganizing the German southern front and making
arrangements to cover the now unavoidable withdrawal of Army
Group 'A' from the Caucasus to the vicinity of Rostov, Sixth Army
had no alternative but to hang on in a situation which had now become desperate. The sin was not that this or that opportunity of
breaking out had been missed, but that the original plan for the
approach march in July 1942 had been so completely bungled. As a
result, General Paulus and his Army were drawn into the vortex of
events and one of the most efficient experts of the old, traditional
General Staff type was deprived of any opportunity of exercising his
operational skill. And now, let General Paulus continue the story.

Walter Goerlitz

[1] In a letter to Captain E. A. Paulus, dated 24 February 1959, General
Hoth, Commander, Fourth Panzer Army, gives it as his opinion that between
19 and 23 December it was Sixth Army's duty to try to fight its way out. The
undue importance attached to the fuel situation, he asserts, had fatal consequences. The decisive point, he says, was not how far Sixth Army could get,
but the vital need to smash the Soviet encircling ring. Major v. Zitzewitz, Army
Headquarters Liaison Officer with Sixth Army, affirms that Paulus was in
favour of a break-out and mentions a telephone conversation of his own with
AHQ, in which he said: 'Do you people intend to leave us here to rot?'

The basic facts of the Sixth Army's operations at Stalingrad (Phase II) by Field-Marshal Friedrich Paulus

(*Vide* Phase I, page 215)

On 12 December 1942 Fourth Panzer Army[1] began its attack from the Kotel'nikovo area. It succeeded in reaching a point within 50 kilometres of the south-western front of the cauldron, where it first came to a halt and then had to retire. My repeated and urgent requests to be allowed to break out and meet Fourth Army, or, alternatively, to follow it in its retreat (which, of course, would have entailed the abandonment of the Volga front) were rejected by Army Headquarters.[2]

By the end of December, it was clear that the attempt to relieve Sixth Army had failed. At that time, my Army was still capable of fighting – to a limited degree and for a limited period. The causes of our loss of fighting efficiency were the steady stream of casualties and the increasing exhaustion of the troops as the result of shortage of rations. At this juncture, it was still possible to fly out the wounded. For our inability to conduct normal, full-scale operations lack of fuel supplies was primarily responsible. For both these reasons I submitted urgent demands to Army Group and Army Headquarters for an immediate and massive increase of the supplies of fuel, food and ammunition (in that order) that were being flown in by air, emphasizing at the same time that these were essential, if it were later decided that the Army should fight its way out.

At the same time I issued fresh orders to my Corps Commanders

[1] At the outset the relieving force consisted of: 6 Panzer Division, at full strength (General Raus), 23 Panzer Division, under strength and battle-worn (General v. Vormann), and VI and VII Corps of the Fourth Rumanian Army. The Rumanian 'Popescu Cavalry Corps' (5 and 8 Rumanian Cavalry Divisions) was detailed to protect the flank of the main attack by LVII Panzer Corps.

[2] Here the Field-Marshal is over-simplifying very greatly. The problem was how to make 'Wintergewitter' and 'Donnerschlag' – two separate operations with different objectives – merge into one single operation. Vide pp. 273 et seq. At this juncture Paulus' requests were being addressed to Army Group rather than to Army Headquarters.

to make preparations for a break-out, with the infantry divisions linked to the six motorized and Panzer divisions. As at that time we had an exceptionally large number of motor vehicles at our disposal, it would have been quite possible to put the mass of the infantry – including their wounded – on a mobile footing. We still had more than 200 tanks. (Note by author: he had only sixty!) The one essential was that enough fuel for an 80 kilometre move should be flown in to us.

Army Group's answer was that Sixth Army was to stand fast and at all costs to hold the Volga front, that measures were in hand for the launching of a fresh relieving operation, for which powerful Panzer forces were being concentrated from all the other fronts and that arrangements had also been initiated for an air-lift on a major scale (Air Transport Fleet).[1]

On 1 January 1943, we received a signal from Hitler which ran more or less as follows: 'Every man of the Sixth Army can start the New Year with the absolute conviction that the Fuehrer will not leave his heroic soldiers on the Volga in the lurch and that Germany can and will find the means to relieve them.'

III. General Hube's Mission

On 8 January, the Red Army dropped leaflets from the air containing an ultimatum. At that time the fronts of the cauldron were all still intact. I told my Corps Commanders that there was no question of capitulation; and I should add that not one of them had ever mentioned such a possibility.

The deciding factors which led to the rejection of the ultimatum were not only the orders issued by higher authority, but also and, indeed, primarily the report brought back by General Hube regarding Supreme Command's intentions.[2]

General Hube brought back with him details of Army Head-

[1] On 15 January Field-Marshal Milch was given plenipotentiary powers by Hitler and placed in charge of the Stalingrad air lift.

[2] An SS Corps was, in fact, in readiness – but too late. General Hube arrived at Fuehrer Headquarters on 29 December. The plan, he was told, was to send the SS Panzer Corps, consisting of the fully-equipped 'Leibstandarte Adolf Hitler' and 'Das Reich' Panzer Divisions, to relieve Stalingrad. Hitler, however, did not ask how long Sixth Army could hold out, but simply said that it must do so.

quarters' new relief operations, which were to be launched from the west. From western Europe, from Germany itself and from all the other fronts the movement of Panzer and motorized formations, he said, was already in progress. Supplies by air were being reorganized on an entirely new and broader basis. Like the winter crisis of 1941–2 at Kharkov, the battle of Stalingrad, Hube was convinced, would be transformed into a great victory.

Thus, while previously the relief of the Sixth Army had been the foremost objective, now two further major aspects were being emphasized: continued resistance by Sixth Army was an essential prerequisite to the creation of a new front in the southern sector of the eastern theatre of war; and coupled with it, a new major offensive was under consideration.

Thanks to Hitler's instructions regarding the maintenance of secrecy, I had not been put in the picture either as regards the detailed situation in the middle and lower Don areas, or as regards the strength of the reserves said to be standing by, in readiness to attack. All I was told was the bald fact that Army Group 'A' had started to withdraw from the Caucasus on 1 January. General Hube's report and a statement in the same vein made by the Army Group Commander[1] placed upon me the obligation to hold out at all costs – or to be prepared to accept responsibility, *vis à vis* not only Supreme Command, but also the whole of the German people, for the collapse of the southern sector and with it the disintegration of the whole of the eastern front. That was my view, and that was the view which I expressed to the General Officers under my command.

As the stabilization of the southern sector had not yet been achieved, I became even more convinced that any premature disengagement, which would set free six enemy armies and at the same time leave the Stalingrad-Tikhoretsk railway, of such vital importance to him, in enemy hands, would have gravely jeopardized both the creation of a new German front and the withdrawal of Army Group 'A' from the Caucasus.[2]

[1] i.e. Field-Marshal v. Manstein. In *Lost Victories*, pp. 352 et seq. (Methuen), he describes how greatly impressed General Hube, who had given Hitler an unvarnished picture of Sixth Army's position, had been with Hitler's assurances that the Army would be relieved and that the air lift would be increased.

[2] As far as Sixth Army is concerned, once the attempt at relief had been

IV. Defence of the cauldron against the main Russian attack

On 10 January, the approximate date expected by Sixth Army, the Russian main attack began. By 13 January the western front had been pushed back to the valley of the Rossoshka, which, together with the Pitomnik airfield, fell into enemy hands on 15 January.

Two small, subsidiary airstrips near Gumrak still remained available, and these, according to the Air Force, would enable supplies still to be flown in. By 17 January the cauldron had been reduced to half its original size. The battle, when due consideration is given to the physical condition of the troops, can be said to have been conducted so far according to plan. Moreover, the apparatus of command was still intact.

Nevertheless, thanks to the ever increasing want and to the fears engendered by the thought of captivity, the Army began to exhibit symptoms of a psychosis of increasing severity. As far as captivity was concerned, we had all, leaders and men alike, fallen victims to the voice of propaganda. It is this, I think, that was responsible for the wording of the unfortunate Army Order issued on 20 January. In addition to an appeal to stand together as comrades in arms and not to desert, the order contained a warning against the uncertainties of captivity, which held promise of nothing but death from starvation or cold, or life as a prisoner under deplorable and degrading conditions.[1]

Prior to this, individual staffs (LI Army Corps and XIV Panzer Corps) had submitted requests for permission to break out in groups westwards, south-westwards and southwards. The idea behind the request was to save as many men as possible from captivity. After earnest consideration I came to the conclusion that the suggestion was not a practical one and for this reason, and especially out of consideration for the wounded who could not be moved, I felt obliged to reject it.

---

abandoned – an absolutely correct appreciation of the situation. But this does not alter the fact that it was faulty planning by Supreme Headquarters that had landed Sixth Army in this situation. Anyone who fails to draw a sharp distinction here between cause and effect will never arrive at a correct appreciation either of the situation as a whole or of Sixth Army's situation in particular.

[1] When the Field-Marshal wrote these notes, he obviously had no idea of the fate that had befallen the German prisoners of war in the USSR.

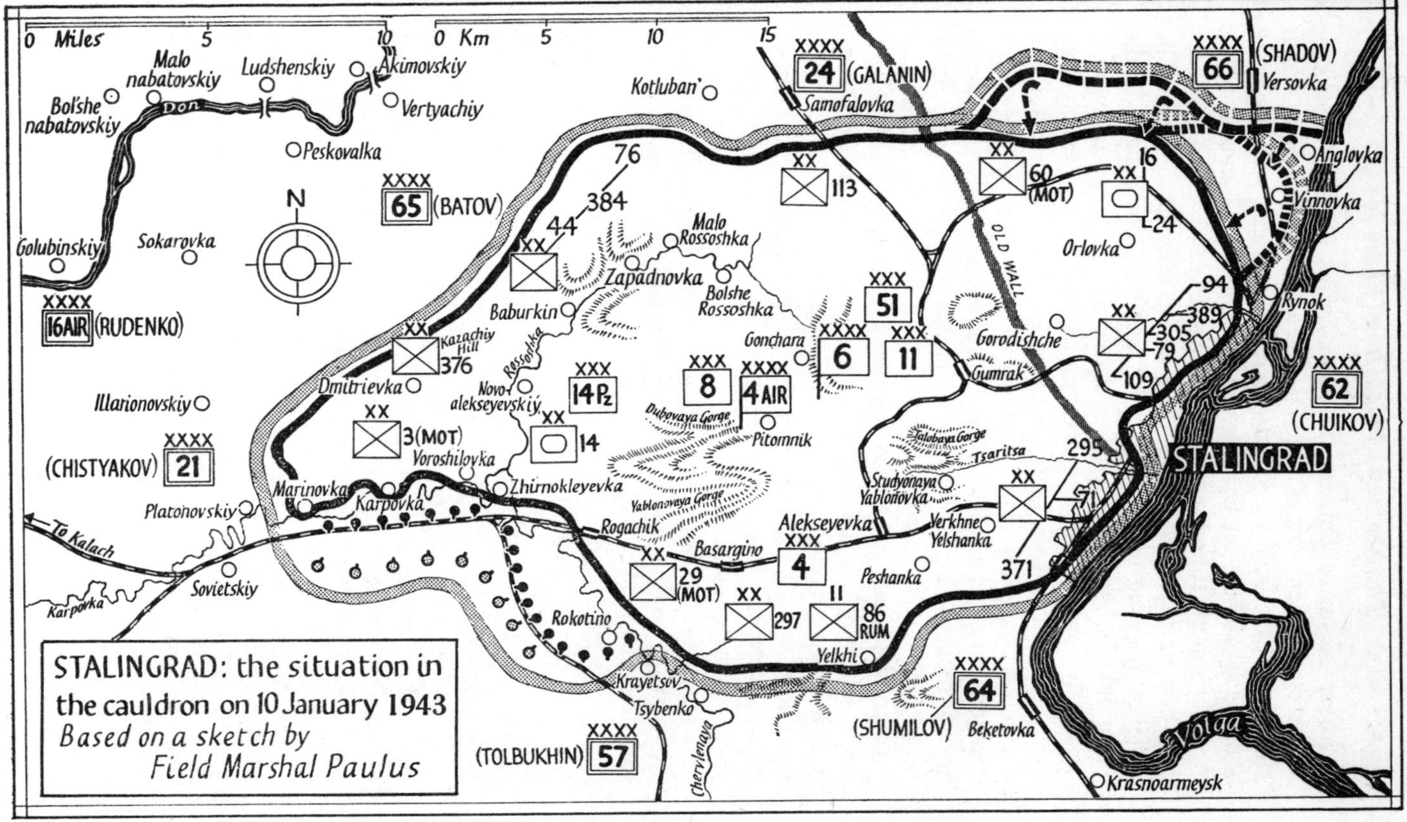

MAP 7

STALINGRAD: the situation in
the cauldron on 10 January 1943
Based on a sketch by
Field Marshal Paulus

About 19 or 20 January, numerous signs of disintegration – understandable in view of the suffering and deprivations to which the troops have been subjected – became apparent, particularly in those sectors where the fighting was fiercest.[1] This I knew not only from the reports submitted to me, but also from what I saw with my own eyes on my all but daily tours of the main battle areas. The suffering imposed upon my men by long weeks of hunger, in the bitter cold and without a roof over their heads, made an ever increasingly burdensome impression on me, and I felt it was my duty once again to approach higher authority, and on 20 January I sent the following signal simultaneously to Army Group and Army Headquarters: 'As a result of the catastrophical supply situation as regards food, fuel and ammunition, the fighting capacity of my Army is sinking rapidly. I have 16,000 wounded unprovided for. Except on the Volga front, we have no prepared positions, no living shelters, no wood. Signs of disintegration are becoming increasingly apparent. I again request liberty of action and permission to conduct operations as I see fit, and when operations no longer possible, to take such steps as I can to ensure attention for the wounded and to avoid complete annihilation.'[1]

A report on the same lines but with more detailed information was sent by hand of Army Headquarters Liason Officer, who left the cauldron by air.[2]

Army Headquarters' reply was in the following terms: 'Capitulation out of the question. Your Army is fulfilling an historical function by holding out to the last and thus making possible the creation of a new front in Rostov area and the withdrawal of Army Group from Caucasus.'

On 21 or 22 January the Commodore of an Air Transport unit reported his arrival at my Headquarters, saying that he had come to see what the situation was inside the cauldron. He told me that his unit had been transferred from the Mediterranean to Rostov and

---

[1] On the great value of Sixth Army's resistance vide v. Manstein, *Lost Victories*, pp. 362, et seq.

[2] i.e. Major v. Zitzewitz, who states that he flew out on the evening of 20 January. On the 21st he saw Field-Marshal v. Manstein, who advocated surrender by Sixth Army. On the 22nd he submitted his report to Hitler in his Wolfsschanze headquarters.

was ready to go into action. He said that with one daily sortie he could fly in far more than 300 tons, that he already had over 100 aircraft, some of them the latest giant model, and that another 100 were on the way to join him. He was too late. The next day the last of our airfields fell into enemy hands. . . .

Report by Major Thiel, Commander III Bomber Group 27, on his visit to General Paulus on 19 January 1943

Extract from the diary of Field-Marshal Milch, Director, Air Transport operations, Stalingrad

20 January. 1605. Heard report by Major Thiel and Squadron Leader Meyer, III Bomber Group.

Landed 1100 hours, 19 January, in Stalingrad. Large number of enemy fighters over fortress area, but none flying at less than 3,000 feet. When aircraft landed it at once came under artillery fire and was hit.

Gumrak landing strip usable by day. Three craters immediately south of it and two craters at its end. Any movement on airstrip is followed at once by bombing by three U-2s, which maintain constant patrol over the area.

When visibility deteriorates, these Russian aircraft disappear.

Commanding the airstrip is Lieutenant Kolbenschlag. His orders, generally speaking, are badly carried out. The men are too apathetic. On landing, Thiel at once reported to General Paulus. In Thiel's opinion, landing on airstrip is practicable only by day. General Paulus told him (in these words): 'The Air Force won't believe what my Staff tell them and they've let the whole show down.' Major Thiel pointed out lack of any proper ground organization – no unloading party available. The aircraft, which had landed at 1100 hours, had still not been unloaded at 1600 hours! (This agrees with reports from other aircrews.)

Since, as a result of the above-mentioned difficulties, the landing, unloading and turning-round of twenty-five aircraft per hour is not possible, we shall not be able to fly in the requisite 200–300 tons per day. General Paulus was very agitated and said: 'You are talking to dead men. We remained here on the Fuehrer's orders, and the Air Force has let us down and not fulfilled its promises.' (Extract ends.)

During the fighting of the next few days, the size of the cauldron continued to diminish. On 24 January the western front was withdrawn to the edge of the city itself. I had earlier moved my command post from Gumrak to the battle headquarters of 71 Infantry Division, and on the afternoon of 23 January I moved again into the southern sector of the city, which is the objective of the main enemy attack.

By 24 January supply by air was possible only by means of air drops. This situation had been foreseen by Army Headquarters, who have directed that, in the event of the army being split up into groups, these groups will carry on the fight independently, keeping in touch by wireless with Army Group and Army Headquarters. Accordingly, the following have been appointed as Group Commanders, should the need arise: Northern group – General Strecker; central group – General Heitz; southern group – myself.

Northern group was cut off on 26 January, central group on 29th. Thus, in accordance with Army Headquarters instructions, my command over the northern and central sectors of the cauldron came to an end. Resistance by the utterly exhausted troops in the central and southern sectors (including the Army Staff) ceased on 31 January. The northern sector continued to fight on until early on 2 February.

I submitted Sub-Sections I-VI of these 'Basic Facts' to General v. Seydlitz, commanding LI Corps, on 5 August 1945, and to General Strecker, commanding XI Army Corps, on 8 September 1945. These officers have accepted as accurate the account I have given, both as regards their own personal roles, and as regards the situation as a whole, in so far as they were in a position to judge it.

Signed: v. Seydlitz. 9 September 1945

Strecker. 9 September 1945.

Paulus.

Appendix to the basic facts, Sixth Army's operations at Stalingrad (Phase II)

(*Vide* Phase I, page 226)

After the failure to relieve Stalingrad, in reply to reiterated requests for permission to fight my way out and for the despatch by air of supplies to enable me to do so, I received, at the beginning of January 1943, a letter from Field-Marshal v. Manstein, the gist of which was as follows: '... I fully understand and share your anxieties about Sixth Army. Nevertheless, higher authority is better placed to view the situation as a whole and to decide what measures must be adopted; and higher authority, too, bears the responsibility. Your duty is to carry out the orders given to you to the best of your ability. For whatever happens afterwards you bear no responsibility. ...'

The fact that the GOC-in-C, Army Group, supported the orders issued to me by Army Headquarters had considerable influence on my own attitude. Field-Marshal v. Manstein enjoyed the reputation of possessing a highly qualified mind of outstanding strategic ability and of being a man both willing and able to stand up to Hitler.

III. Co-operation with subordinate Commanders

Throughout the whole period of our encirclement, close contact was maintained between my subordinate Commanders and myself. There was a constant exchange of views on the situation and the measures to be taken – sometimes directly with divisional commanders at crucial moments in the battle. These conferences usually took place either when I was visiting the various command posts or when individual commanders visited me in my own headquarters. At no time were any regular General Officers' conferences held, nor, in the circumstances, would it have been possible to do so.

On the question of an independent break-out, contrary to the explicit orders of Army Group and Army Headquarters, Generals Heitz, Strecker, Hube and Jaenecke were emphatically opposed to any such action, while General v. Seydlitz was in favour.

Not one of my subordinate commanders approached me with the suggestion that we ought to accept the Russian demand for surrender made on 8 January. On this question of a cessation of hostilities, it was not until 20 January that the subject was raised for the first time by Generals v. Seydlitz and Pfeffer (who had recently been flown in to take command of IV Army Corps in place of General Jaenecke, wounded and evacuated by air). Generals Heitz, Strecker and Hube, on the other hand, adhered to their attitude of no surrender to the very end.

About this time, as a result of what I had myself seen and after much thought, I called a conference with my Chief of Staff and my GSOs I and II, Operations, to discuss the question. Only my GSO I was in favour of continuing the fight. I therefore decided once again to summarize the conditions prevailing in the cauldron and call upon higher authority to make the ultimate decision. As far as I can remember, General v. Seydlitz saw the draft of this signal at my battle headquarters. In it I said that the troops under my command had reached the limit of human endurance and suffering. At the same time I discussed with my closest advisers the steps to be taken, should permission to surrender be received. The answer to my signal was the telegram quoted on page 264, in which it was stated that Sixth Army had been given 'the historic task' of holding out to the very end and of thus saving the whole front.

The subject of capitulation was next raised on 25 January, when General v. Seydlitz visited my battle headquarters on the south bank of the Tsaritsa, and then again on 27 January, when I visited Generals Schloemer and v. Daniels (divisional commanders) in the command post they had set up in the town prison. All I could do was to point out that the general situation did not permit us to surrender, but rendered it imperative that we should hold out for just as long as we possibly could.

How sharply divided opinions among senior officers were regarding the situation and the fighting capabilities of the troops is well illustrated by one example: On 30 January, the very eve of capitulation, General Korfe with elements of 295 Infantry Division counterattacked and recaptured a block of barrack buildings which they had just previously lost to the enemy.

Except for those mentioned above, no other divisional commander approached me on the subject of surrender.

IV. Notes on certain individual aspects, in amplification of the above

1 EVACUATION FROM THE CAULDRON BY AIR

In view of the many individual attempts to get out of the cauldron somehow or other, great importance, from the point of view of morale, was from the outset attached to the regularization of evacuation by air. As Army Commander I at once issued strict instructions on the subject and took steps to ensure that they were obeyed.

Evacuation by air was governed by the following guiding principles:

A. With the sanction of the Army Commander

(1) All badly wounded, then less serious cases – final decision to be made by the Medical Officer stationed at the airfield. In all, some 42,000 wounded were thus evacuated.

(2) Army couriers. Only officers unfit for further service and civilian officials were to be nominated by Corps and Divisions. Final decision to be made by the Army Chief of Staff. In January 1943 this was altered. From then onwards only officers whose services were required by Army Group or Army Headquarters for duty outside the cauldron were so employed.

(3) (After prior concurrence of Army Group.) The Staffs of the following divisions, which had either ceased to exist or had been broken up, were flown out:

- (a) Staff, 384 Infantry Division, for employment on the Chir. Quartermaster's Branch (three aircraft) were shot down.
- (b) Staff, 94 Infantry Division, for duty at Morozovsk.
- (c) Staff, 79 Infantry Division, to Rostov, to raise a new 79 Division.

B. By Order of Army Headquarters

Certain categories, such as officers on the Staff College List, commanders, technical NCOs and specialists of the Panzer arm and a number of officers detailed by name.

2 APPOINTMENTS AND PROMOTIONS

In view of the situation, it was considered desirable that appointments which fell vacant should be filled from officers already serving with Sixth Army and that these officers should be granted the rank of the appointment which they assumed. The GOC-in-C, Sixth Army, was authorized to make promotions up to the rank of Lieut-General, in accordance with detailed guiding principles laid down by Personnel Branch, Army Headquarters.

V. The mental and physical condition of the troops

Our initial attacks had made heavy demands on the stamina of the troops and had very considerably weakened their powers of physical endurance. The major Russian offensive had then imposed upon them burdens and strains of a severity which they had never experienced before. These hardships varied greatly from front to front. Those troops who remained in their old positions were well-found, both from the fighting point of view and as regards their supplies of food and stores. But those who, in the process of creating the cauldron, were called upon to occupy new, unprepared positions in the snowbound Steppes between the Volga and the Don were from the outset exposed to exceptionally heavy hardship. They had no material with which to build shelters or dugouts, no firewood, no cooking facilities, very little water and wholly inadequate winter clothing.

Those units of XI Army Corps which had originally been in position west of the Don had, in addition to all this, suffered severe casualties in fighting their way back across the river and into their new positions on the western front of the cauldron.

The problem of getting supplies to the troops withdrawn from the eastern sector of the cauldron and hastily pitch-forked into the new south-western front in process of creation, had been greatly complicated by the fact that these troops had been torn out of their own divisional areas and were thus deprived of the smoothly working system of food distribution which had previously served their needs.

In spite of all this the fighting spirit of the men, initially, was wholly admirable. They had faith in their leaders and took it for granted that their hopes of relief would be fulfilled. Otherwise, they felt sure, they would never have been left where they were. These hopes were further strengthened when Fourth Panzer Army advanced to their relief at the beginning of December, and when that attack failed, fresh promises from Army Headquarters awakened fresh hopes.

It was only from 10 January onwards, when the main Russian attack was launched, that morale and hope began to falter. The men then tended to become apathetic and slack, and more and more of them, exhausted and dispirited, began to seek refuge in the cellars of Stalingrad. Many voices were raised against the pointlessness of carrying on the struggle, though an equal number sternly demanded that we should fight on.

Thanks not only to the reports I received, but also to the visits I paid almost every day to subordinate staffs and command-posts, I always had a clear picture both of the situation and of the conditions under which the troops were fighting and living.

Although the scale of rations, and particularly the bread issue, was wholly inadequate from the very beginning of the siege, distribution was effected in a comparatively orderly manner until about the middle of January. But when the last airfield fell into enemy hands on 24 January, the system broke down completely. Issues bore no relation to ration strengths, and the large number of men separated from their units and holding on in the town itself received scarcely any rations at all.

Contrary to my strict orders, some units hoarded rations instead of distributing them – a fact that did not come to light until the very end; and by that time, of course, it was no longer possible to make any distribution of these 'black' rations.

The system of dropping supplies by parachute, which was started on 25 January, proved useless. The volume dropped was far too small, and any systematic collection and distribution was found to be no longer possible. A considerable portion of the supplies thus dropped fell into enemy hands.

In view of the increasingly difficult food situation, once the Russian offensive had started, I gave orders, about 10 January or shortly after, that all Russian prisoners of war were to be concentrated in the western sector, near the Pitomnik airfield, and ordered to return to the Russian lines. As, just about that time, my western front was heavily attacked and thrown back, I had no opportunity of seeing for myself that this order was carried out. It was only later, in captivity, that I learnt that the handing over of these prisoners had not taken place. They had set off for the Russian lines, but had then turned back.

A pressing problem was that of medical attention. Although the total number of wounded flown out (see IV 1, above) was large, it was not nearly large enough, and on 24 January evacuation by air stopped altogether.[1] The hospitals were completely full, and no alternative accommodation was available anywhere. The cellars in Stalingrad itself were crammed with men, and every hour brought a fresh stream of sick and exhausted men into the city. Drugs, medicines and bandages became increasingly scarce.

A further affliction which adversely affected the morale and health of the troops was that in the closing stages it was no longer possible to bury the dead, for the men had by that time become too exhausted to be able to dig graves in the hard, frost-bound ground.

The realization of the inconceivable torments which my officers and men were suffering weighed heavily on me when it came to making decisions. In the struggle between obedience to orders which emphasized in most compelling terms that every added hour of resistance was of vital importance, on the one hand, and the promptings of common humanity, on the other, I felt at the time that obedience had to take precedence. The responsibility placed upon the Sixth Army and the contribution it was being called upon to make towards the creation of a new front in the southern sector imposed on us the obligation not voluntarily to give up the struggle in Stalingrad and thus add to the sacrifices we ourselves had already made even greater sacrifices on the part of those who were striving to restore the situation.

---

[1] The figure of 42,000 officers and men quoted was made up of approximately 35,000 wounded and 7,000 'specialists' of all kinds, ranging from General Officers to technical maintenance personnel of Panzer units. According to his notes, the Field-Marshal placed the strength of Sixth Army in the cauldron on 23 November 1942 at 220,000 men. Russian statistics state that between 10 and 29 January 16,800 prisoners were taken and that when Stalingrad capitulated a further 91,000 fell into their hands – a total, that is, of 107,800 prisoners of war. When the 42,000 flown out is added to this, the losses suffered by Sixth Army during the siege must have amounted, therefore, to 72,200 killed or died of wounds, sickness, starvation or cold.

Red Square, Stalingrad

The ruins of Stalingrad

Refugees leaving Stalingrad

*The Stalingrad Cauldron (Phase II): documents and signals: 'Wintergewitter' or 'Donnerschlag'?
Relief, break out or wait? December 1942*

Secret
0700 hours, 22 December 1942
(By wireless telephone)
From Sixth Army

To The Chief of the General Staff Army Headquarters

Ref: Chief of General Staff's No. 4068/42

1 Ration strength on 18 December: 249,600, including Rumanians (13,000) auxiliary volunteers (19,300) and wounded (approximately 6,000).

2 Battle strength: In front line (approximate figures), infantry 25,000, pioneers, 3,200. These do not include the following who are also in the main battle zone: Regimental and Battalion Staffs, heavy infantry weapons, anti-aircraft and assault guns, tanks, Army troops (pioneers, artillery, construction battalions, M-G battalions, etc.), Air Force and anti-aircraft units, Rumanians and volunteers.

Full and precise figures have been called for and will be submitted in a few days. Delay in submitting is due to difficulty of making an accurate check. Movement by day is no longer possible in battle zone, and data in possession of Army and Corps Staffs have been destroyed. For these reasons returns have previously not been called for.

3 (a) Fuel

'Otto' fuel (petrol) 133 cubic metres.
Diesel oil 12 cubic metres.

Running stocks held by Corps are negligible and amount to barely 0.1 per cent of authorized daily consumption.

(b) Food

Stock situation on 20 December. (Half-rations scale)

Bread	..	..	..	up to 24 December
Butter, fats	..	..	,, 25	,,
Main meal	..	..	,, 26	,,
Evening meal	..	..	,, 26	,,
Drinks	..	..	..	,, 27 ,,
Tobacco	..	..	,, 28	,,

(c) Ammunition

In percentage of authorized scale: (Here follow figures for various weapons, from anti-aircraft guns up to heavy howitzers, which vary from 79 per cent to 35 per cent.)

Stocks in Army reserve are low and include 3,000 rounds for light field howitzers, 900 rounds for heavy field howitzers and 600 rounds for other guns up to 10-cm.

4 Health

Nourishment for troops unsatisfactory to bad. Men have been on half rations since 26 November, and bread issue, since 8 December, has been reduced to 200 grms per day. Physical condition of the troops is therefore deteriorating. Under present conditions they are incapable of undertaking long marches or engaging in offensive action without a large number falling out. Since 21 November there have been fifty-six deaths in Army area attributable to a large extent, according to Medical Officers, to malnutrition. Number of sick amounts to 2,000. (These are included under 'wounded' in para (1) above.)

5 From 23 November to 18 December, daily average volume of supplies received by air – 85 tons. It is only in the last few days that there has been any material improvement. From 19–21 December daily average has been 225 tons.

Signed................

Secret
No. 421026/42
0415 hours, 23 December 1942
General Staff (Op. Is/b)
Army Headquarters.
(Despatched by teleprinter, 0650 hours, 23 December 1942.)

From Chief of the General Staff Army Headquarters

To Field-Marshal v. Manstein, GOC-in-C, Army Group Don

PERSONAL & IMMEDIATE

Ref: Army Group Don's No. Ia 0374/42.

Following from Fuehrer, begins:

The railway junction Morozovsk and the two air bases at Morozovsk and Tatsinskaya will be held and kept in operation at all costs.

For this purpose, 11 Panzer Division has been released. To replace it, Fuehrer agrees that units of LVII Panzer Corps be transferred across the Don. LVII Panzer Corps' bridge-head, however, must be held against the time when the offensive can be resumed from it. Efforts must be made to clear the east bank of the Don from the mouth of the Aksay to the mouth of the Chir, in order to relieve forces on the Don west bank.[1]

Army Group Don will report measures being taken. Consignment of Tiger tanks destined for Army Group Don will cross frontier at Brest by first trains on 23 December. Ends

signed Zeitzler

AHQ teleprinter signal No. 421026/42, dated 23 December 1942 (received 1305 hours) forwarded herewith,
Please acknowledge receipt.
This signal was repeated by wireless.

signed Scholze
Lieutenant,
Cipher Officer,
Army Group Don.

Secret
(By hand of Officer only)
No. Ia. 0374/42
Headquarters,
Army Group Don.

From Headquarters, Army Group Don
To Chief of the General Staff, Army Headquarters

(1) *Food*

(a) In the present heavy fighting under severe climatic conditions the minimum required to maintain the fighting strength of the troops is 2,500 calories per man per day. (500g bread, 90g tinned meat, 100g vegetables, 90g evening meal, 50g fats, 50g sugar, 20g salt and seasoning, 15g drinks, 25g tobacco – total (including packing) 1,130g.) For ration strength of 250,000 men this equals 282 tons per day.

[1] A euphemestic way of denoting the abandonment of relief operations.

(b) Horses at present on strength – 7,300 troop horses and 15,700 pack and transport animals. If all are slaughtered, Sixth Army considers it would have enough meat to last until 15 January, and no tinned meat would be required before that date. This would reduce the daily air lift to 255 tons.

Infantry divisions, however, would thereby be immobilized, except for such assistance as could be given to them by motorized formations. Preservation of the 7,300 troop horses is therefore considered highly desirable, in order that at least a portion of the heavy weapons and the divisional artillery should remain mobile. This would necessitate supply by air of 22 tons (3 kilos per horse) of fodder per day. The period during which horse flesh would provide the meat ration would be proportionately decreased.

2 *Ammunition*

For purely defensive purposes (exclusive of any major action) 100 tons daily.

3 *Fuel*

For distribution of supplies and defensive action by Panzer and anti-arcraft units – 75 tons per day.

4 Total air-lift volume required to maintain Sixth Army in its fortress position is therefore 550 tons per day.

Teleprinter conversation between Field-Marshal v. Manstein and General Paulus.

1740–1820 hours, 23 December 1942

v. Manstein. Good evening, Paulus. Yesterday you reported to Army Headquarters that you had enough fuel for a 20-kilometre sortie.[1] Zeitzler says would you please re-check and confirm this? What I have to tell you is this: The enemy is apparently putting in more and more troops against Fangohr,[2] with the result that the

[1] Paulus had reported on 19 December that his Panzers could not sortie more than 20 kms without risking being unable to get back, if the relief operations failed.

[2] Major-General Fangohr, Chief of Staff, Fourth Panzer Army, used here as camouflage to denote that Army.

latter has been forced to remain more or less on the defensive. Apart from that, the position on the left flank[1] means that I shall have to withdraw troops from Fangohr and further weaken him. What effect that will have on the co-operation between him and yourself you will yourself realize. Now – if, during the next few days we could fly in a limited amount of fuel and supplies, do you think, if the worst came to the worst, that you could lay on Operation 'Donnerschlag'? I don't want an immediate answer. Think it over and get in touch with me again, please, at 2100 hours. I may add that to keep Sixth Army adequately supplied, which by my reckoning means 550 tons a day, for any length of time is going to be extremely difficult – particularly in view of what has happened on the left flank. Over.

Paulus. 'Donnerschlag' has become more difficult than it was, because during the last few days the enemy has been digging in on the south and south-western front and, according to wireless intercepts, seems to have concentrated six armoured brigades behind these new positions. Preparations for 'Donnerschlag' – reliefs, distribution of fuel and so on – would take six days. From here, of course, I can't tell whether there's the slightest chance of the Army being relieved in the fairly near future, or whether we shall have to try 'Donnerschlag'. *If the latter – then the sooner the better.*[2] But it must be clearly realized that it will be a very difficult operation, unless Hoth manages to tie down really strong enemy forces outside. Am I to take it that I am now authorized to initiate Operation 'Donnerschlag'? Once it's launched, there'll be no turning back. Over.

v. Manstein. I can't give you full authority today. But I hope to get a decision tomorrow. The main point is – are you confident that Sixth Army could fight its way out and through to Hoth, if we come to the conclusion that adequate supplies over a long period could not be got to you? What do you think? Over.

Paulus. In that case, I'd have no option but to try. Query – is the envisaged withdrawal of forces from Kirchner's area going to take place? Over.

v. Manstein. Yes – today. How much fuel and supplies would you require before launching 'Donnerschlag' and on the assumption

[1] The collapse of the Italian Army on the Don.
[2] Author's italics.

that once the action began, further supplies to meet day to day requirements would reach you? Over.

Paulus. 1,000 cubic metres of fuel and 500 tons of food. If we get that, all my armour and motor vehicles will have enough. Incidentally, we are expecting attacks on our west and south-west front tomorrow.

v. Manstein. Well, that's the lot. Good luck, Paulus.

Paulus. Thank you, Sir. And good luck to you, too.

> Teleprinter conversation
> CHRISTMAS.
> Between General Schmidt, Chief of Staff, Sixth Army, and General Schulz, Chief of Staff, Army Group Don. 24 December, 1705–1715 hours.

My dear Schmidt, the thoughts of the Field-Marshal and all of us are with Sixth Army. I haven't much news for you. Fangohr is still on the defensive. The enemy is apparently bringing up reinforcements against him all the time. Nothing much from the Chir front. 11 Panzer Division put in an attack westwards from Morozovsk and has halted the enemy advance – for the time being, anyway. We've still had no decision about you people from Army Headquarters. The Field-Marshal told me to say that you'd better make up your minds that the answer will be Operation 'Donnerschlag'. We're hoping for better weather . . . (mutilated) all available . . . to fly in the fuel and food you require. What's your news? Over.

Schmidt. Can aircraft still take off safely from Tatsinskaya?

Schulz. So far – yes. Alternative airstrips have also been made.

Schmidt. Will Fangohr be able to hold the Myshkova sector?

Schulz. We very much hope so. But he may have to decrease the present size of the bridge-head a little.

Schmidt. Has a Panzer division been taken away from him to the west bank of the Don?

Schulz. Yes. We had to transfer one division to the west bank for the defence of Morozovsk. Tomorrow, however, the SS Division Viking will start reaching the Salsk area by road and rail. We have also asked urgently for very considerable reinforcements for the Army Group. AHQ's answer hasn't come in yet. I think that's all I have to tell you. Once more then – very best wishes for Christmas from the Field-Marshal and all of us.

                                        Secret
                                        No. Ia 0376/42
                                        24 December 1942
                                        Headquarters, Army Group Don.
IMMEDIATE   By hand of Officer only.
    To The Chief of the General Staff, Army Headquarters
From The General Officer Commanding-in-Chief, Army Group
                        Don
Ref: Telephone signal of 1730 hours, 24 December 1942.
Ref: Para 1. As already reported, Sixth Army will require six days to make the necessary arrangements for a break-out. For this purpose, 1,000 tons[1] of fuel and 500 tons of food must be flown in. Given good weather this can and must be done. Whether the attempt will succeed no one can say. But unless Sixth Army can be adequately supplied in its fortress, there is no alternative. If everything possible is to be done to ensure success, Hoth must be reinforced by III Panzer Corps as soon as possible and at the last moment by 16 Motorized Infantry Division, and then with First Panzer Army he must go over to the offensive as quickly as he can.
Ref: 2. Paulus can move, provided we send him the fuel and food mentioned above. If the weather is good, six days will suffice both for this and for III Panzer Corps to move up. What he (Paulus) can take with him will depend on the physical condition of his troops and the horse situation (divisional artillery). In any case, however, all waggon transport not required for the actual battle and all immovable material will have to be abandoned.
Ref: 3. According to Sixth Army reports, the stamina of the troops has decreased very considerably, and on the present scale of rations it will inevitably continue to do so at an increasing speed. It might

---

[1] Translator's note. The signal says '1,000 *tons*'. But Paulus himself said (p. 278) '1,000 cubic metres'. Bulk liquid measures are usually expressed in cubic metres. 'Tons' here is probably a misprint.

be possible to provide for the men for a little while longer, but then they would be quite incapable of fighting their way out. The end of this month is, in my opinion, the last possible date.

Ref: 4. I do not think it will be possible to send either 7 Panzer Division or SS Viking Division to the Army's right wing, since both these divisions will be required to maintain our hold on the Donets and on the Donets-Don-Chir arc. Apart from that, 7 Panzer Division would in any case arrive too late to be of any use to Hoth.

Ref: 5. In the current situation, I do not welcome the placing of another Army Group under my command. Nevertheless I think it must be done, though I must ask for complete liberty of action in the conduct of subsequent operations. In this connection, I feel bound to point out that the situation as a whole has now developed to such an extent, both as regards Sixth Army and as regards Army Groups 'A' and 'B', that the major decisions now under consideration are being taken too late. May I suggest that you consider what would happen if we were commanding on the other side? . . .

> (signed) v. Manstein
> Field-Marshal,
> General Officer Commanding-in-Chief, Army Group Don.

The Stalingrad Cauldron (Phase II) as seen from the air: extracts from the War Diary of Air Fleet 4 and the personal diary of General v. Richthofen, GOC-in-C, Air Fleet 4: relief—'Wintergewitter' or 'Donnerschlag'?

12 *December* 1942. Good, clear weather. At 0430 hours Fourth Panzer Army's attack under General Hoth got off to a smooth start. Air force units are co-operating. . . .

v. R(ichthofen) had a conference with v. Manstein. Subject: lack of co-operation and the general situation. v. R(ichthofen) regards the situation as critical. He is urging Zeitzler to reinforce the army and to give us back the air formations which have been seconded from us. Expressed his views very forcibly to Jeschonnek over the telephone and said: 'My faith in our leadership is rapidly sinking to zero.'

13 *December*. Many fog patches, strong wind. v. R(ichthofen) to Semichmaya, where Fourth Panzer Army and LVII Panzer Corps are attacking. Divisions, he says, are all attacking too late, because they wait for a Russian counter-attack that never comes. 'Of any real attempt to pour forward, to press on towards Stalingrad – not a trace! Here they're all "shilly-shallying about" against enemy forces that are known to be weak. The GOC (i.e. General Kirchner, commanding LVII Panzer Corps) has only a very sketchy idea of how precarious the situation at Stalingrad is; but in any case, his heart is not in the job.'

14 *December*. Very bad weather, misty, fine rain, warm. Except for small air-lift to Stalingrad (80 tons fuel), no flying possible.

15 *December*. Ground fog. Air reconnaissance and intervention in land battle both impossible. We managed nevertheless to fly 70 tons into Stalingrad. Russians are attacking Fourth Panzer Army from every direction and are throwing our people back on to the Aksay. There's nothing we can do to help. Sixth Army's chances are becoming slimmer and slimmer.

16 *December*. v. R(ichthofen) notes: Today 27 and 51 Bomber Squadrons were taken away from us. This means that tomorrow's attack will be robbed of a third of its air support. That we should get as far as the Aksay was obvious from the start, since up to that point the Russians have nothing but outposts. It was in the area immediately beyond the river that the battle began in earnest, and it is from this area that our troops are now being thrown out.

Tomorrow's attack goes in against an enemy who has proved his superiority. That it will succeed in achieving a real break-through is more than doubtful. Further to reduce its striking power by robbing it of one third of its air support means that we are abandoning Sixth Army to its fate – and that is plain murder. I said as much to Jeschonnek and formally disclaimed all responsibility. Deluding himself with stupid arguments, he won't believe me. He insists that, with the Italians scattered to the four winds, Sixth Army couldn't be rescued anyway. Tried to prove to me that I myself had consistently drawn attention to the importance of this sector of the front and had always advocated that it should be strengthened. But he forgets not only that I was always of the opinion – and still am – that Sixth Army ought to be withdrawn from the Volga and got out of the cauldron, but also that I had insisted that to continue to support the Italians, once our relief operations had started, would be impossible. I told v. Manstein all this. We both feel the same – that we're like a couple of attendants in a lunatic asylum! . . .'

17 *December*. A sudden sharp frost. Tanks can now get a move on. v. R(ichthofen) again touring round, but, as he puts its, 'Devoid of any optimism. We must just blunder on and do our duty.' Bad news from the Italian sector. Two divisions have broken and fled in panic.

18 *December*. Despairing telegrams from Sixth Army to Air Fleet regarding food situation. These have been sent on to Air Force Headquarters. . . .

' . . . In the evening a long discussion with v. Manstein on the subject of Sixth Army fighting its way out. To fly in the volume of stores demanded just can't be done. We had a heart-to-heart talk about the lack of drive in the conduct of operations and the general situation. v. Manstein told me that a report is being submitted to Hitler this evening, recommending that Sixth Army be ordered to fight its way out. He seemed to regard Hitler's agreement as a foregone conclusion.'

19 *December*. v. Manstein today ordered Sixth Army to break-out south-westwards . . . 154 aircraft carried 289 tons of supplies to Stalingrad. . . .

' . . . But now the Fuehrer has ordered that Stalingrad will be held' (notes v. R(ichthofen)). 'In this connection, I learned from v. Manstein and Zeitzler that at the final conference on the subject the Reichsmarschall had expressed the view that the supply situation wasn't nearly as bad as it was made out to be. Apart from the fact that it would do his figure a power of good to spend a little time in the cauldron, I can only assume that my reports are either not read or are given no credence. In the old days, one could have done something about it, but nowadays one is treated like a silly kid and has no say at all!'

Stalingrad, a brief survey in retrospect
by Field-Marshal Paulus

The whole of the Stalingrad complex consists of three phases:
(1) The Drive to the Volga.

Within the framework of the war as a whole, the 1942 summer offensive represented an attempt to achieve by further offensive action what we had failed to achieve in the late autumn of 1941 – namely, to bring the eastern compaign to a swift and victorious conclusion – which, after all, was one of the primary objects of the sudden onslaught on Russia – in the expectation that this would lead to our winning the whole war.

In the minds of the military commanders, it was this purely military aspect that was predominant. This basic attitude regarding Germany's last chance of winning the war dominated all our military thinking during the two phases ahead.

(2) With the launching of the Russian November offensive and the encirclement of the Sixth Army and part of the Fourth Panzer Army – some 220,000 men in all – the emphasis shifted from 'the victorious conclusion of the Russian campaign' to the question: how can we avoid being completely defeated in the east and thus losing the whole war?

It was this latter that was uppermost in the minds of both the commanders and the rank and file of Sixth Army, while higher authority – Army Group, Army and Supreme Headquarters – still believed, or at least pretended to believe, that we still had a chance of ultimate victory.

As a result, there arose a sharp divergence of opinion regarding plans for the further conduct of operations and the methods to be employed to implement them. Since higher authority, adhering still to the more optimistic appreciation mentioned above and promising immediate support, had forbidden Sixth Army to try to fight its way out during the first phase of the battle of encirclement (when it could quite easily have done so), the Army subsequently had no alternative but to stand and fight. Any other, independent action on its part might well have led to complete disorganization and the subsequent dissolution of the whole of the southern sector of the eastern theatre of war. Had that happened, not only would all hope of ultimate victory have been irremediably destroyed but very swiftly all possibility of avoiding decisive defeat and the consequent collapse of the whole eastern front would have disappeared.

(3) In the third phase, after the attempt to relieve Sixth Army had foundered and the promised help had failed to materialize, our sole objective was to gain time and thus to make possible the creation of a new front in the southern sector and the rescue of the very strong German forces operating in the Caucasus.

If we did not succeed in this, then the magnitude of our defeat in the eastern theatre would alone have sufficed to ensure our losing the whole war.

By this time, the higher authorities themselves had also adopted the line that we must 'hold out at all costs', if the worst were to be avoided. The question of the resistance to be offered by the Sixth Army culminated therefore in the following problem: As I myself saw the situation and, even more, as the situation was depicted to me by those above, total defeat could be avoided only if Sixth Army fought on to the very last. All the more recent wireless signals were couched in the same sense – 'every additional hour counts' and (repeatedly from the neighbours on our right) 'How much longer can Sixth Army hang on?'

From the time the cauldron was formed, and more particularly after the failure of Fourth Panzer Army's attempt to relieve us at the end of December, I, as the Army Commander, was confronted with violently conflicting considerations.

On the one hand were the stream of strict orders to hold fast, the repeated promises of help and admonitions of increasing urgency that I must be guided by the situation as a whole. On the other hand there was the purely human aspect of the increasing and incredible hardships and suffering which my troops were being called upon to endure and which inevitably caused me to ask myself whether the time had not come for me to give up the struggle.

But, deeply though I sympathized with the troops committed to my care, I still believed that the views of higher authority must take precedence; that Sixth Army must accept its agony, must make all the sacrifices demanded of it, if by so doing, we would ensure – as they themselves were convinced we should – that the even greater number of their comrades in neighbouring armies would be rescued and saved.

I believed that by prolonging to its utmost our resistance in Stalingrad I was serving the best interests of the German people, for, if the eastern theatre of war collapsed, I saw no possible prospect of a peace by political negotiation.

To have stepped on my own responsibility out of the general framework, to have acted deliberately against the orders given to me would have entailed the acceptance of a sequence of responsibilities: at the outset, by breaking out, I should have been responsible for the fate of my neighbours; later, by prematurely giving up the fight, for that of the southern sector and with it the whole of the eastern front; and that would have meant – or so it least it seemed – that I should have been responsible to the German people for the loss of the whole war. In that case they would not have hesitated to place on me the whole blame for everything that had happened in the eastern theatre.

And (with the future outcome still hidden from us) what convincing and valid arguments could the Commander of the Sixth Army have produced in support of his disobedience of orders in the presence of the enemy?

Does the fact that his troops are in a position that is hopeless, or threatens to become so, give a Commander the right to refuse to obey orders? In the case of Stalingrad, it could by no means be asserted with certainty that our position was hopeless or even – except at the very end – that it threatened to become so. How, then, could I later have demanded obedience, or even felt justified in doing so, from one of my subordinates in a situation of, in his opinion, similar danger?

Does the prospect of his own death or the probable destruction or capture of his troops release the Commander from his soldierly duty to obey orders?

That is a question which each individual must today leave to his own conscience to answer.

At the time of which I am writing, neither the nation nor the Armed Forces would have understood my acting in this manner. It would have been an unequivocal, revolutionary, political act against Hitler. Furthermore, it is at least possible that, by abandoning Stalingrad contrary to orders, I should have been playing into Hitler's hands and given him the opportunity of castigating the cowardice and disobedience of his Generals and putting upon them the whole blame for the military defeat that was looming larger and larger.

I should, too, have prepared the ground for a new myth, that of the Stalingrad stab in the back, to the great detriment of the German people's ability to form an accurate picture of the history of this war and to draw the conclusions that it is so important that they should draw.

The possibility of initiating a *coup d'état*, of deliberately inviting defeat, in order to bring about the downfall of Hitler and his National-Socialist régime as obstructions to the ending of the war never entered into my deliberations, nor, so far as I am aware, was any such idea ever mooted by anyone anywhere within the limits of my command.

Such ideas not only played no part in my deliberations, but would also have been wholly out of keeping with my character and outlook. I was a soldier, and I believed that it was by obeying orders that I could best serve my people.

As regards the responsibility of my subordinate commanders, they, tactically speaking, were under the same compulsion to obey my orders as I myself was, in the broader sphere, to carry out the strategic conceptions imposed upon me.

The responsibility – *vis à vis* the officers and men of the Sixth Army and the German people – for having obeyed orders and resisted till we could do no more and collapsed is mine and mine alone.

Friedrich Paulus,
Field-Marshal.

Epilogue

••

'We are surprised to find you here! Why didn't you fly out in good time? Why didn't your Supreme Command ensure that so valuable a man was flown out? We would never have allowed so prominent a man to fall into enemy hands like this!'

These were the questions and remarks with which four senior Russian officers, Generals Shumilov, Rokossovski, Voronov and Vassilievski, greeted Paulus when he was taken prisoner.

Paulus replied that the German conception of military ethics demanded that a Commander should share the fate of his troops. To have deserted them at the last moment and abandoned them to their misery would have been unthinkable.

Regarding the question why the Commander-in-Chief of the Sixth Army had continued to the very end to obey the orders of Supreme Headquarters, one of the Soviet Generals remarked that that was only to be expected and that he could not have done anything else. General Rossovski himself said: 'What we don't understand is why you continued to accept Hitler's political leadership.' This remark, according to his son, made a deep and lasting impression on the Field-Marshal and later he referred to it again and again.

When he was marched off into captivity, he was convinced – and with every justification – that not only could his countrymen, his Fuehrer and his country not hold him blameworthy in any way, but also that his Army and he himself had given their utmost in a desperate situation in the service of their land. It was fate, in the shape of the faulty planning and execution of the whole of the summer offensive of 1942, that had placed Sixth Army and its Commander in a situation in which, after a certain and precisely definable moment, their continued resistance, even though it involved the sacrifice of the whole Army, became of vital importance to the German front – at least in the southern sector. This fact cannot be too strongly emphasized, and it was a fate which no mutiny or disobedience of orders would have helped them to escape. Those who do not appreciate this are ignoring the facts of the case. And in this connection, all that can be said in defence of those numerous writers of varying prominence who have devoted themselves to the story of 'The Betrayed Army' is, that they have produced novels but have not written history.

This brings us to the present time. The sole object of this book, however, is to make a contribution to the history of the Second World War in the shape of a treatise concerning a battle which, admittedly, was not the military turning-point of the eastern campaign – that came with the German defeat at Kursk and Bielgorod in the summer of 1943 – but which, in both German and Soviet eyes, constituted the politico-psychological turning-point of the whole war. Just when the collapse of his country, of the National Socialist Party, of his people and its armed forces was imminent, Field-Marshal Paulus made a decision which was incomprehensible to many Germans in general and to innumerable old soldiers in particular; and it is just for this very reason that fairness demands some concluding remarks on his career up to his death after great suffering in 1957.

For reasons unknown to us, Field-Marshal Paulus was kept in Soviet captivity for a very long time. He had been in a number of prisoner of war camps. Except for one disgraceful scene, when he was subjected to scorn and derision on arrival at his first camp, he was treated correctly; indeed, by Russian standards, more than correctly – and very differently to the rest of the officers and men of the Sixth Army!

But captivity as a prisoner of war in Soviet Russia has a character of its own. Hitler regarded the Second World War, and particularly the campaign against Soviet Russia, as a war between world ideologies. But the Russian were and still are far the greater adepts at waging ideological warfare. In the prisoner of war camps of the totalitarian Powers, the captors almost invariably did their utmost to win their captives over to their ideological way of thinking; then again, not infrequently the shock caused by defeat manifested itself in the prisoners in the form of a politico-ideological metamorphosis. This applies equally to both German and allied prisoners (e.g. the case of Lascar) in Soviet camps and to Soviet officers and men in the National Socialist camps, as is shown by the case of General Vlassov and his socialistic Great Russian Freedom Movement.

As far as the more senior ranks of the German Corps of Officers is concerned, it must be remembered that the conflict between the traditionalists and the revolutionaries had never been really settled. When it became plain that defeat was inevitable, and under the ægis of a Hitlerian regimentation that daily became more arbitrary and despotic, this wound opened afresh. Hitler, who acted as a catalyst on every accepted standard in the German way of life, dominated, though he remained invisible, the conflicts that arose in the Soviet camps. Even here his sinister influence was the cause of fresh rivalries and friction.

In the summer of 1943, senior officers of the Sixth Army, with General v. Seydlitz at their head, founded in co-operation with German communist emigrants in Russia the Bund Deutscher Offiziere (The Federation of German Officers), as part of the 'Nationalkomitee Freies Deutschland' (National Committee of Free Germany), which was then in process of creation. The attitude of the Soviet Government – whether it initially regarded this Committee as a genuine partner, against the possibility that Germany might overthrow Hitler and conclude a premature peace, or whether it looked upon it as just one more diversionary tool in its hands – is of no importance. But in the minds of a large number of German officers it conjured up the idea of a united front for the creation of a new order in Germany. It was a utopian idea, like all those other conceptions of a Right and Left wing 'united anti-fascist front', which sprang up in so many of the resistance movements all over Europe, but which, in practice, was doomed to swift extinction.

Field-Marshal Paulus, eagerly though the Russians tried to convert him, hesitated for a very long while before he decided to co-operate with the National Committee. For a long time he doubted whether there was really any sense in prisoners of war indulging in political activities. It was only at the end of July or the beginning of August 1944, when the first news of the 20 July plot reached him and he heard that old and trusted friends like Field-Marshal v. Witzleben, Generals Hoepner and Fellgiebel and Major v. Stauffenberg had had the courage to try to overthrow Hitler, that he made up his mind. And he did so on 8 August 1944, the day upon which v. Witzleben and Hoepner were tried by the Peoples' Court in Berlin, convicted and hanged.

Through the medium of appeals, Paulus tried to rally the German armies in the east, whereupon the Gestapo promptly arrested the whole of his family at home. It was, in any case, too late. As far as the Soviet High Command was concerned, victory was now only a question of time, and there was no longer any need for a genuine alliance with the National Committee.

For Paulus, however, there was another aspect which exercised his mind. He had always been a meticulous and logical thinker, and he had always striven to differentiate with painful precision between right and wrong. Now, when the true character of the Hitler régime was revealed to him, he found himself confronted with the question whether there had been any justification whatsoever, either morally or under the accepted code of international ethics, for the unprovoked attack on Soviet Russia. Germany, he concluded, had been in the wrong, and he felt that he himself bore a share of her guilt in that, as a Principal Staff Officer, he had prepared the plans for this sudden onslaught. And because he was conscious of this feeling of personal guilt, he felt he could not refuse, when called upon by the Soviet prosecution, to appear as a witness against the senior commanders of the German Armed Forces at the Nuremberg trial.

There was yet another aspect which influenced him. He had, to his personal cost, ample evidence of the extent to which the justly famous *esprit de corps* of the German Corps of Officers had degenerated. Long before the legend sprang up (after the catastrophe) that Paulus had not had the courage to emulate the feat of Yorck, another story was being bandied round: 'Paulus failed and let us down completely.' As far as Hitler and the leaders of both State and Armed Forces were concerned, the Generals, Officers and men of the Sixth Army were dead from the moment they were marched off into captivity. No one ever mentioned them again. It could never be admitted that the forces led by Hitler had lost a battle to the Bolsheviks. Generals who lose a vital battle often suffer a cruel fate. But in this case contemptible and shabby contumely had been added. All these things left a feeling of deep bitterness in Paulus' soul, for he had believed in all sincerity that he had done his duty as he had been commanded to do it. And now, he found, no one had the courage to stand and speak in his defence.

It can safely be assumed that a responsible Commander-in-Chief like Paulus, who reached his conclusions only after meticulous consideration, would not frivolously change his conclusions, once they had been reached. His change of outlook was not primarily an acceptance of communism as a way of life, but rather a military conclusion to which he had come and a foreign policy he had evolved which, he hoped, would be for the good of his people. Germany's sole hope of peaceful regeneration, he felt, lay in a close co-operation with the Soviet Union. He chose the East in preference to the western democracies and to all the efforts to create a defensive system being made by a western German State that was rapidly consolidating its position.

And to this attitude he adhered after he had been released from Soviet captivity. He chose Dresden as his place of residence, and there he remained, a respected, but at times and in the eyes of conventional S E D officials, a somewhat strange guest of the 'German Democratic Republic'.

As has already been stated, the object of publishing the Field-Marshal's military papers is to make a contribution to the history of the war, and not to raise the question of a divided Germany. It is perhaps fitting, therefore, to close this narrative with a final note on what ultimately befell him.

Elena Constance Paulus died in Baden Baden in 1949. She had never seen her husband again. Paulus himself was not vouchsafed many years in his materially extremely comfortable refuge in Dresden.

In 1955–6 he fell victim to a species of organic cerebral sclerosis which led to the complete paralysis of the muscles but left the intellect unimpaired, and against which medical science is power-less. Of this disease he died in 1957. During the whole of his painful and fatal illness, he displayed the same steadfastness and composure in the face of the inevitable as had characterized his military career and the crises with which it confronted him.

Walter Goerlitz

Index